890044

Drive Right

A Responsible Approach   Eighth Edition

Authors

Margaret L. Johnson

Owen Crabb

Richard Kaywood

Arthur A. Opfer

Ronald L. Budig

Reading Consultant

Robert A. Pavlik

Scott, Foresman and Company
Editorial Offices: Glenview, Illinois

Regional Offices: Sunnyvale, California • Tucker, Georgia
Glenview, Illinois • Oakland, New Jersey • Dallas, Texas

Reviewers and Contributors

ISBN: 0-673-22450-3 (hardcover)
ISBN: 0-673-22451-1 (softcover)

Copyright © 1987,
Scott, Foresman and Company
Glenview, Illinois.
All Rights Reserved.
Printed in the United States of America.

Drive Right

A Responsible Approach   Eighth Edition

Contents

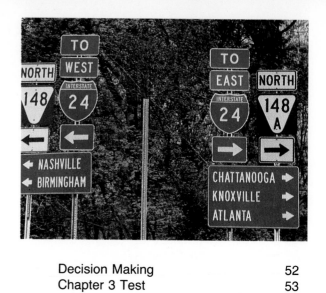

Unit 1
The Driving Task

Chapter 1
You Are the Driver

Chapter 2
Basic Car Control

Chapter 3
Signs, Signals, and
Roadway Markings

Chapter 4
Making Safe Driving Decisions:
The IPDE Process

As a beginning driver, you might feel confused when looking at a group of signs such as this. However, each sign provides important information and helps keep the highway transportation system running safely and efficiently. Signs such as these are only one part of the highway transportation system. People are the most important part of this system.

In this unit you will learn about your role as a driver in the highway transportation system. You will also learn what signs and signals mean, and how to use your car's controls. Finally, you will learn an organized, thinking-doing process to help you become a safe, responsible driver.

Chapter 1
You Are the Driver

You're the Driver!

Imagine you are a driver in this scene. Despite the great number of vehicles, each driver seems to be cooperating to make the system work.

Assume that you are in the right-hand lane. Your traffic light is about to turn green. Is the pedestrian in a dangerous position?

Is the street on which the two yellow cabs are moving a one-way or a two-way street?

Can the white car ahead of you make a right turn? Why or why not?

Knowledge, attitudes, and skills are essential to safe driving. Each driver must cooperate and share the roadways with others in the highway transportation system.

This chapter describes the different parts of the highway transportation system. You will learn about your role and responsibilities as a driver in this system. You also will learn how driver education can help you develop the knowledge, attitudes, and skills necessary for safe driving.

Objectives

1–1 A System for Driving

1. List the three parts and explain the purpose of the highway transportation system (HTS). (4)
2. List the agencies that regulate the HTS. (5)

1–2 What Drivers Do: The Driving Task

3. Explain how the driving task involves social, physical, and decision-making skills. (6)
4. Explain the four steps of the IPDE process. (7)

1–3 Driving Responsibilities

5. Tell how your attitude can affect your driving. (8)
6. Explain your driving-related financial responsibilities. (8)
7. List examples of breakdowns in the HTS. (8)
8. Explain why saving fuel is important. (9)

1–4 Driver Education and Responsible Driving

9. Explain driver education as a first step toward responsible driving. (10)
10. Explain why driver education is an ongoing process. (10)

1–1 A System for Driving

You look forward to the day when you can earn a driver's license. Your license should be a symbol that you are becoming more mature. You have greater independence to participate in a wider range of activities. Your license represents a new responsibility.

The Highway Transportation System

As you learn to drive, you join other drivers as part of the *highway transportation system*—the HTS. The HTS is a complex system composed of three parts: people, vehicles, and roadways. The purpose of the HTS is to move people and goods from one place to another in a safe, efficient, and economical manner. These pictures show some of the people, vehicles, and roadways of the HTS.

Of all transporation systems, the HTS is the most complex. It has the greatest variety of users—drivers, motorcyclists, bicyclists, and pedestrians. However, these users receive less training when compared to other transportation system users. For example, airplane pilots undergo extensive training and testing compared to the relatively brief training period of most HTS users.

People The people who use the HTS by walking, driving, or riding are called *roadway users*. Most roadway users are drivers of cars. Other roadway users include passengers, pedestrians, cyclists, and drivers of trucks, vans, buses, and emergency vehicles.

Many roadway users utilize the HTS to travel to and from their jobs or school. Others, such as truck drivers, perform their jobs while using the HTS. Still others travel the HTS for pleasure.

Roadway users include all age groups, from preschool children to senior citizens. Their physical, mental, and emotional conditions range from excellent to very poor.

Most roadway users utilize the HTS responsibly and cooperatively. Some do not. Some people use the HTS while distracted by personal problems. Still others drive when they are tired, ill, or intoxicated. You must learn to compensate for roadway users who cannot or will not perform in a safe, responsible manner.

Vehicles Consider the vast number and different kinds of vehicles using the HTS. The smallest and least protected is the bicycle. At the other extreme is the semi-trailer truck

weighing many tons. In between are motorcycles, cars, vans, buses, campers, and farm and construction vehicles.

Some vehicles are older cars with many miles on them. Others are shiny new models just off the assembly line. They represent a wide range of steering, accelerating, and braking performance, as well as different safety equipment. Their running conditions vary according to the way they have been maintained.

Roadways Roadways vary from dirt roads to multilane expressways. In between are

congested city streets, rural highways, and mountain roadways with steep grades and sharp curves.

Traffic controls and roadway maintenance range from excellent to nonexistent. Such adverse conditions as darkness, rain and snow, fog, wind, and potholes can further complicate the driving task. As more and more people use these roadways, driving skills and cooperation become increasingly important.

Regulating the HTS

The most important element in the regulation of the HTS is the driver who obeys traffic laws. Driving is a privilege granted by each state through a license. You earn a license by passing a state examination. In accepting a license, you also accept the responsibility to obey traffic laws.

Many private agencies and departments of federal, state, and local government also help regulate the HTS. The federal government has established the National Highway Safety Act, a set of traffic-safety guidelines. Using these guidelines:

► Federal and state legislatures pass laws which make up the *vehicle code*.

► State and local police enforce the laws.
► State departments of motor vehicles or licenses set up rules and regulations for the control of drivers and motor vehicles.
► Courts decide whether drivers charged with violating the laws are guilty or innocent.
► Local, county, and state highway and traffic engineers maintain the roadways and traffic controls.

Review It

1. What are the parts of and the purpose of the HTS?
2. What agencies help regulate the HTS?

5

The *driving task* includes all the skilled actions you must take to drive safely. These actions must be based on sound judgment and correct decisions. To perform the driving task safely, you must:

► apply seeing skills and stored knowledge to interpret traffic scenes correctly.
► identify situations and respond correctly at the proper time.
► judge time-space relationships that constantly change.
► coordinate hands and feet with seeing and other senses to control your car.
► obey traffic laws, signs, and signals.
► understand your car's functions well enough to know its limitations and to keep your car in good running condition.

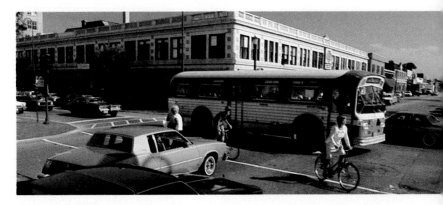

Social Skills
Driving is largely a social task. Like other social tasks, driving requires skills in interacting and cooperating with people, such as those in the picture. Courtesy is an important part of the social task. A courteous driver obeys traffic laws and is thoughtful of other roadway users. Without courtesy and cooperation, safe and efficient movement in the HTS would be impossible.

For the most part, other people on the roadways will be strangers to you. They bring their own problems and levels of skills to the driving task. Some roadway users might be tired; their reactions might be slower than usual. Others might be angry or distracted by personal problems. Still others, especially at night, might have been drinking. Part of your social task as a driver is your obligation to carefully observe the behavior of other roadway users. You then must adjust for mistakes made by them.

Physical Skills
You must learn basic physical skills well enough so they become almost automatic. You then can concentrate on the social and decision-making driving skills.

Beginning drivers often pay too much attention to the physical part of the driving task. They might ignore the social and decision-making skills needed for safe driving. They think good driving is merely skillful maneuvering of their vehicles. Hands turn the steering wheel and feet push the pedals. However, hands and feet respond only when they receive directions from the brain.

Decision-Making Skills
Since the brain controls driving, safe driving is mainly a mental, decision-making task. The physical skills of either turning a wheel and applying a brake or an accelerator pedal are of little use if done at the wrong time. Deciding where and when to steer, brake, and accelerate is essential to being a safe driver.

Only after you master the decision-making skills of driving can you become a skillful driver. An organized, thinking-doing process can help you master decision-making skills.

The IPDE Process

The *IPDE process* is an organized, thinking-doing process you can use when driving. The four steps of the IPDE process pictured here are:

► *Identify* information in the driving scene, such as potential hazards.
► *Predict* where possible conflicts can occur.
► *Decide* what actions to take and when and where to take them to avoid conflicts.
► *Execute* the correct response as the situation requires.

With practice, the IPDE process can become a habit that helps protect you from driving conflicts. Protecting yourself and others from dangerous and unexpected changes in the driving environment is *defensive driving*. The IPDE process can help you become a defensive driver so you:

► anticipate the actions of other roadway users.
► avoid conflicts before they occur.
► adjust to changing weather and roadway conditions.

Review It

1. How does the driving task involve social, physical, and decision-making skills?
2. What are the four steps in the IPDE process?

Identify the oncoming car and the driveway ahead.

Predict the car might turn across your path into driveway.

Decide that you will slow and be prepared to stop.

Execute by taking foot off accelerator and braking gently.

When your state first issues you a driver's license, you are considered a mature person with basic driving skills. In some states, no distinction is made between the behavior required of you, as a beginning driver, and the behavior of a person with years of driving experience. Each driver is expected to obey the law and avoid conflicts

Along with your license to drive comes your responsibility to be a safe driver. Your responsibility includes protecting the passengers in your vehicle. You also are expected to help protect other roadway users, like those in this picture.

Attitude

Your attitude toward driving will affect your willingness to learn safe-driving habits. This same attitude also will influence your behavior behind the wheel.

Some drivers confuse recognition as a skillful driver with attention-getting which results from creating a disturbance. These drivers seek attention by reckless actions, such as "peeling" away from a STOP sign, only to come to a screeching halt at the next STOP sign.

Work for recognition rather than attention. Earn the respect of others by showing a mature, responsible attitude. Your reward could be the freedom to drive—a freedom granted by the state and other roadway users—because you have earned their trust.

Financial Responsibility

As a driver, expect to pay your fair share of driving-related expenses. Vehicle-related costs include buying fuel as well as maintaining and insuring your car. You also are financially responsible by state law for any damage you cause to other people and their property.

Breakdowns in the HTS

A breakdown occurs when any part of the HTS does not work properly. Traffic tie-ups and collisions are two examples of HTS breakdowns. Your judgment is a factor in avoiding or minimizing these breakdowns.

Roadway repairs, collisions, and such adverse weather as rain, snow, fog, or ice can tie up traffic. Drivers involved in a tie-up are responsible for driving in a safe, cooperative manner.

A *collision* occurs when a vehicle hits another object. A collision is a more serious HTS breakdown than a traffic tie-up. Collisions, particularly at high speeds, often have tragic results.

Collisions Do Not Just Happen

A more accurate term for "accident" is collision. Most collisions do not just happen; they are caused. The causes of collisions can be determined. Steps can be taken to eliminate many of the causes.

Causes of Collisions   Driver error is the main cause of most collisions. Frequently, these errors occur because a driver violates a traffic law. Other causes include adverse weather conditions and defects in vehicles and roadways. Think about possible causes for the collision shown here.

Many collisions have multiple causes. For example, a car skids in the rain and crashes through a guardrail. An investigation reveals that the car was traveling too fast for the curve and conditions of the roadway. Contributing to the collision was the absence of a warning sign, "Roadway Slippery When Wet," and the poor condition of the car's brakes. While the wet roadway and poor brakes added to the problem, the primary cause of the collision was driving too fast for conditions.

Social and Economic Loss
Collisions have serious social and economic effects. Traffic collisions cost the national economy an estimated 45 billion dollars in property damage, time away from a job or school, medical fees, and insurance premiums each year. The cost of family disruption, shattered career plans, mental anguish, and physical suffering cannot be measured in dollars.

Age Groups in Collisions
Traffic collisions are the leading cause of death for young people 16–19 years old. Drivers in this age group represent less than 10 percent of the U.S. population. However, young drivers account for about 17 percent of all traffic deaths.

Lack of experience is a major factor in young drivers' poor driving records. Increased risk-taking, overexposure to night driving, and increased use of alcohol and other drugs also contribute to unfavorable driving records. However, many young people have proven they can be responsible drivers.

Fuel Conservation
Decreasing fuel supplies and higher prices have caused many drivers to decrease the amount they drive. Occasional fuel shortages have created long lines of motorists waiting to "fill up" at service stations.

The continuing focus on pollution and conservation of natural resources demands that you remember your responsibility to save fuel. You can learn driving habits that save fuel and also save you money.

Review It
1. How can your attitude affect your driving performance?
2. What are the financial responsibilities of driving?
3. What are some causes of collisions?
4. Why is it important to conserve fuel?

1–4   Driver Education and Responsible Driving

As you begin this course, you probably are thinking of the benefits a driver's license can bring you. You are eager to learn the facts and skills needed to earn your license.

A Beginning

A driver-education course can teach you a great deal about safe driving. Completing a driver-education course does not guarantee you will become a good driver. That is a decision you must make each time you drive. However, driver education can help you build a firm foundation of knowledge, attitudes, and skills for safe and energy-efficient driving. For example, these students are learning about a car's controls.

You learned that driving is a combination of decision-making, social, and physical tasks. In driver education you can learn thought processes that will help you drive responsibly and safely. You can learn to cope with traffic problems in various environments, during adverse weather conditions, and in different emergencies.

Some lessons will deal with your responsibility for protecting other roadway users and passengers in your car. Other lessons consider the importance of your physical and emotional conditions while driving. Facts about basic car control, maneuvers, and maintenance will be discussed. Information will be given about saving fuel, insuring a car, planning a trip, and exploring career opportunities.

A Continuous Process

Keep in mind that this course cannot teach you everything you will ever need to know about safe driving. As long as you drive, you will continue to learn. Advancements in automotive technology and changes in the HTS make driver education a continuous process.

Driver education can help establish a foundation for safe driving. It can open the door to a lifetime of safe, responsible, and enjoyable use of your vehicle.

Review It

1. What can you learn from driver education?
2. Why is driver education a continuous process?

Safe Driving Tips

Be a Fuel Saver

Advancements in Traffic Safety

An important objective of driver education is to keep drivers aware of issues that can directly affect their driving. Look in this location of each chapter for information on safe driving tips, traffic-safety advancements, and fuel-saving tips.

The information will relate to the chapter topics. In Chapter 10 on Highway Driving, for example, you will read tips on saving fuel during highway driving. Use this information to become a responsible driver in the highway transportation system.

Chapter Summary

1. The parts of the highway transportation system (HTS) are people, vehicles, and roadways. The purpose of the HTS is to help move people and goods safely, economically, and efficiently from one place to another (1–1)
2. Federal, state, and local agencies regulate the HTS. (1–1)
3. Driving is a combination of social, physical, and decision-making skills. You make decisions, carry out decisions, and interact and cooperate with other roadway users. (1–2)
4. The IPDE process has four steps: *identify* information from the driving scene; *predict* possible conflicts; *decide* on necessary, safe actions; *execute* the decision. (1–2)
5. Your attitude when driving determines whether you will seek attention through reckless actions, or earn the respect of others through mature, responsible driving. (1–3)
6. You are financially responsible for such driving-related costs as fuel, car maintenance, insurance, and any damage you might cause to other people and their property. (1–3)
7. Causes of HTS breakdowns include roadway repairs, adverse weather, and collisions. (1–3)
8. Fuel conservation is important because of fuel expense, decreasing supplies, and continuing focus on conserving natural resources and reducing pollution. (1–3)
9. Driver education can help build a firm foundation of knowledge and skills for safe, responsible, and fuel-efficient driving. (1–4)
10. Advancements in automotive technology and changes in the HTS make driver education a continuous process. (1–4)

Think About It

Study a newspaper report of a traffic collision. List the multiple causes that might have contributed to the collision.

Decision Making

You are driving and observe the traffic ahead as pictured in situations 1 and 2. For each picture, *identify* the possible problem. Then *predict* what might happen. Finally, *decide* what action you should take to keep the problem from becoming worse.

1.

2.

3. What might be the causes of this collision? What social and economic effects might this collision have on the drivers?

4. Why should this driver wait before driving?

Chapter 1 Test

Multiple Choice Copy the number of each sentence below on a sheet of paper. Choose the answer that best completes each statement.

1. The purpose of the highway transportation system (HTS) is to
   (a) create greater freedom for roadway users.
   (b) replace the railroad system. (c) move people and goods in a safe, efficient, and economical way. (d) compete with other transportation systems. (4)
2. You judge where possible points of conflict might occur in this step of the IPDE process:
   (a) identify. (b) predict. (c) decide. (d) execute. (7)
3. Most states require all drivers to be financially responsible so that they can
   (a) have a bank account. (b) pay for car repairs. (c) pay for any damage they cause to other people and their property. (d) borrow money to buy a car. (8)
4. The major cause of collisions is
   (a) driver error. (b) poor weather conditions.
   (c) vehicle defects. (d) roadway defects. (9)
5. Saving fuel is important because
   (a) fuel is expensive and supplies are decreasing. (b) beginning drivers waste more fuel.
   (c) many service stations have closed. (d) the U.S. must produce all of its own energy. (9)

Completion Copy the number of each sentence below. After each number, write the letter of the word or words that complete the sentence correctly.

6. The ____ is the group of laws that regulate the HTS. (5)
7. The driving task includes social skills, physical skills, and ____. (6)
8. A ____ is prepared to adjust for the mistakes of other roadway users. (7)
9. Your ____ is important in determining how safe a driver you will be. (8)

10. A better term to describe when a vehicle hits another object is ____ rather than *accident*. (8)
    a. attitude
    b. collision
    c. decision-making skills
    d. defensive driver
    e. financial responsibility
    f. vehicle code

Vocabulary Copy the number of each phrase below. Match the definition in List A with the term it defines in List B.

List A
11. people who use the HTS (4)
12. a complex system that includes people, vehicles, and roadways (4)
13. all the skilled actions you must take to drive safely (6)
14. the steps of the driving task (7)
15. locate potential hazards (7)
16. judge where possible conflicts can occur (7)
17. protecting yourself and others from dangerous and unexpected changes in the driving environment (7)
18. determine what actions to take and when to take them (7)
19. perform proper car control responses to avoid possible conflicts (7)
20. result of a vehicle hitting another object (8)

List B
a. collision
b. decide
c. defensive driving
d. driving task
e. execute
f. highway transportation system (HTS)
g. identify
h. IPDE process
i. predict
j. roadway users
k. vehicle code

Chapter 2
Basic Car Control

You're the Driver!

You are soon to become a driver like the person in this picture. Before you actually drive, you must understand how a car's controls and other devices operate. You also must know the procedures to follow when starting, moving, and stopping a car.

What should you check before entering the car?

Once in the car, what should you check before starting the engine?

Where is the odometer? What does it tell you?

Where is the horn?

Does the car have an automatic transmission or a manual transmission?

If the car has a manual transmission, what control is there that is not needed for an automatic transmission?

This chapter explains the instruments, devices, and controls on a car. You also will learn the procedures for starting, moving, and stopping both automatic transmission and manual transmission cars.

Objectives

2–1 *Instruments, Controls, and Devices*

1. Identify each gauge or warning light on an instrument panel and explain its function. (16)
2. Describe the function of each control used to operate a car. (18)
3. Explain the use of safety, communication, and comfort devices. (20)

2–2 *Getting Ready to Drive*

4. List in order the checks you should make when preparing to drive. (22)
5. Tell how to enter a car from the street side. (22)

2–3 *Driving a Car with Automatic Transmission*

6. Explain how to use each gear. (23)
7. Tell the correct procedures to start, move, and stop the car. (24)

8. Explain the correct way to leave a car from the street side. (27)

2–4 *Driving a Car with Manual Transmission*

9. List the procedures for starting, moving, and stopping a stick-shift car. (29)
10. Define downshifting. (30)

Instrument Panel

Before beginning to drive, you must know the location and operation of the car controls and devices for safety, comfort, and communication. You also must know what the warning lights and gauges tell you. Read the car owner's manual to learn the location and operation of the car's instruments, devices, and controls.

The location of the gauges and warning lights can vary from one car model to the next. No matter where the gauges and warning lights are located, their purposes are the same. You can make sure warning lights are working if they light when the ignition switch is turned to "On."

This instrument panel is one example of the location of the gauges and warning lights in a car. The numbers on the picture above correspond to the gauges and lights explained on this and the following pages.

Safety-Belt Light (1) When you turn the key, the safety-belt light comes on to remind occupants to fasten their safety belts. On many cars, the light remains on for a few seconds when the engine is started, even if belts are fastened.

Speedometer (2) This instrument tells how fast the car is traveling. Speed is indicated in both miles per hour and kilometers per hour.

Odometer (3) The *odometer* is usually located near the speedometer. The odometer shows the total number of miles the car has been driven. Some cars have separate trip odometers that can be set back to zero to record the number of miles driven during a period of time.

Fuel Gauge (4) The fuel gauge shows the amount of fuel in the tank. Never let the fuel tank get below one-quarter full; you risk running out of fuel.

Try to keep the tank at least half full in cold weather to help prevent fuel-line freeze. This problem can occur when moisture condenses and freezes inside the tank and fuel line. Ice particles can block the fuel line and stop the fuel flow.

Temperature Light or Gauge (5) This light or gauge warns you if the coolant in the engine gets too hot. If overheating occurs, stop at the nearest safe place. Turn off the engine, and wait for it to cool. Have the cooling system checked as soon as possible.

Oil-Pressure Warning Light or Gauge (6) This light or gauge warns you when the engine oil is not circulating at the right pressure. However, it does not tell you the amount of oil in the engine. Use the oil dipstick to check the engine's oil level.

Stop immediately if the light or gauge indicates trouble. Losing oil pressure can cause serious and expensive damage to your car's engine. Have the system checked before you continue.

Alternator Warning Light or Gauge (7) Your car's electrical system is in trouble if this light comes on or the gauge shows "discharge." The alternator is not making enough electricity to run the car. If too little electricity is being made, the engine must use stored electricity from the battery.

The *alternator warning light* or gauge warns that the battery is being used. The more electricity used, the sooner the battery will be dead. Turn off as many electrical devices as possible, and have the system checked without delay.

Brake-System Warning Light (8) The brake-system warning light serves two purposes. First, the light reminds you to release the parking brake before moving the car. Second, should the light come on while you are pressing the foot brake, it means that part or all of the brake system is not working properly. If this light turns on, slow down, brake gradually to a stop, and have the car towed. Do not drive the car until the problem has been corrected.

Turn-Signal Indicators (9) These indicators are usually two small green arrows, each of which flashes to show the direction of the turn. The indicators will stop flashing automatically when the turn signal is cancelled.

High-Beam Indicator (10) This light glows when the high-beam headlights are on. The light is off when you are using only low-beam headlights.

Car Controls

The characteristics and locations of car controls often vary from one car model to another. However, each control performs the same function in all cars. The numbers in the pictures on pages 18–20 match the controls explained.

Steering Wheel (11) The steering wheel controls the direction of the front wheels. The car moves right when you turn the wheel right. The car moves left when you turn the wheel left. The car's response to these turns is the same when moving forward and backward.

Some cars have adjustable steering wheels for better comfort and control. Many cars are equipped with power steering, an option that makes the steering wheel easier to turn. If the engine stalls in a car equipped

with power steering, you can still steer, but will have to use more effort to do so.

Selector Lever (12) In a car with automatic transmission, move the *selector lever* to choose forward or reverse gears. This control is located on the steering column, as shown in the picture, or on the floor to the right of the driver's seat.

Gear-Shift Lever (13) In a car with manual transmission, shift gears by moving the shift lever to the desired position. This lever usually is located on the floor to the right of the driver. In some cars, it is located on the steering column.

Ignition and Starter Switch (14-15-16-17-18) This switch is usually located on the steering

column. The picture above shows all the positions. Get ready to start the engine by putting the key into the *ignition switch*. Turn the key to the right one notch, to the "On" (15) position. The warning lights should light, and the fuel gauge will register. Turn to the "Start" (16) position to start the engine. When the switch is turned backwards to "Lock" (17), both the shift lever and steering wheel are locked and the key can be removed. Turn to "Lock" only when the selector lever is in PARK. Turn the key to "Accessory" (18) to

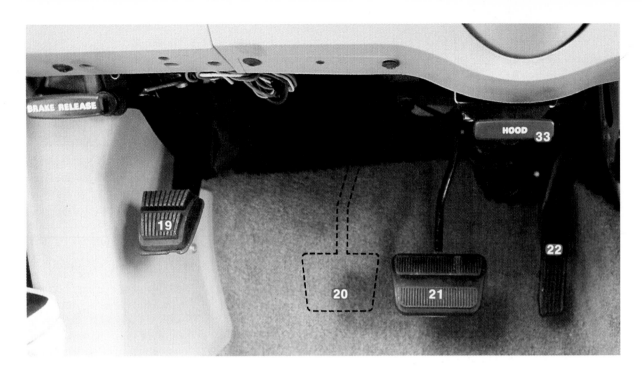

operate the radio and other electrical equipment without running the engine.

Parking Brake (19) The *parking brake* keeps the car in place when it is parked. If the foot brake fails while driving, use the parking brake to slow the car.

The parking-brake pedal is located on the far left in many cars. Push down on the pedal to set the parking brake. Pull the parking-brake release lever on the left side under the instrument panel to release the parking brake.

In other cars, the parking brake is a lever located on the floor to the right of the driver's seat. Pull the lever up to set the parking brake. Push the button at the tip of the lever, and lower the lever to release the brake.

Clutch Pedal (20) In a stick-shift car, the *clutch pedal* is to the left of the foot-brake pedal. Pushing this pedal down lets you shift gears.

Foot-Brake Pedal (21) Pushing down on the *foot-brake pedal* slows or stops the car. Pumping this pedal also turns on the brake lights in the back of the car. Tapping the pedal lightly makes the brake lights flash without slowing the car.

Power brakes reduce the physical effort you must make to stop the car. However, power brakes do not shorten your stopping distance.

Accelerator Pedal (22) The *accelerator* controls the speed of the car. The accelerator pedal is located to the right of the foot-brake pedal. Pushing the

accelerator pedal down increases speed; releasing it slows the car.

The accelerator pedal also activates the *automatic choke* in many cars. The choke adjusts how much air enters the engine when starting the car. A closed choke reduces the amount of air, making it easier to start the car when the engine is cold. To close the choke, press the accelerator pedal to the floor once, then release it. After the engine has warmed up, tap the accelerator to open the choke and reduce engine speed. Cars with fuel-injection engines do not have automatic chokes.

Caution: Closing the automatic choke when the engine is warm can make starting difficult.

Devices for Safety, Communication, and Comfort

These devices are located where you can easily reach them. Locate and understand the operation of the following devices on any car you drive.

Safety Belts (23) A properly fitted safety belt helps keep the wearer from:

► being thrown from the car during a sudden stop or collision.
► hitting a part of the car during a sudden stop or collision.

Fasten your safety belt to a snug fit before starting the engine. Some states now require drivers and front-seat passengers to wear safety belts.

Passive Restraints The term *passive restraint* describes a safety device that works without any action by the car occupants. The automatic safety belt is one type of passive restraint. This belt is connected from the door to the center of the car.

The air bag is a second type of passive restraint. In a collision, air bags inflate on impact in front of the driver and front passengers.

Head Restraints (24) Most cars have *head restraints,* padded devices on the backs of front seats. Head restraints help reduce whiplash injuries if your car is struck from the rear.

Inside and Outside Rearview Mirrors (25-26) The inside mirror (25) shows you the view through the rear window. The left outside mirror (26) shows a view of the roadway to the left and rear of your car. Each area that the mirrors cannot show is a *blind spot*. The dark areas in the picture below are blind-spot areas. Glance over both shoulders to check these areas before changing lanes.

Windshield Wipers and Washers (27) One switch usually operates both the wiper and the washer to clean the outside of the windshield. A container under the hood of the car holds windshield-washing solution or water. Use a windshield antifreeze solution in winter to prevent freezing.

Emergency Flasher Control (28) This switch usually is located on the instrument panel or the steering column. When the *emergency flasher* is on, both front and rear turn-signal lights flash at the same time. These lights warn others that your vehicle is a hazard or that you are in trouble.

Light Switch (29) The light switch is usually a knob on the left side of the instrument panel. In some cars, the light switch might be at the end of the turn-signal lever.

This device controls headlights, taillights, parking lights, and side-marker lights. It also controls instrument panel, license plate, and dome lights. Pull the knob one notch to light the parking and side-marker lights. Pull the knob to the second notch to light the headlights. All other lights, except the dome light, are on in both positions. In most cars, turn the knob to control both the dome light and the instrument panel light.

Turn-Signal Lever (30) This lever is on the left side of the steering column. Move the lever up to signal a right turn and down to signal a left turn. The turn signal stops flashing after a turn when the steering wheel is straightened. You might have to cancel a signal manually if a turn is slight. Hold the lever up or down lightly to signal a lane change.

Dimmer Switch (30) On many cars, you change the headlights from low to high beam by moving the turn-signal lever toward the steering wheel. On other cars, the switch is a floor button.

Cruise Control (31) Use the *cruise control* to set the car's speed for highway or expressway driving. This optional device is usually a button on the end of the turn-signal lever or on the steering wheel. When cruise control is set, you can remove your foot from the accelerator pedal; the car's speed will stay constant. Tap the foot-brake pedal lightly to cancel cruise control.

Use cruise control with caution. It reduces the amount of control you have over speed adjustment and might lull you into a false sense of security.

Horn (32) The horn usually is located on the steering wheel. Know how to use the horn on each car you drive as to not hunt for it in an emergency.

Hood Release Lever (33) Many cars have a *hood release* lever under the instrument panel. Pull the lever to release the hood lock. This lever might be located near the parking-brake release lever. Be careful not to pull the wrong lever when releasing the parking brake.

Heater, Air Conditioner, and Defroster (34) The heating and air-conditioning systems warm or cool the inside of the car. The defroster helps keep the inside of the windshield, side windows, and rear window free of moisture. Many cars have a separate switch for a rear-window defroster.

Sun Visor The sun visor is located above the windshield. When pulled down, it helps cut glare so you can see better.

Seat Adjustment Lever The seat adjustment lever is usually at the lower front or left side of the driver's seat. In cars with bucket seats, both front seats have an adjustment lever. Adjust the seat so you are in a comfortable position.

Review It

1. What warning does the temperature gauge or light provide?
2. What action should you take if the oil-pressure warning light or gauge indicates trouble?
3. How can you check for cars in blind-spot areas?

Follow certain procedures before you enter a car to drive. Begin by checking both the outside and inside of the car before driving. The procedures for getting ready to drive are given below. Develop a habit by practicing the procedures in the same order every time you get ready to drive.

Outside Checks

1. Walk around you car and make a "circle check." Look for objects around the car and in the path you intend to take.
2. Glance at the tires to see they are inflated properly.
3. Make sure that the windshield, windows, headlights, and taillights are clean.
4. Check the back window ledge for loose objects. Remove them before driving.

Getting into the Car

1. Whenever possible, enter the car from the curb side. You lessen your risk of being struck by another vehicle.
2. If you enter from the street side, have your keys in your hand. Avoid searching for them as you stand near oncoming traffic. Walk around the front of the car as the driver in the first picture is doing. You then face oncoming vehicles and reduce your risk of being hit. Do not open the door if an oncoming vehicle is near.
3. Get in quickly and close the door.

Inside Checks

1. Lock all doors.
2. Put the key in the ignition switch. Sit with your back firmly against the seat.

3. Reach for the accelerator and brake pedals with your foot to judge a comfortable distance.
4. Move the seat forward or backward so you are within comfortable reach of all controls and devices.
5. Adjust the head restraint to reach the middle of the back of your head.
6. Adjust the inside rearview mirror so it reflects the area to the rear.
7. Adjust the outside rearview mirror so you can see the area to the left and rear of the car.
8. Fasten your safety belt as the driver above is doing. Ask all passengers to fasten theirs.

Review It

1. What are three outside checks to make before entering the car?
2. Why should you walk around the front of the car when entering from the street side?

Learning the steps for starting, moving, and stopping an automatic transmission car is not difficult. Practice each step in the correct order so that the procedures become a habit.

Selector Lever Positions

The *shift indicator* shows the gear positions. It is located on the steering column, on the instrument panel, or by the floor selector lever. The shift indicator in the picture above shows the car is in PARK. The picture to the left shows a floor-mounted lever. The indicator shows the car is in DRIVE.

Park (P)   This gear position locks the transmission. Always shift to PARK when you stop driving. Never shift to PARK when the car is moving. You can remove the key from the ignition only when the lever is in PARK.

Reverse (R)   Use this gear for backing. Never shift to REVERSE while the car is moving forward. Expensive damage to the transmission can result.

When you shift to REVERSE, the back-up lights turn on. These lights warn others that you are backing. At night, back-up lights help you see where you are backing.

Neutral (N)   This position allows the wheels to roll. Shift to NEUTRAL when you are stopped in traffic for more than a few minutes. If the engine stalls while the car is moving, shift to NEUTRAL (not PARK) to restart the engine.

Drive (D)   This position is for normal forward driving.

Low (L^1 and L^2, or 1 and 2) Both LOW positions are for slow, hard pulling and for going up or down steep hills. LOW^2 also is used when driving in snow. Use LOW^1 when going up or down extremely steep grades and when pulling very heavy loads.

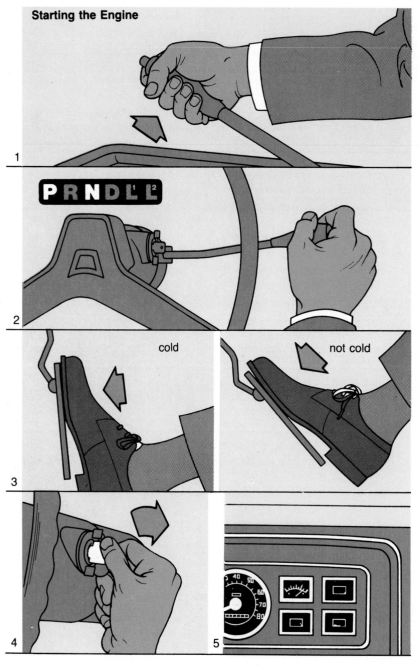

Starting the Engine

Starting the Engine

Use this procedure to start the engine. These pictures correspond to the steps.

1. Make sure the parking brake is set.
2. Make sure the selector lever is in PARK or NEUTRAL.
3. If the engine is cold, use your right foot to press the accelerator to the floor *once* to set the automatic choke. If the engine is not cold, simply press the accelerator lightly and hold it. (Check this procedure in your car owner's manual. The starting procedure for an engine with fuel injection differs from this starting procedure for an engine with a carburetor.)
4. Turn ignition switch to "On." Continue turning key forward to start the engine. Release key as soon as engine starts.
5. With the engine running, check the gauges. Check the fuel supply. Make sure that the electrical and oil-pressure systems are working properly.

Caution: Never try to start the engine when it is already running. Expensive damage to the starter can result. If the engine has not started, the alternator light will be red, or the gauge will show "discharge." Press lightly on the accelerator to check whether or not the engine is running.

Steering the Car

Several factors contribute to proper steering of a car. Tracking and hand positions are two important factors.

Hand Positions Firmly grip the wheel on each side in a balanced position. Imagine the steering wheel is the face of a clock, as shown here. One balanced position for steering control is at the 10 and 2 o'clock position. Some drivers prefer the 9 and 3 o'clock position. Regardless of your hand position, always keep the knuckles of your hands outside the rim of the wheel. Notice the driver's hands and relaxed arm positions in the picture.

Tracking Steering a car in its intended path of travel is called *tracking*. Look well down the road ahead of you.

Make only small turns of the wheel in order to track. Beginning drivers often overcorrect steering errors by turning the wheel too much. Avoid watching the steering wheel or a hood or fender ornament as a tracking guide. Once you know how to make steering adjustments, you will make them automatically. You then can concentrate on the total driving task.

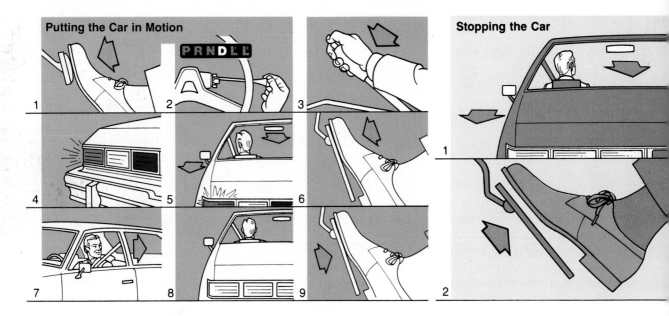

Putting the Car in Motion

After starting the engine, follow this procedure to move the car. Each numbered step is pictured above.

1. With the engine idling in PARK, press down the foot-brake pedal.
2. Move the selector lever to DRIVE.
3. Release the parking brake while continuing to hold the foot-brake pedal down.
4. If you are going to move away from the curb, use the turn signal to alert other drivers.
5. Check for traffic ahead and in both rearview mirrors. Glance over your left shoulder. See if any vehicle is approaching from the rear.
6. When the street is clear, press gently on the accelerator.
7. Quickly check again over your left shoulder for traffic.
8. Cancel the signal, if necessary.
9. As you reach your desired speed, let up a little on the accelerator. Adjust your speed to traffic conditions.

Caution: Always press down on the foot-brake pedal and come to a full stop before shifting to any gear. This action keeps your car from moving before you are ready.

Stopping the Car

The center pictures above show the numbered steps to follow when stopping your car:

1. Check traffic in both mirrors before slowing down.
2. Let up on the accelerator.
3. Tap foot brake lightly to signal for a stop.
4. Push down gradually and firmly on the foot-brake pedal. Ease up slightly on the brake pedal just before stopping. This action helps you make a smoother stop. Leave the selector lever in DRIVE if you plan to start moving again immediately. Otherwise, shift to PARK.

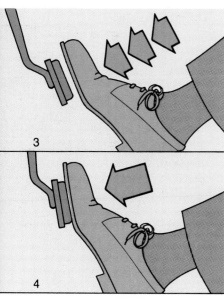

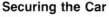

Securing the Car

This procedure for securing the car applies to cars with either automatic or manual transmissions. The numbered pictures correspond to the steps:

1. Once you have stopped, continue to keep pressure on the foot brake.
2. Shift to PARK in an automatic or to REVERSE in a stickshift.
3. Set the parking brake, and turn off all accessories.
4. Turn off the ignition switch, and remove the key. Release the foot brake.
5. Unfasten your safety belt.
6. Close the windows, and lock all doors except yours.

Leaving the Car

Leave the car from the curb side whenever possible. You avoid the risk of opening the door into moving traffic.

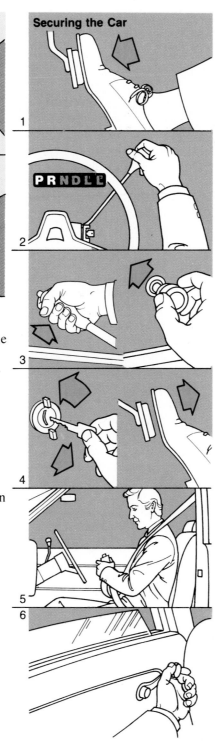

Securing the Car

If you do get out on the street side, follow these steps:
1. Check both inside and outside mirrors.
2. Glance over your left shoulder for approaching traffic before opening the door.
3. Make sure you have the keys in your hand so you do not lock them inside the car.
4. When it is safe, open the door and get out quickly.
5. Lock the door. Walk around the rear of the car to the curb as shown above. You then face approaching traffic and reduce your risk of being hit.

Review It

1. What is the purpose of each gear in an automatic transmission?
2. What are the correct procedures for moving and stopping the car?
3. What should you do immediately after you turn off the ignition? Why should you leave the car from the curb side if possible?

2–4 Driving a Car with Manual Transmission

Learning to drive a car with manual (stickshift) transmission is not difficult. You must learn to coordinate the clutch, accelerator, and gear-shift lever.

Selector Lever Positions

Most stickshift cars have either a four-speed or a five-speed shift pattern. REVERSE is usually in the upper left corner, or in the lower left or right corner. Note the typical patterns of gear positions for four- and five-speed transmissions shown here.

Fourth gear is used for highway driving, and fifth gear for higher speeds. These gears save fuel because they take less power to keep the car moving.

Using Stickshift Gears

Neutral (N) This position is the crossbar of the pattern. Have your car in this gear when standing still or when starting the engine.

First (1) Use FIRST gear to start the car moving up to a forward speed of 10 to 15 mph. Use FIRST gear also to pull very heavy loads and drive up or down very steep hills.

Second (2) Use SECOND gear to bring the car up to a forward speed of 15 to 25 mph. Use SECOND gear also for hills or driving on snow or ice.

Third (3) Use THIRD gear to accelerate to speeds in the range of 25 to 35 or 40 mph.

Fourth (4) In a four-speed transmission, use FOURTH gear for highway driving. Shift to

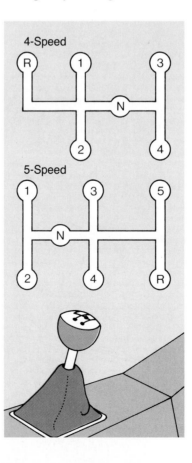

FOURTH gear at speeds of 35 to 40 mph.

Fifth (5) In a five-speed transmission, use FIFTH gear to drive at higher speeds on level roadways.

Reverse (R) Use the REVERSE gear for backing. Never shift to REVERSE while the car is moving forward. Expensive damage to the transmission can result.

Using the Clutch

Always press the clutch pedal to the floor before starting the engine, before shifting, or before coming to a stop. Shift smoothly from one position to the next. The speeds given here for shifting are only guidelines. Read your car owner's manual; transmissions vary greatly.

Caution: The term *riding the clutch* means resting your left foot on the clutch pedal while driving. This practice causes needless clutch wear.

Starting the Engine

Follow these steps to start a car with manual transmission:

1. Be sure parking brake is set.
2. Press clutch pedal to the floor with your left foot.
3. Put gear-shift lever in NEUTRAL.
4. Depress accelerator part way and hold. (Set choke if engine is cold.)
5. Turn on ignition switch, and check warning lights.
6. Turn key forward until engine starts, and then release.
7. Check gauges.

Putting the Car in Motion

Once the engine is running, use these steps to put the car in motion. Each numbered step is pictured here.

1. Press clutch pedal to the floor.
2. Move gear-shift lever to FIRST.
3. Depress foot brake, and release the parking brake.
4. Check traffic in both mirrors, and signal to leave the curb.
5. Check traffic ahead, and in rearview mirrors. Check to the rear by glancing over your left shoulder.
6. If the road is clear, accelerate gently and gradually and release clutch slowly. Releasing the clutch suddenly causes the car to jerk forward. The engine can stall. The point where the engine takes hold and the car starts to move is called the *friction point*.

7. Hold the clutch momentarily at the friction point.
8. Continue gradual acceleration, and let the clutch up all the way.

Shifting from First to Second

At about 10 to 15 mph follow these steps to shift from FIRST to SECOND:

1. Press the clutch down.
2. Release the accelerator.

3. Move gear-shift lever to SECOND. Pause slightly as you go across NEUTRAL into SECOND. This action helps you shift smoothly.
4. Accelerate gently as you slowly release the clutch. Hesitate briefly at the friction point.

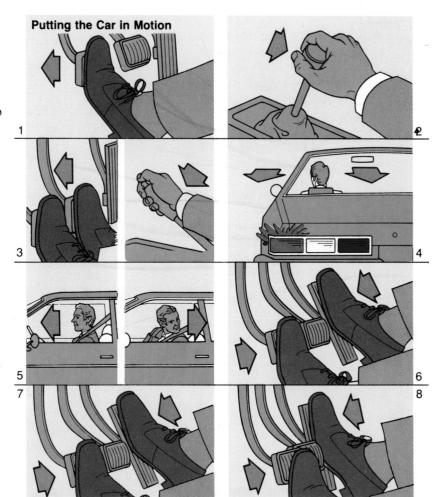

Putting the Car in Motion

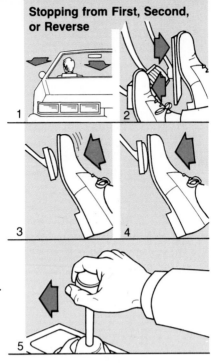

Stopping from First, Second, or Reverse

Stopping from First, Second, or Reverse

The first set of pictures corresponds to these steps:

1. Check traffic in mirrors.
2. Press the clutch pedal down while releasing accelerator.
3. Tap the brake pedal lightly to signal for a stop.
4. Press the foot brake gently.
5. Shift to NEUTRAL when stopped.

Shifting to Third, Fourth, and Fifth

Once you have accelerated to the higher speed ranges described on page 28, follow these steps to shift gears:

1. Press the clutch down.
2. Release the accelerator.
3. Shift to the desired gear.
4. Accelerate gradually while releasing the clutch smoothly.

Stopping from Higher Gears

When stopping from THIRD, FOURTH, or FIFTH, first use the brake to slow down before depressing the clutch. The engine helps slow the car. The second set of pictures corresponds to these steps:

1. Check the mirrors for traffic.
2. Let up on the accelerator.
3. Tap the brake lightly to signal for a stop.
4. Brake gradually to about 15 to 20 mph.
5. Press the clutch pedal down.
6. Brake to a smooth stop.
7. Shift to NEUTRAL when stopped.

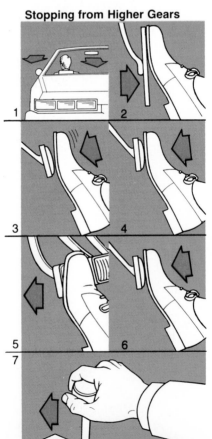

Stopping from Higher Gears

Downshifting

The term *downshifting* means shifting from a higher to a lower gear. The engine has greater pulling power in lower gears than in higher ones. If you have slowed to around 30 mph in FOURTH gear, you must downshift to THIRD in order to regain speed. Follow these steps to downshift:

1. Depress the clutch and shift to THIRD. Accelerate gradually while releasing the clutch smoothly.
2. Accelerate to 35 or 40 mph. Depress the clutch, and shift back to FOURTH.

You can downshift for added control, as when slowing before a sharp turn. However, be sure to complete the downshift before starting the turn. You also can downshift to gain extra pulling power when climbing long or steep hills. Use a lower gear to go down long or steep hills to save wear on the brakes. The engine helps slow the car. Let the clutch out after every downshift.

Review It

1. What are the steps for starting the engine and moving the car in FIRST gear?
2. What is the difference between the procedures for stopping from lower gears and stopping from higher gears?

Advancements in Traffic Safety

Automotive engineers work to make cars safer for drivers and passengers. One new safety device is a third brake light. This red light is positioned inside or outside at the center of the rear window. When you tap the foot-brake pedal, this third brake light shines at the same time the regular brake lights do.

This higher, center light serves as an "attention getter" for drivers behind because of the light's eye-level position. Traffic-safety engineers consider this brake light an effective device to help reduce the number of rear-end collisions.

Chapter Summary

1. Each gauge on the instrument panel gives important information about how your car is operating. Check the gauges and warning lights often. (2–1)
2. Car controls enable you to operate your car safely and efficiently. (2–1)
3. Other devices such as safety belts, mirrors, and lights provide safety, communication, and comfort for a car's driver and occupants. (2–1)
4. Make all outside checks before entering your car. Enter your car safely, and then make all inside checks. (2–2)
5. Walk around the front of your car to enter from the street side. This practice lets you see traffic approaching from the rear. (2–2)
6. PARK holds the car when stopped. REVERSE backs the car. NEUTRAL lets wheels roll. DRIVE is for normal forward driving. LOW is for harder pulling. (2–3)
7. Learn the correct procedures for starting, moving, and stopping a car with automatic transmission. With practice, each of these procedures will become a habit. (2–3)
8. Walk around behind the car when leaving from the street side. This practice lets you see traffic approaching from the rear. (2–3)
9. To start, move, and stop a stickshift car in FIRST gear, first check traffic. Use the clutch, the accelerator, and brake pedal. Signal, and then shift. Learn the procedures in correct order to that they become a habit. (2–4)
10. Use downshifting for added control and for extra pulling power when climbing long, steep hills. (2–4)

Think About It

1. What steps can help a driver track in a straight line?
2. Why is fastening the safety belt the last step of the inside checks, before starting the engine?

Decision Making

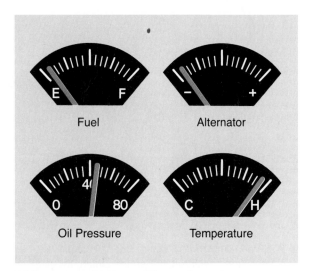

Fuel   Alternator

Oil Pressure Temperature

1. While you are driving at different times, four gauges on your instrument panel might look like the pictures above. What does each gauge indicate? What problems might you have? What should you do?

2. This driver is going to enter the car and drive. Identify the incorrect procedure the driver is following. Explain why the procedure is unsafe. What error should the driver correct? What safety checks should the driver make?

3. What step did this driver forget while getting ready to drive? Why was this error serious? What steering problems might this driver have? How could the driver achieve more controlled steering?

4. You are preparing to turn this very sharp corner. You are driving a four-speed car in FOURTH. What should you do before entering the turn? Describe the procedure you would use.

Chapter 2 Test

Multiple Choice Copy the number of each question below on a sheet of paper. Choose the letter that best answers each question.

1. If an automatic-transmission car stalls during driving, what must you do to restart it?
   (a) shift to NEUTRAL   (b) shift to LOW   (c) get a jump-start   (d) set the automatic choke   (23)
2. How do you know the engine is on?
   (a) check the exhaust pipe   (b) try to drive
   (c) turn on the radio   (d) press lightly on accelerator   (24)
3. What should you do in a car with automatic transmission just before shifting to DRIVE?
   (a) fasten your safety belt   (b) press down on the foot-brake pedal   (c) engage the clutch
   (d) check fuel gauge   (26)
4. Which way should you walk around a car when getting out on the street side?
   (a) toward the front of the car   (b) either way
   (c) toward the rear of the car   (d) neither way   (27)
5. When stopping from FOURTH in a stickshift car, which pedal do you press first?
   (a) clutch pedal   (b) accelerator   (c) foot-brake pedal   (d) dimmer switch   (30)

Completion Copy the number of each sentence below. After each number, write the letter of the word or words that complete the sentence correctly.

6. Use the ____ to choose forward or reverse gears in an automatic-transmission car.   (18)
7. An air bag is an example of a ____.   (20)
8. When the ____ is set, you can remove your foot from the accelerator; car speed will stay constant.   (21)
9. Steering a car in its intended path of travel is called ____.   (25)
10. When stopping from REVERSE in a stickshift car, depress the ____ first.   (30)

a. brake pedal
b. clutch pedal
c. cruise control
d. passive restraint
e. selector lever
f. tracking

Vocabulary Copy the number of each phrase below. Match the definition in List A with the term it defines in List B.

List A
11. shows miles driven   (17)
12. indicates trouble in electrical system   (17)
13. operated by a key to start the engine   (18)
14. keeps car in place while parked   (19)
15. controls amount of air to engine when starting the car   (19)
16. pedal that controls speed of car   (19)
17. pedal that slows or stops the car   (19)
18. area not shown in rearview mirrors   (20)
19. padded supports that help reduce whiplash injuries   (20)
20. lever that unlocks hood of car   (21)
21. warns that vehicle is a hazard   (21)
22. device that shows the different driving gears and the gear being used   (23)
23. driving with foot resting on clutch pedal   (28)
24. point where engine begins to move a stickshift car   (29)
25. shifting from a higher to a lower gear   (30)

List B
a. accelerator
b. alternator warning light
c. automatic choke
d. blind spot
e. downshifting
f. emergency flasher
g. foot-brake pedal
h. friction point
i. head restraints
j. hood release
k. ignition switch
l. odometer
m. parking brake
n. riding the clutch
o. seat adjustment
p. shift indicator

Chapter 3
Signs, Signals, and Roadway Markings

You're the Driver!

Driving would be next to impossible without signs, signals, and roadway markings. These controls help traffic to flow smoothly.

Imagine that you are driving on the street shown here. The red traffic light is about to turn green. You want to continue straight ahead.

Have you stopped at the right place?

Are you in the best lane to continue straight?

Will you have to stop for other vehicles that intend to turn?

How might pedestrians create a problem for drivers?

What is the purpose of the two white parallel lines in front of you?

Do these traffic lights have a special signal for drivers turning left?

To be a safe driver, you must know what signs, signals, and roadway markings mean. This chapter discusses these controls and how to respond to them.

Objectives

3-1 Traffic Signs

1. Explain the meaning of the eight shapes and eight colors used for traffic signs. (36)
2. Describe the actions to take at STOP, YIELD, and speed-limit signs. (36)
3. List five situations where warning signs might be used. (39)
4. Explain how guide signs and international signs help you when driving. (41)

3-2 Traffic Signals

5. Describe what to do at a red light, a yellow light, and a green light. (43)
6. Describe the action to take when you approach a flashing red signal or a flashing yellow signal. (44)
7. Explain how arrows and lane signals control traffic. (45)
8. Describe the actions to take with pedestrian signals and officer's signals. (46)

3-3 Roadway Markings

9. Describe the difference between broken yellow lines and broken white lines. (47)
10. Explain the purpose of rumble strips and raised roadway markers. (49)
11. List six types of special roadway markings. (50)

3–1 Traffic Signs

Shapes

Octagon:
Stop

Triangle:
Yield

Vertical Rectangle:
Regulatory

Pentagon:
School

Round:
Railroad Crossing

Pennant:
No Passing

Diamond:
Warning

Horizontal Rectangle:
Guide

You will see hundreds of different traffic signs while driving. While traffic signs serve many purposes, each traffic sign has a specific color and shape.

Colors and Shapes

Note the eight sign colors and eight sign shapes shown here. Each color and sign shape has a special meaning. By knowing the meaning of these colors and shapes, you can tell the meaning of a sign at a distance.

Each traffic sign has a specific purpose. A *regulatory sign,* such as a STOP sign, controls traffic. A *warning sign* alerts you to possible hazards and road conditions. A *guide sign* gives directions.

Regulatory Signs

Regulatory signs tell you about laws that you must obey. These signs usually are white squares or rectangles with red or black lettering. Some regulatory signs, such as STOP and YIELD signs, have unique shapes.

Stop Sign   A STOP sign is used on a road that crosses a main highway or a through street. The STOP sign is a red octagon with white letters.

Colors

Red:
Stop, yield, or prohibited

Yellow:
Warning

White:
Regulatory

Orange:
Construction or detour

Black:
Regulatory

Green:
Guide

Blue:
Motorist service

Brown:
Public recreation and cultural interest

Always come to a *full stop* at a STOP sign. Once stopped, always yield the right of way to pedestrians or other vehicles in or approaching an intersection. To *yield* means to allow others to use an intersection before you do. Using the *right of way* means you accept the privilege of immediate use of the roadway. If another driver must slow or stop after you leave a STOP sign, then you have not yielded the right of way.

The location of a STOP sign or stop line helps you decide where to stop. If there is only a STOP sign, stop before entering the intersection. Stop where you can see approaching traffic, but stop before you reach any crosswalk. The lower left picture shows where to stop when a stop line is present. Stop just behind the stop line and before entering a crosswalk.

If you cannot see cross traffic clearly after stopping, as shown in the lower right picture, move ahead slowly and stop again. Make sure the way is clear before driving into the intersection.

At some intersections, STOP signs are posted at all four corners. Each STOP sign might be posted with a small sign that says "4-way." Follow these steps at a 4-way stop:

1. The driver who stopped first should be allowed to go first.
2. When cars at right angles stop at the same time, the driver on the right should be allowed to go first.
3. Signal your intention to proceed by moving forward slowly before entering the intersection.
4. Keep looking for traffic to the left and right while driving through the intersection.

Yield Sign Always slow or stop, and give the right of way to cross traffic when approaching a red and white triangular YIELD sign. Proceed through the intersection when it is safe to do so.

Car colors in traffic model photographs represent:
Yellow: action car
White: other cars in motion
Blue: parked cars

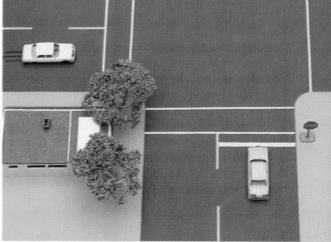

Speed Limit Signs The speed limit sign pictured below is designed to restrict travel to safe speeds. Collisions and fuel consumption have been reduced as a result of setting 55 mph as the maximum speed limit in some areas.

Speed limits are set for ideal conditions. When traffic, roadway, or weather conditions are not ideal, you must obey the *basic speed law*. This law states that you may not drive faster than is safe for existing conditions, regardless of posted speed limits.

A *minimum speed limit* is set on some roadways, such as highways and expressways. This speed limit tells you not to drive slower than the given speed unless conditions are bad. If conditions are bad, follow the basic speed law and drive slower than the minimum speed limit.

Advisory speed limits are set for special conditions such as sharp curves. In some areas, special speed limits are set for different times of the day. For example, school zones have special speed limits during school hours.

Turns and Lanes

One Way

Parking and Passing

Pedestrians and Trucks

Other Regulatory Signs Look at the signs to the left. These signs are used to:
- ► direct traffic to turn or go straight.
- ► direct one-way traffic.
- ► control parking and passing.
- ► restrict pedestrians or truck traffic.

Red-lettered words on a white sign usually tell what *not* to do. Black-lettered words usually tell what you *can* do. Some signs have a black symbol in a red circle and crossed by a red, diagonal slash. The red circle and bar indicate that a certain action is prohibited.

Warning Signs

A warning sign helps you avoid surprise situations. Most warning signs are diamond-shaped. Warning signs have black symbols or lettering on a yellow or orange background.

Diamond-Shaped Warning Signs Yellow, diamond-shaped signs such as these warn you of a danger ahead. Be prepared to slow or stop when you see a warning sign.

Side Road (left)

Divided Highway

Road Narrows (from right)

Handicapped Crossing

Left Curve

Pedestrian Crossing

Signal Ahead

Cross Road

Two Way Traffic

Hill

Divided Highway Ends

Fire Station

Slippery When Wet

Deer Crossing

Equestrian Crossing

Farm Machinery Crossing

Merging Traffic (from right)

Low Clearance

School Signs A school zone sign, showing two children, is posted within a block of a school. A school crossing sign shows children in a crosswalk area. This sign is posted near intersections or crossings used by children. Notice the difference between these two signs shown below.

Use extra care in a *school zone*. Children might dart out into the street without looking. They might ride bicycles on the wrong side of the street or take other unexpected actions. Be ready to obey a crossing guard's directions in a school zone.

School Zone   School Crossing

No-Passing Signs A yellow, pennant-shaped sign with black letters, as shown below, can be posted on the *left* side of the roadway. The sign appears at the start of a no-passing zone and shows you at a distance where a no-passing zone starts. A no-passing sign is used together with a solid yellow line on the roadway. If you intend to pass, you must complete your pass before reaching this sign.

Railroad Signs This round, yellow sign, with a black X and two R's, warns that you are approaching a railroad crossing. Look at the railroad sign below. This sign is posted about 250 feet before a railroad crossing in a city. It is posted about 750 feet before a railroad crossing in a rural area. Note the white crossbuck sign that is posted at all railroad crossings. Flashing red lights and crossing gates might be added to alert you when a train is coming.

Construction Signs Orange, diamond-shaped or rectangular signs alert you to construction zones. Orange, triangular warning signs might be used on a construction vehicle to warn that the vehicle is slow moving. Be alert in a construction zone, such as the one in the top left picture. Be ready to slow, stop, or drive around workers and trucks. Follow the directions from any worker directing traffic.

Guide Signs

A guide sign provides information. Guide signs highlight routes, intersections, service areas, and other points of interest or information.

Route Signs   Local, state, national, and interstate routes are posted with route signs. Notice below how route signs vary according to the type of roadway. All the signs tell you about route numbers. Notice in the picture to the right how route signs can be combined with information about a city's streets. Use this information to plan ahead and adjust your route as needed.

Interstate routes have red, white, and blue route signs. Notice to the right how a special numbering system is used for interstate routes. Study the illustrations to learn this numbering system.

U.S. Route Marker

State Route Marker

County Route Marker

Interstate Route Marker

An east-west route is even numbered. A north-south route is odd numbered.

A three-figured route that starts with an odd number leads into a city.

A three-figured route that starts with an even number goes around a city.

Other Guide Signs   You will see a wide variety of guide signs in addition to route signs. Note below that green signs provide information on destinations ahead and distances to be traveled. Blue signs highlight highway services such as fuel, food, lodging, and nearby hospitals. Brown signs direct you to recreation areas or cultural points of interest.

International Signs

These international signs tell their messages with symbols rather than words. Drivers who travel from country to country can read these signs without learning several languages. The United States has adopted several *international symbols* for use in highway signs. More and more of these symbols will be used as international travel increases.

Review It

1. What do the eight shapes and eight colors of traffic signs stand for?
2. What actions should you take at STOP, YIELD, and speed-limit signs?
3. What are five situations where warning signs might be used?
4. What information do guide signs and international signs provide?

Stop

Railroad crossing

Yield

No bicycles

Falling rocks

Speed limit

No U-turn

Minimum speed

Road narrows

Expressway

First-aid station

Gas station

3-2 Traffic Signals

Traffic lights, arrows, flashing signals, lane signals, and pedestrian signals are used to help traffic flow smoothly. Each of these devices is a *traffic signal*.

All traffic signals have specific colors. Each color has a specific meaning. Red means stop. Yellow means caution; you must be ready to stop. Green means go; you can proceed *if the way is clear and safe*.

Traffic Lights

Various combinations of traffic lights are placed at intersections to control traffic. Remember the following types of lights so you will be familiar with them while driving.

Red Light   The first picture shows a red light. You must come to *a full stop* at a red light. Stop behind the stop lines, crosswalk, or before entering the intersection.

Yellow Light   The second picture shows a yellow light. Make every reasonable effort to stop at an intersection for a yellow light. Sometimes you might be too close to stop safely when a yellow light appears. You then will have to go through the intersection.

Green Light   The third picture shows a green light. Cross traffic is stopped. You can proceed only if the intersection is clear of traffic. When going through a green light, check traffic to the left and right before entering the intersection. When approaching a light that has been green for some time, be prepared for the light to turn yellow, then red.

Traffic Light Locations   Look for traffic lights beside or over a roadway or at the intersection the lights control. The red light in a traffic signal is always mounted on the top or to the left. The yellow light is in the center. The green light is on the bottom or to the right.

Computerized Traffic Lights
Computerized traffic-light systems are often used to control the flow of traffic. A computer coordinates traffic lights at several intersections. With this system, traffic can flow for several blocks at or near the speed limit without stopping.

Traffic lights also can be set to change when traffic approaches. A sensor in the roadway detects traffic. This system can be used where most of the traffic comes from one direction, such as a left-turn lane.

Right-Turn-on-Red Many states have laws that allow drivers to make a right turn when facing a red light. Follow these steps when making a *right-turn-on-red:*

1. Come to a *full stop.*
2. Make sure it is legal to turn on a red light. Some areas prohibit turning right on a red light. Some intersections have signs to prohibit a right-turn-on-red.
3. Let pedestrians and other vehicles (including bicyclists) clear the intersection.
4. Complete your right turn only if the intersection is, and will remain, free of traffic. *If in doubt, do not turn.*

Right-turn-on-red laws have helped reduce fuel consumption and travel times. However, pedestrian accidents have increased at some intersections where turning right on a red light is permitted. The top picture shows that you must wait for pedestrians to clear the crosswalk before you turn right on a red light.

Pedestrians also must protect themselves. They must not assume that every driver knows how to make a safe turn at a red light. *As a pedestrian, do not cross until you are sure it is safe to do so.*

Flashing Signals

A *flashing signal* is used to caution drivers or to tell them to stop. These signals are used at intersections and other hazardous locations.

Note the flashing red signal in the middle picture. Make a *full stop* when you come to a flashing red signal. A STOP sign and stop line can be used with this signal. After you stop, proceed if the intersection is clear.

When you see a warning sign and flashing yellow signal, as shown in the bottom picture, slow down. Be prepared to stop.

GO left only. Be sure that oncoming traffic does not run the red light.

GO right only. Yield to pedestrians and vehicles already in the intersection.

GO straight ahead only after yielding to vehicles and pedestrians within the intersection.

WARNING. The red arrow is about to appear.

STOP. You may not go in this direction.

Arrows

Traffic must flow in the direction that an arrow is pointing. Look at the arrows above. When you come to a green arrow pointing to the left or right, turn in that direction. Remember first to yield to other traffic and pedestrians. Turns are prohibited when an arrow points straight ahead.

A yellow arrow warns you that a red arrow is about to appear. Be prepared to stop or to clear the intersection quickly.

Always stop at a red arrow. Do not proceed until the arrow changes to green.

Lane Signals

Sometimes traffic in towns and cities needs to go in one direction during one time and in the opposite direction at other times. This shared use of lanes occurs on some streets and expressways to control morning and evening rush-hour traffic. In these situations, lights hang overhead to show whether or not a lane can be used at a specific time. Each light is a *lane signal.*

The picture below shows that you may drive in a lane with a green arrow over it. The traffic flow should be normal.

If your lane has a yellow X over it, move to a lane labeled with a green arrow. The yellow X warns you that the lane is about to be closed to traffic going in your direction.

If your lane has a red X over it, move as soon as possible to a lane that has a green arrow over it. The red X warns you that the lane is closed to traffic going in your direction.

Pedestrian Signals

A *pedestrian signal* is used at an intersection with heavy traffic. These signals or symbols are mounted near traffic lights as seen in the top picture. Pedestrians may cross at an intersection when they face a WALK signal or symbol. Pedestrians must clear the intersection or wait on a curb when the DON'T WALK signal or symbol flashes or remains lit.

Normally, the WALK signal or symbol and the green traffic light will be on at the same time for pedestrians and drivers going in the same direction. The DON'T WALK signal or symbol usually begins to flash its warning just before the yellow light appears for drivers. If you approach an intersection and see the DON'T WALK signal or symbol flashing, predict that your green light will soon change.

Officer's Signals

You must obey signals given by a traffic-control officer, even if the officer's signals contradict the traffic signal. A hand held up with the palm toward you means stop. A hand waving you on means to go. Signals can be given at dawn, dusk, and night with lighted wands as shown in the bottom picture.

Review It

1. What should you do when you approach a red light? a yellow light? a green light?
2. What action should you take as you approach a flashing red signal? a flashing yellow signal?
3. How can lane-signal arrows help control traffic?
4. How do pedestrian signals and officer's signals help you when driving?

3–3 Roadway Markings

A *roadway marking* gives you a warning or direction. These markings are usually lines, words, or figures painted on the roadway. Sometimes special markings are used on curbs and other surfaces.

Yellow Line Markings

The broken yellow line is used to separate two-way traffic. It also means a driver may pass when no traffic is coming from the opposite direction, as the driver of the yellow car in the left picture is doing.

The driver of the yellow car in the middle picture may not pass. The solid yellow line indicates that passing on that side of the roadway is not allowed. Passing is allowed when the solid yellow line ends. Turning left across a solid yellow line into a driveway or alley is allowed if there is no oncoming traffic.

The right picture shows how solid double yellow lines divide traffic and prevent passing. Drivers may make left turns across these lines if there is no oncoming traffic.

White Line Markings

Broken white lines separate lanes of traffic that are moving in the same direction. You may cross these broken lines when changing lanes.

Solid white lines keep drivers in their lanes and restrict lane changing. Do not cross solid white lines. White arrows are used in lanes to tell you when and where to turn. If you are in a lane with an arrow and the word ONLY, you *must* continue in the direction of the arrow as shown in the top picture. You may turn or go straight if there is a curved and straight arrow in your lane.

Solid white lines, as shown in the bottom left picture, also are used along the side of a roadway to mark the edge of the roadway. These lines help you to better see the edge of the roadway at night.

Notice the crosswalk in the bottom right picture. Some crosswalks have diagonal or perpendicular lines to highlight the area. You must yield the right of way to pedestrians in crosswalks.

A solid white line across your lane can be used as a stop line. Stop lines show where to stop for a STOP sign or a traffic light.

Rumble Strips and Raised Roadway Markers

Notice the rumble strips, short sections of corrugated roadway, in the bottom left picture. Rumble strips alert you to hazards through the noise your tires make when you drive over the strips. Rumble strips warn of an upcoming hazard such as a major or dangerous intersection or a tollgate.

On some highways, it is hard for some drivers to see the driving lane at night. Raised roadway markers are used in such situations. These devices, shown in the bottom right picture, are small reflectors. When these markers are struck by headlight beams, they shine and highlight the driving lane.

Raised roadway markers are color coded. White markers are used at the edge of a roadway or lane. Yellow markers might be used on the left edge of an expressway. If you are driving and see red roadway markers, pull off the roadway immediately. These red markers warn that you are driving in the wrong direction. Turn your car around and drive in the opposite direction.

Other Roadway Markings

No-parking zone curb markings, like the one shown in the top left picture, might be red, yellow, or white. No-parking zones often are near fire hydrants and intersections.

Yellow lines mark obstructions on two-way roads. White lines are used on one-way roads, as seen in the middle left picture.

Notice the marking for the school crossing in the bottom left picture. When you see this white marking, watch for children in the area.

The white roadway marking shown in the top right picture shows you where an exit ramp starts. Do not make a last-minute decision to cross this area.

The railroad roadway marking shown in the middle right picture warns you that a railroad crossing is ahead. Do not pass near railroad crossings.

The bottom right picture shows a parking space reserved for handicapped drivers. Check for signs that say HANDICAPPED PARKING ONLY and signs with the handicapped parking symbol. Check also for this symbol painted on a parking space before pulling into a space. Only handicapped drivers should use these spaces.

Review It

1. What is the basic difference between broken yellow lines and broken white lines?
2. What are the functions of rumble strips and raised roadway markers?
3. What are the functions of six types of roadway markings?

Advancements in Traffic Safety

Traffic engineers in some cities are experimenting with pedestrian signals for the blind. A recently developed device creates a steady sound when the WALK light is on. The device emits a pulsing sound when the DON'T WALK light is flashing or remains lit. The pitch of the sound indicates whether the street runs in an east-west or a north-south direction. The volume of the sound increases and decreases as surrounding traffic noise increases and decreases.

Chapter Summary

1. The eight traffic sign shapes are octagon, triangle, round, vertical rectangle, pentagon, pennant, horizontal rectangle, and diamond. The eight traffic sign colors are red, white, black, yellow, orange, green, blue, and brown. (3–1)
2. Come to a full stop at a STOP sign. Slow down or stop at a YIELD sign. A speed limit sign shows the safe maximum or minimum speed. (3–1)
3. A warning sign warns of a hazard ahead, a no-passing zone, a railroad crossing, a school crossing or zone, or a construction zone. (3–1)
4. Guide signs give information on routes, intersections, services, and points of interest. International signs use symbols rather than words. (3–1)
5. Stop at a red light. Prepare to stop or clear the intersection at a yellow light. Proceed on a green light if the intersection is clear. (3–2)
6. Stop at a flashing red signal. Slow down and be prepared to stop at a flashing yellow signal. (3–2)
7. Traffic must flow in the direction that a green arrow is pointing. A yellow arrow warns that a red arrow is about to appear. Stop at a red arrow, and wait until a green arrow appears. Drive only in the lanes over which green lane signals appear. (3–2)
8. The WALK signal or symbol and the green light appear at the same time for drivers and pedestrians going in the same direction. The DON'T WALK signal or symbol usually flashes just before the yellow light appears. Obey a traffic-control officer's directions, even if they contradict the traffic signals. (3–2)
9. Broken yellow lines separate two-way traffic. Broken white lines separate lanes of traffic going in the same direction. (3–3)
10. Rumble strips and raised roadway markers alert drivers of possible hazards. (3–3)
11. Six roadway markings are: no-parking curb markings, handicapped parking spaces, road obstruction markings, railroad markings, school crossings, and beginning of an exit ramp. (3–3)

Think About It
Pedestrian accidents have increased with drivers making right turns at red lights. What problems can be created for drivers and pedestrians by right-turn-on-red laws?

Decision Making

1. What is the speed limit in this situation? What speed law might make driving at 45 mph illegal?

2. Can you use the left lane ahead? Why might lane signals be used on this street?

3. The orange signs ahead are used to warn drivers about what condition? What mistake has this driver already made?

4. You want to pass the vehicle ahead. Is it safe and legal to pass?

Chapter 3 Test

Multiple Choice Copy the number of each sentence below on a sheet of paper. Choose the letter that best completes each statement.

1. The color of a regulatory sign is
   (a) red. (b) white. (c) blue. (d) brown. (36)
2. When you see a pennant-shaped sign, you must
   (a) stop. (b) yield right of way. (c) not pass.
   (d) watch for trains. (40)
3. When you approach a flashing yellow signal, you should
   (a) slow down. (b) watch for a traffic-control officer. (c) pass. (d) stop immediately. (44)
4. A yellow X over a lane tells you to
   (a) drive in that lane. (b) move to a lane with a red X. (c) move to a lane with a green arrow.
   (d) pull off the roadway. (45)
5. When a traffic-control officer holds up a hand with the palm facing you, you should
   (a) go through the intersection. (b) stop.
   (c) back up. (d) yield right of way. (46)

Completion Copy the number of each sentence below. After each number, write the letter of the word or words that complete the sentence correctly.

6. The ____ of a traffic sign can tell you the meaning of the sign. (36)
7. You must come to a full stop at a ____. (37)
8. A ____ in a red circle and crossed by a red bar prohibits a certain action. (39)
9. Lanes of traffic moving in the same direction are separated by ____. (48)
10. A large white X with two small R's painted on the roadway warns that a ____ is ahead. (50)

a. black symbol
b. broken white lines
c. broken yellow lines
d. railroad crossing
e. STOP sign
f. shape and color

Vocabulary Copy the number of each phrase below. Match the definition in List A with the term it defines in List B.

List A

11. informs you of traffic laws (36)
12. privilege to use the roadway first (37)
13. to allow another driver to go first (37)
14. slowest legal speed that you can drive in ideal conditions (38)
15. requires speed to fit conditions (38)
16. alerts you to possible hazards (39)
17. area where schoolchildren might be (40)
18. gives directions and other information (41)
19. symbols used on signs rather than words (42)
20. a traffic light, arrow, flashing signal, lane signal, or pedestrian signal (43)
21. flashing traffic light that indicates stop (red) or caution (yellow) (44)
22. permits a right turn at a red signal light (44)
23. signal that tells whether or not a lane may be used (45)
24. traffic signal saying WALK or DON'T WALK (46)
25. lines, words, and figures painted on the roadway (47)

List B

a. basic speed law
b. flashing signal
c. guide sign
d. international symbols
e. lane signal
f. maximum speed limit
g. minimum speed limit
h. pedestrian signal
i. regulatory sign
j. right of way
k. right-turn-on-red
l. roadway marking
m. school zone
n. traffic signal
o. warning sign
p. yield

Chapter 4
Making Safe Driving Decisions: The IPDE Process

You're the Driver!

Imagine you are the driver of the car approaching the intersection in this picture. What features of the situation should you identify as creating possible hazards?

Should you predict the light will stay green so that you can go through the intersection without stopping?

Based on your prediction, what action should you take?

What actions do you predict the oncoming driver might take?

What path of travel would you use if the person at the car opens the door?

What decisions might you make?

How can you communicate your decision to drivers behind you?

You reduce your risk of collisions by using an organized system of thinking. This very important chapter presents the IPDE process, an organized system for safe driving. The IPDE process will help you analyze traffic situations, develop your ability to make wise decisions, and then execute safe driving actions.

Objectives

4–1 *The IPDE Process*

1. Name the four steps of the IPDE process.   (56)
2. Describe an orderly visual search pattern.   (56)
3. Define selective seeing and give one example of it.   (57)
4. Explain how knowledge and experience help you make accurate predictions.   (60)
5. List three elements about which you must make predictions.   (61)
6. Name the three decisions you must make when applying the IPDE process.   (62)
7. List the four most important actions you can take to avoid conflict.   (64)

4–2 *Safe Path of Travel*

8. Name the four requirements for a safe path of travel.   (66)
9. Explain what is meant when you separate hazards, minimize a hazard, and compromise space.   (67)

4–3 *Using the IPDE Process*

10. Describe the IPDE process as a complete process.   (69)
11. List four factors that can lengthen the IPDE process.   (70)

4-1 The IPDE Process

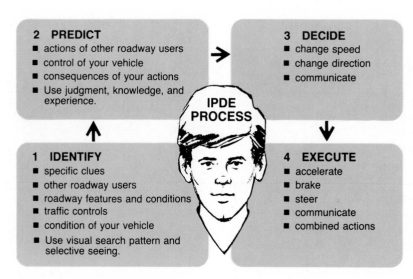

2 PREDICT
- actions of other roadway users
- control of your vehicle
- consequences of your actions
- Use judgment, knowledge, and experience.

3 DECIDE
- change speed
- change direction
- communicate

IPDE PROCESS

1 IDENTIFY
- specific clues
- other roadway users
- roadway features and conditions
- traffic controls
- condition of your vehicle
- Use visual search pattern and selective seeing.

4 EXECUTE
- accelerate
- brake
- steer
- communicate
- combined actions

The driving task is primarily a thinking task. Your hands and feet do only what your brain tells them to do. Safe driving depends, to a great extent, upon your ability to correctly "read" and analyze traffic situations. Being able to see well does not ensure you will identify all the critical clues or make the correct responses.

Most responsible drivers use some kind of system that deals with all traffic possibilities they will encounter. As a result, these drivers have fewer close calls and collisions than those who do not use an organized system.

The *IPDE process* is an organized system of seeing, thinking, and responding. The IPDE process can help you develop a safe and successful driving system. There are four steps in the IPDE process:

1. Identify
2. Predict
3. Decide
4. Execute

To process information properly, you must identify hazards and clues and predict possible points of conflict. Then you must decide how to avoid conflict and execute the correct actions. Study the IPDE steps above and learn the key words that are a part of the IPDE process.

Identify

The first step of the IPDE process is *identify*. This step involves much more than just seeing. When you identify, you give meaning to what you see. You must know when to look, where and how to look, and what to look for. Notice the children playing in the yard in the picture above. The driver of the car should identify them and predict they might run into the street.

Orderly Visual Search Pattern

You can use any of several visual patterns to help develop your own identifying process. An *orderly visual search pattern* is a process of searching critical areas in a regular sequence. Using an orderly visual search pattern, you look for clues in certain areas in a systematic manner. You must practice this process continually so that it becomes a habit.

Below is one example of an orderly visual search pattern for straight-ahead driving:

1. Glance ahead.
2. Check rearview mirror.
3. Glance ahead again.
4. Search the sides of the roadway, intersections, and driveways.
5. Glance ahead again.
6. Check speedometer and gauges.
7. Glance ahead again.

All glances should only last an instant. Once your orderly visual search pattern becomes a habit, you will be able to adjust it for any maneuver or driving environment.

Where and How to Look Different driving environments and traffic situations present a variety of visual search problems. As you gain driving experience, you learn what kinds of traffic situations and events are most important to identify.

The three guidelines below are part of the Smith System. This set of good searching habits can help you learn where and how to look. This system helps you develop a more effective visual search pattern.

▶ **Aim high in steering** To "aim high" means to look far ahead as you drive. Keep your view up rather than looking down at the area in front of your car.

In city traffic, try to look at least a block ahead. On highways and expressways, look as far ahead as possible. The picture above shows the distance ahead you should be looking on an open highway. Look across hills and curves, as this driver is doing. Identify conditions and possible conflicts in the distance.

▶ **Keep your eyes moving** As part of an orderly visual search pattern, take selective glances. Glance near and far, to the right and left, in the mirrors, and at the instrument panel. Be sure to look ahead again after each glance to the sides, rear, and instrument panel.

▶ **Get the big picture** Try to be aware of the whole traffic scene. This awareness results from aiming high in steering and keeping your eyes moving. Getting the big picture is the

mental process of putting together the critical clues that your eyes selected and identified as they moved.

What to Look For
Knowing how, when, and where to look does little good if you do not know what to look for. Develop the technique of *selective seeing* in your identifying process. Selective seeing means that you select and identify only those events and clues that pertain to your driving task.

Not all hazards and important clues are easy to identify. Signs, neon lights, stores, and billboards contribute to a complex traffic scene. Note below how difficult it can be to identify a clue, the traffic light, as you approach the intersection.

Search for Specific Clues Use your visual search pattern to look for specific driving-related clues. When searching parked cars on a street, you might identify an important clue such as front wheels turned toward the street as the top picture shows. You also might identify the vapor coming from the exhaust pipe, as well as a driver sitting in the car. These clues give meaning to the situation. They indicate that the car might enter your path of travel.

As your searching skills improve, so will your ability to select the more important areas to search. You will identify the driving-related objects and events that might affect your path of travel.

The kinds of clues you search for will change in different driving environments. In city driving, search for such areas and events as intersections, parked cars, pedestrians, and traffic. On open highways, search areas much farther ahead. Look for crossroads, slow-moving vehicles, and animals. During expressway driving, search the other lanes ahead, behind, and beside you.

Regardless of the environment, always look for other roadway users, roadway features and conditions, and traffic controls in every situation. Be aware of these clues. Evaluate them as part of your ongoing driving task.

Look for Other Users Search the traffic scene for other roadway users who might affect your planned path of travel. Watch for movement of other users, especially in areas that have shadows and shade.

Look for different sizes and shapes of users, such as bicyclists, pedestrians, animals, and other vehicles. Imagine you are the driver in the second picture. You might not see the child if you are not searching for critical clues.

Look for other users' problems as well as your own. Another driver might swerve into your lane in an attempt to pass or avoid other vehicles. You might see that an oncoming driver's lane is partly blocked. That driver might have to cross into your lane. Help the oncoming driver by pulling to the right to help the driver pass safely.

Look for Roadway Features and Conditions The roadway itself is another important area to watch. Identify intersections, hills, and curves early. Be aware ahead of time that the width of your lane might be reduced. Some reasons for changes in roadway features and conditions are:

▶ **Change from multilane to single lane** Multilane roadways often narrow into single-lane roadways. Identify signs warning you of this change early enough to position your car in the through lane.

Roadway repair is a frequent cause of lane closure. When you see signs indicating roadway repair ahead, move into the through lane as soon as possible. The driver stopped in back of the barricades in the picture above did not move to the through lane early enough. Therefore, the driver had to make an unnecessary stop. Always try to avoid this type of stop in moving traffic.

▶ **Change in width of lane** Standing water, patches of snow, potholes, or objects in the roadway can narrow your lane space. Identify these conditions early so you have more time to plan a path around them.

▶ **Roadside hazards** Your identification process should keep you looking constantly for pedestrians, bicyclists, parked cars, and animals. Watch for shopping center entrances and exits, roadside stands, and restaurants. Other users can appear suddenly from almost any location and can cause your lane space to be reduced.

▶ **Roadway surface** Identify the roadway surface and condition each time you begin to drive. Be prepared to adjust your driving for wet, snow-covered, icy, or gravel roadways.

Look for Traffic Controls Learn to look in different places for traffic controls. At major intersections, controls can be overhead, in the center of the intersection, or on the four corners. Identify traffic controls as early as possible so you are ready to make correct responses.

Predict

Once you have identified a possible hazard, *predict* how this hazard might create a conflict. When you predict, you interpret the information you have identified. You predict where possible points of conflict can occur. You try to foresee what might happen and how it might affect your planned path.

How to Predict

Predicting involves what is happening, what could happen and, if it does happen, how it might affect you. To predict, you must evaluate the situation and make a judgment about the possible consequences. The more complex a situation is, the more difficult it is to identify and predict.

Imagine you are driving the car on the right in this picture. You should predict that one of the bicyclists might swerve or fall. If so, predict that the oncoming car might enter your path in order to avoid the

bicyclist. Your ability to predict and make sound judgments will improve as you gain knowledge and experience.

Knowledge The basic part of your driving knowledge comes from your study of traffic laws and driver-education materials. Whenever you drive, you build up knowledge by gathering more information and learning from others. The more you drive, the more you relate new knowledge to what you have already learned.

Experience In addition to knowledge, experience helps you improve your ability to predict accurately. Exposure to a variety of driving experiences provides a solid base for making sound judgments later.

Judgment Making a judgment about a traffic situation involves measuring, comparing, and evaluating. As you drive, you judge speed, time, space, distance, traction, and visibility. You make judgments about your own driving performance as well as the actions and performance of other roadway users. Make every effort to develop the ability to make sound judgments that lead to accurate predictions.

What to Predict

Nearly all predictions that you as a driver make are related to three elements in the traffic scene. You must predict:
► actions of other roadway users.
► your control of your vehicle.
► consequences of your actions.

Predicting Actions of Other Roadway Users   It is easy to make wrong predictions about the actions of other roadway users. Do not assume that others will always take the correct action. Predict that other drivers or pedestrians will make mistakes. By doing so, you are prepared to adjust your actions to compensate. Be prepared for the worst.

The most important types of predictions to make concerning the actions of others are:
► **Action**   What action will the other roadway user take? Is more than one action possible?
► **Time**   When will the action be taken? Where will I be then?
► **Space**   Where might the other roadway user go? Will some of my planned space be used?
► **Point of Conflict**   Where might our paths cross?

Imagine that you are the driver approaching the intersection in the first picture. Predict that the pedestrians on your right will start to cross in front of you. Predict that the oncoming car signaling for a right turn might turn left across your planned path. By making these predictions, you are prepared to slow, swerve, or stop, thus avoiding a collision.

Predicting Control of Your Vehicle   You need time and space to complete any maneuver. Different traffic, roadway, and weather conditions can change the amount of time and space needed.

In the second picture, the driver first identifies that the roadway is slick. The driver then predicts that stopping for the traffic signal will take longer than if the roadway were dry. Based on this prediction, the driver slows and brakes earlier.

Predicting Consequences of Your Actions   In most traffic situations you have a choice of actions to take. While there is not always one correct action, there is usually one best action. You must compare and judge the possible consequences before deciding on the best action to take.

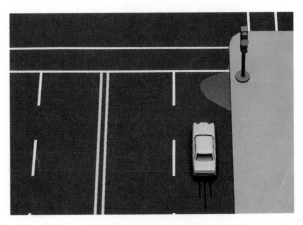

Decide

You have identified a situation and predicted a possible conflict. Now you must *decide* how to avoid the conflict. Your decision might be to change speed, change direction, communicate your plans to others, or it might be a combination of these actions.

Decide to Change Speed Any decision you make is influenced by your own speed and the speed of other vehicles. Many drivers think that slowing down is the only way to avoid a conflict. In many situations, you will decide to accelerate rather than to slow down. Base your decision on your evaluation of the situation and the possible consequences.

The driver of the yellow car in the left picture below judged time and space correctly. The driver decided to accelerate and provide space for the passing driver to return to the right lane. The driver avoided a conflict with the passing and on-coming cars.

Decide to Change Direction Deciding to change direction means you change your position on the roadway. You might change lanes or swerve to the left or right.

In order to have space, use the fourth guideline of the Smith System: Leave yourself an out at all times. "Leaving yourself an out" means you have an *escape path,* a place to go in case of a possible conflict. Having an escape path

means that you keep an area of space all around your car. This area is called a *space cushion.* A space cushion lets you more easily position your vehicle where you want it.

Adjust your direction to improve your space cushion. The right picture below shows the space cushion of the yellow car in multiple-lane traffic.

Decide to Communicate The decision to communicate with others helps reduce a possible conflict. Use the fifth and last guideline of the Smith System: Make sure others see you. This guideline means telling others where you are and what you plan to do. You can communicate with others by using lights, horn, car position, eye contact, and body movement.

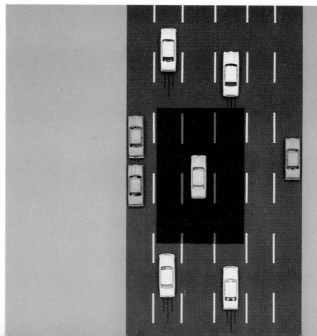

Lights Use lights to give messages to other roadway users:

► **Brake lights** Brake-light messages tell drivers behind that you are slowing, stopped, or standing still. Tap the brake pedal to signal for a stop. This signal warns drivers behind that you intend to slow or stop.

► **Turn-signal lights** These lights give the message, "I plan to turn or change lanes."

► **High-beam and low-beam headlights** These lights inform others that you are approaching. Use low-beam headlights during poor weather conditions that reduce visibility. In the top picture, the driver of the oncoming van realizes that visibility is poor. Even though it is daylight, the driver uses headlights to ensure being seen.

► **Taillights** Taillights tell drivers behind where you are. Keep taillights clean. Taillights will stay on when headlights are on.

► **Emergency flasher lights** Flasher lights convey the messages, "I am in trouble," or "I cannot move," or "I am moving very, very slowly."

► **Back-up lights** White back-up lights let others know you are backing up or you intend to back up.

► **Parking lights** These lights warn other drivers that you are parked along the side of the roadway. Do not use parking lights when you are driving.

Horn Some drivers fail to use the horn when it is needed. A light tap on the horn lets others know you are there. In an emergency, a loud blast might be needed.

Car Position Where you position your car in a lane can be a helpful communication to others. Moving to the right side of the lane indicates that you might turn right. Moving toward the center line indicates that you might turn left.

Eye Contact Try to develop eye contact with other roadway users as much as possible. You can communicate many messages this way. If there is the possibility of a conflict, check to see if the other person is looking at you.

Some vehicles, such as the one in the bottom picture, have darkly tinted windows that make eye contact nearly impossible. Do not depend on eye contact alone to communicate to other roadway users. Eye contact often helps reduce the risk of conflict; it does not guarantee against conflicts.

Body Movement Waving your hand can tell another driver to proceed, or tell a pedestrian to cross in front of you. However, if you signal a pedestrian to proceed, you are responsible for the pedestrian's well-being in the roadway.

In an emergency, raise your right hand and wave it side to side. Seeing this signal through your rear window can alert the driver behind you. Taking this action while tapping the brake pedal rapidly is a combined message for an emergency stop.

Execute

Carrying out your decision in order to avoid conflict is the *execute* step in the IPDE process. In most cases you will execute routine maneuvers and actions. Many will be for use of defroster, heater, windshield wipers, gearshift lever, and other controls. However, more important actions you will execute frequently are:

► accelerate
► brake
► steer
► communicate.

Accelerate   Executing the decision to accelerate means you have judged the speed and use of space by others. You might accelerate to get out of another driver's way or to avoid an obstruction in the roadway.

Deciding to accelerate also means that you are aware of the acceleration capabilities of your vehicle. Remember that different vehicles have different acceleration capabilities. Consider your own vehicle's capabilities before executing a decision to accelerate.

Brake   When you have decided to decelerate or brake to reduce risk, you should have already considered the surface of the roadway. The amount of braking needed will vary with the situation, the speed of your

car, the condition of the roadway, and the condition of your brakes. When braking suddenly, check for vehicles to the rear.

Avoid locking the brakes in an emergency stop. Locked brakes make steering impossible since wheels must be turning to provide traction for steering. Some cars have braking systems that do not lock. This system prevents loss of steering control.

The driver in this picture has braked to avoid striking the children. The wet roadway, the speed of the car, and the amount of braking will determine the result of the driver's response. By using a visual search pattern, the driver might have predicted the actions of others. The driver could have reduced the need for emergency braking.

Combined Actions You will often need to execute a combination of actions. Sometimes you might need to accelerate and steer at the same time. In other situations, you might need to brake, communicate, and steer at the same time.

If you were the driver in the bottom picture, you would be in that situation. In order to avoid an open car door, you should signal, brake, and steer around it. The precision and timing with which you execute these actions determines whether or not a conflict would occur.

Review It

1. What are the four steps of the IPDE process?
2. What is an "orderly visual search pattern?" Give an example of an orderly visual search pattern.
3. What three major elements should you always look for in any driving environment?
4. How do knowledge and experience affect your ability to predict?
5. What are three elements about which you must predict?
6. What are the three decisions you make in the decide part of the IPDE process?
7. What are four actions you can execute to avoid conflict?

Steer When you decide to steer away from a conflict, execute just the amount of steering needed. Oversteering can cause you to lose control of your car, especially at higher speeds. Higher speeds also require more space for your maneuver. Keep an adequate space cushion around your car. You reduce risk by having an escape path to use.

Communicate In many instances your only action will be to communicate. Communicate early enough to give the other person enough time to complete the IPDE process. Study the top picture. The driver in the stopped car is not sure the car behind will stop in time to avoid a rear-end collision. The stopped driver is communicating with both an arm signal and brake lights.

Many drivers assume the roadway ahead will always be clear and safe. This assumption is very risky and does not show good judgment. You should not expect trouble-free driving all the time. Hazards or possible conflicts will often occur in your planned path.

As you develop your IPDE process, you will be better assured a *safe path of travel,* a path that is free of hazards and conflict when you use it. Consider four important requirements needed to maintain a safe path of travel. These requirements are visibility, traction, space, and traffic flow.

Visibility

About ninety percent of all traffic information you gather is received by your eyes. Regardless of how good your vision is, limited visibility will affect your IPDE process at times. Two important visibility factors are:

► **Sight Distance** Your *sight distance* is the distance you can see ahead. The longer this distance is, the more time you have to identify possible conflicts. Your sight distance can be shortened, though, by curves, hills, large vehicles, weather, buildings, trees, or even a dirty windshield.

The driver in the left picture below is following the truck too closely and has sacrificed sight distance. The driver should reduce speed to compensate for shorter sight distance and to have more time for the IPDE process.

► **Field of Vision** Your *field of vision* is the area you can see around you while looking straight ahead. The wider your field of vision is, the better chance you have to use the IPDE process effectively.

Field of vision is most important in areas such as intersections, driveways, and other places where other roadway users might cross your path. The parked cars in the right picture below make driveways difficult to see. Vehicles could enter your path before you could identify them. Reduce your speed when your field of vision is narrowed.

Traction

The basic requirement for controlling any vehicle is *traction* between the tires and the roadway. Traction is the result of

friction, a force which keeps tires from slipping when they are stopped or rolling. Traction is actually the gripping power between the tires and the roadway surface. The more traction there is, the greater the gripping power between the tires and the roadway. See Chapter 7 for a complete explanation of traction.

You must continually evaluate the amount of available traction and adjust speed according to conditions. Wet, snowy, icy, and bumpy or gravel roadways all reduce traction. The poorer traction becomes, the lower your speed must be. You will need more time to stop, accelerate, or make maneuvers.

Space

A safe path of travel requires space. By keeping a space cushion all around your car, you will more easily maintain a safe path of travel. When space is limited, it is much more difficult to avoid a hazard. Reduce your speed in such areas of limited space as bridges, narrow lanes with parked cars, or in lanes next to other traffic.

Traffic Flow

The fourth requirement for a safe path of travel is traffic flow. Adjust your speed to traffic conditions so that you keep up with the flow of traffic and avoid unnecessary stops. Look for change in traffic conditions. Be ready to adjust your speed and space cushion accordingly. By avoiding unnecessary stops, you reduce your risk of rear-end collisions.

Use these techniques to manage space, time, and distance to maintain a safe path of travel.

Separate Hazards You might be involved in a possible conflict situation with two or more hazards at the same time. Adjust your speed in order to handle only one hazard at a time, or *separate* hazards.

In this picture, the car driver should try not to meet the approaching truck near the pedestrians. The car driver should adjust speed so that the truck and the pedestrians are handled separately. In this situation, the car driver should reduce speed to allow the truck to pass the pedestrians first. The car would then meet the truck with ample space before passing the pedestrians.

Minimize a Hazard You can *minimize* a hazard to reduce risk by putting more distance between yourself and the hazard. Study the left picture below. As the yellow car approaches the parked car, the driver predicts a door might open. To minimize the hazard, the driver steers away from the door. This action gives the driver more space and thus reduces the danger.

Compromise Space Sometimes hazards cannot be separated or minimized. When this situation occurs, you must *compromise space* by giving as much space as possible to the greater hazard.

The truck in the right picture below might enter the lane of the yellow car to avoid the parked car leaving the parking space. Although the cars on the right present a hazard, the driver of the yellow car should steer right as far as possible. This action gives more space to the greater hazard, the truck.

Compromising hazards is not always possible or successful. Try to handle multiple hazards by separating rather than by compromising.

You can never be completely free of hazards in your planned path of travel. Using the IPDE process can reduce or simplify potential hazards.

Develop the habit of anticipating multiple hazards. Try to have enough control over situations to prevent meeting two or more high-risk hazards at once. By doing so, you will more often be assured a safe path of travel.

Review It
1. What are the four important requirements that help make a safe path of travel?
2. What are three techniques you can use to help maintain a safe path of travel?

4-3 Using the IPDE Process

Learning and using the IPDE process helps you form plans and execute maneuvers to reduce hazards and avoid conflicts. Once you have established an effective IPDE process, you will:

► see more.
► make better judgments.
► make accurate predictions and correct decisions.
► execute maneuvers more successfully.

Putting IPDE into Action

As you begin to develop your IPDE process, you will use the four steps in order. Once you have learned techniques and skills for identifying, you should add the predicting process. Identifying and predicting are linked together as they are put into action. You identify the hazards or events, and then predict how they might affect you. You then perform the third step, deciding. Finally, you execute a maneuver based on the decision.

You might learn each step of the IPDE process separately, but you cannot use the IPDE process successfully if you treat each part as an isolated step. Think of the steps as being combined into one smooth process. As you broaden your driving experience, make a conscious effort to use the IPDE process at all times.

IPDE Must Be Continual

Only through continual practice will your IPDE process become effective and habitual. As you ride with other drivers, practice the process of identifying, and then predicting, the actions of others. Consider different decisions for actions that you might take. Evaluate the consequences of each possible action. This continual practice will help you develop an effective IPDE process which will become a habit.

Selective Use of IPDE

Once you have the ability to apply the total IPDE process,

you will find occasions when it is not carried out to the execute step. You can use the IPDE process selectively.

Notice the driver nearing the crest of the hill in this picture. The driver has identified the curve sign. No other vehicles are visible, but the driver predicts an oncoming car at the crest of the hill. Based on this prediction, the driver has decided on an escape path to the right. Since there was no oncoming car, the driver did not execute the escape maneuver. In this situation, the driver used IPD, but did not use E of the IPDE process.

Sometimes you should begin a new IPDE process cycle before completing the previous one. Imagine you are the driver of the car approaching the workers in the traffic scene shown in the top picture. You identify the workers as hazards, predict their actions, and begin to make a decision. At the same time you identify the truck which might enter your lane ahead. While you carry out your decision regarding the workers, you also decide what action to take if the truck enters your path.

IPDE Takes Time

Remember that the IPDE process takes time. You must have time to identify, time to predict, time to decide, and time to execute. The more complex the traffic situation is, the longer it takes to carry out the IPDE process. The IPDE process takes more time when you must decide among several different actions.

Deciding upon the correct action depends upon the actions of the other users. Study the traffic situation in the bottom picture. Imagine you are the driver who is approaching the bicycle rider. You identify the driver in the parked car. You predict that the car might enter the path of the bicycle.

If the rider swerves or falls, you might decide to brake. If the rider does not swerve or fall, you might decide to steer left, though the oncoming van presents a hazard. You might also decide to brake and swerve at the same time.

These factors also can increase the time it takes to complete the IPDE process:

► You or other drivers might be tired, confused, or impaired.
► The area and situation might be new to you or other drivers.
► You or other drivers might be distracted or preoccupied.

When you are driving, try to keep your mind totally on your driving task. Full attention to all situations is required to use the IPDE process effectively.

Review It

1. What is meant by combining the IPDE steps into one process, and the selective use of the IPDE process?
2. What are four conditions that can cause the IPDE process to take more time?

Be a Fuel Saver

► Develop your IPDE process with a goal of avoiding as many unnecessary stops as possible. Each stop requires additional fuel as you wait to proceed, and then accelerate again.
► Use the technique of separating hazards to avoid unnecessary, fuel-wasting stops.

► Identify necessary stops early. Easing up on the accelerator early when approaching a red light or a STOP sign saves fuel. This action also gives time for the light to change to green, thus avoiding a stop.
► Identify blocked lanes early in order to avoid unnecessary stops. Starting from a stop uses more fuel than just slowing.

Chapter Summary

1. The four steps of the IPDE process are identify, predict, decide, and execute. (4—1)
2. An orderly visual search pattern means searching for clues in a systematic manner. For straight-ahead driving, glance ahead, check rear, glance ahead, search to sides, glance ahead, check speedometer and gauges, glance ahead. (4—1)
3. Selective seeing is choosing only those clues and events that pertain to your driving task. (4—1)
4. Knowledge about traffic laws and driver-education materials helps you learn to identify and predict. Driving experience gives you exposure to a greater variety of situations. Your identifications and predictions become more accurate. (4—1)
5. When applying the IPDE process, predict the actions of other users, control of your own vehicle, and consequences of your actions. (4—1)
6. When applying the IPDE process, you might decide to change speed, to change direction, or to communicate to other roadway users. (4—1)
7. Execute one or any combination of these actions to avoid conflict: accelerate, brake, steer, and communicate. (4—1)

8. You must have these four factors to ensure a safe path of travel: good visibility, good traction, space to make maneuvers, and ability to adjust to the traffic flow. (4—2)
9. Separate hazards, minimize a hazard, or compromise space to reduce the risk of conflict. (4—2)
10. Use the four IPDE steps together as one smooth process. As you gain experience, you will use the IPDE process more selectively. (4—3)
11. These factors can increase the time needed to complete the IPDE process: traffic situation is more complex; driver condition; area or situations are new to the driver; the driver is distracted or preoccupied. (4—3)

Think About It
How might other roadway users, such as pedestrians, use the IPDE process to protect themselves?

Decision Making

1. You are the driver approaching the slow-moving vehicle. How will you use the IPDE process? Which action will you choose? What factors might affect your safe path of travel?

2. How would knowledge and experience help the driver approaching the STOP sign execute a safe stop?

3. What steps should the driver who is approaching the parked car take to reduce risk?

4. The approaching car is entering your lane. What possible conflicts are there? What actions might you take? How can you communicate to a driver behind you?

Chapter 4 Test

Multiple Choice   Copy the number of each question below on a sheet of paper. Choose the letter that best completes each statement or answers each question.

1. What step of the IPDE process helps a driver become aware of problems?
   (a) identify   (b) predict   (c) decide
   (d) execute   (56)
2. What step of the IPDE process tells how to avoid a conflict?
   (a) identify   (b) predict   (c) decide
   (d) execute   (62)
3. "Leaving yourself an out" means
   (a) leaving a door unlocked in case of an emergency.   (b) deciding to change direction.
   (c) parking so that your door is not blocked.
   (d) having an escape path available.   (62)
4. What action reduces the risk of handling two hazards at the same time?
   (a) scan   (b) separate   (c) track   (d) predict   (67)
5. When you do not carry out the entire IPDE process, you have performed a
   (a) selective use of IPDE.   (b) combined action.   (c) point of conflict.   (d) compromise.   (69)

Completion   Copy the number of each sentence below. After each number, write the letter of the word or words that complete the sentence correctly.

6. Being aware of the whole traffic scene means you are getting the ____.   (57)
7. Your ability to predict will improve as you gain in both knowledge and ____.   (60)
8. You interpret the information you have identified during the ____ step of the IPDE process.   (60)
9. The open area you always keep around your car is called a ____.   (62)
10. Carrying out a decision is the ____ step of the IPDE process.   (64)

   a. big picture
   b. execute
   c. experience
   d. identify
   e. predict
   f. space cushion

Vocabulary   Copy the number of each phrase below. Match the definition in List A with the term it defines in List B.

List A

11. an organized system of seeing, thinking, and responding   (56)
12. look at critical areas in a regular sequence   (56)
13. see the clues that pertain to driving task   (57)
14. step in the IPDE process that tells what might happen   (60)
15. path that is free of hazards   (66)
16. distance you can see ahead   (66)
17. area you can see around you while looking straight ahead   (66)
18. gripping power between tires and roadway   (66)
19. reduce risk by putting more space between you and a single hazard   (68)
20. reduce risk by giving as much space as possible to the greater of two or more hazards   (68)

List B

   a. compromise space
   b. execute
   c. field of vision
   d. IPDE process
   e. minimize
   f. orderly visual search pattern
   g. predict
   h. safe path of travel
   i. selective seeing
   j. sight distance
   k. traction

Unit 2
Interacting with Traffic

Chapter 5
Basic Car Maneuvers

Chapter 6
Intersections

Chapter 7
Natural Laws and Car Control

Chapter 8
Interacting with Cyclists

Both the car driver and the bicyclist pictured here are users of the highway transportation system. Each individual must obey traffic laws. Both the car driver and the bicyclist must be familiar with the capabilities of his or her own vehicle and other vehicles. Finally, each individual must cooperate with other roadway users to avoid conflicts.

In this unit you will learn how to maneuver your car in various situations and how natural laws affect car control. You will also learn how to manage different types of intersections. Finally, you will learn how to interact safely with such other roadway users as motorcyclists and bicyclists.

Chapter 5
Basic Car Maneuvers

You're the Driver!

Imagine you are a driver approaching the intersection in this picture. You want to make a left turn.

From which lane should you make the turn?

How could you warn drivers behind that you plan to turn?

What possible hazard do the angle-parked cars on the left present to you?

What clue, besides movement of traffic, tells you that you are on a one-way street?

What problems should you look for as soon as you turn the corner?

If you had wanted to turn right one block after this intersection, which lane would you be in?

If you wanted to angle park on the left side, when would you begin to turn into the parking space?

This chapter explains such basic maneuvers as how to steer, change lanes, turn, and park. Chapter 5 also discusses how to turn your car around and how to start and park on hills. In addition, you will learn when and where to perform these maneuvers.

Objectives

5–1 Steering, Signaling, and Changing Lanes

1. Explain how to steer straight forward and backward. (78)
2. Describe the correct use of hand signals. (79)
3. List the steps for changing lanes. (80)

5–2 Turns and Turnabouts

4. Describe hand-over-hand steering. (81)
5. List the steps for making left and right turns. (81)
6. Explain how to back left and right. (83)
7. Explain how to perform five different turnabouts. (84)
8. List the factors to consider before deciding which type of turnabout to use. (86)

5–3 Parking

9. List the steps for angle and perpendicular parking. (87)
10. List the steps for parallel parking. (88)

5–4 Starting and Parking on Hills

11. Explain how to start from an uphill parking space without rollback. (89)
12. Explain how to park uphill and downhill with and without a curb. (90)

Steering control is critical in every successful driving maneuver. Developing steering control involves these points:
► developing good visual habits
► adjusting speed
► adjusting the steering wheel continually
► judging available roadway space accurately.

Steering Straight Forward

Use a comfortable, balanced hand position when you practice steering straight ahead. Aim high with your visual search. Look far ahead toward the center of your intended path, not at the center line or lane lines. Avoid looking at your hands or feet while driving. When you look down, you cannot see your planned path of travel.

Continually make slight steering corrections as to drive in a straight line. A beginning driver might tend to *oversteer,* or turn the steering wheel too much. When you oversteer, your car can weave from side to side, rather than move forward in a straight line.

Some beginning drivers tend to *understeer,* or turn the steering wheel too little to keep the car in the planned path. If you understeer, you go too far first in one direction, and then in the other direction. Correct understeering by turning the wheel more often, but using only slight movements.

You soon will develop a feel for the space your car occupies. Practice and experience enable you to think of your car as an extension of yourself. You will soon be able to accurately judge the space your car uses while it is moving and the space you need to make various maneuvers.

Steering Straight Backward

Backing your car might feel strange to you when you do it for the first time. Before backing your car, look back to make sure your path is clear. Do not rely on the rearview mirrors. Follow these steps to back correctly:
1. Hold the brake pedal down, and shift to REVERSE.
2. Turn your body to the right, and put your right arm over

the back of the seat. Look back through the rear window. This driver is in the correct position for backing straight.
3. Put your left hand at the top of the steering wheel at the 12 o'clock position.
4. Release pressure on the brake pedal just enough to allow the car to creep backward slowly. In most cases, the idling speed in an automatic-transmission car allows the car to move back without accelerating.
5. Move the top of the steering wheel in the direction you want the back of the car to go. Make only small steering corrections.
6. Keep your foot over the brake pedal while the car moves back. Glance quickly to the front and sides to check traffic. Continue looking back through the rear window as you brake to a smooth stop.

Backing a Stickshift Car You can back slowly in a stickshift car by carefully controlling your use of the clutch pedal. Follow these steps for backing in a stickshift car:

1. Push the brake and clutch pedals down.
2. Shift to REVERSE.
3. Release the brake, and let the clutch come out slowly to the friction point.

Holding the clutch at the friction point allows the car to back at a slow, controlled speed. Releasing the clutch suddenly causes the car to jerk back quickly, or even continue backing if the engine does not stall.

Most stickshift cars can move slowly in REVERSE with the clutch at the friction point and with no acceleration. When this backing procedure is possible:

► Keep your right foot over the brake pedal, ready to stop.
► When stopping, push the clutch pedal down and brake to a stop.
► Glance quickly to the sides to check traffic, but continue looking back until you stop.

Signaling

Signaling with turn-signal lights and arm signals is very important when you plan to turn, change lanes, enter traffic, slow suddenly, or stop. Always signal well in advance of any maneuver so other drivers have time to react.

Even though cars have turn-signal devices, a combination of turn lights and hand and arm signals will be more effective at times. Hand signals are easier to see in bright sunlight. At night, however, turn lights are easier to see. A waving arm signal gets attention during an emergency stop. Should the turn-signal device not work, you must use hand signals.

Notice the hand and arm positions in these pictures. The first shows the left arm and hand pointing up for a right turn. The second shows the left arm and hand extended straight out for a left turn. The third shows the left arm extended downward, indicating slow or stop.

When using arm signals, use your right hand to maintain steering control. Make any arm signals well before you enter a turn. Return your left hand to the steering wheel before executing a turn. Use both hands on the steering wheel when executing a turn.

Right Turn

Left Turn

Slow or Stop

Changing Lanes

Changing lanes properly is an important maneuver on a roadway with two or more lanes of traffic moving in your direction. You might need to change lanes before making a right or a left turn. Changing lanes also sometimes gives you a better position in, or a broader view of, the traffic flow.

Steering control is a critical factor as you learn the lane-changing maneuver. Oversteering, a common error, can cause your car to turn too sharply as you start to enter the adjoining lane. The first picture shows an incorrect path for changing lanes. At higher speeds, this oversteering error could cause you to lose steering control.

Execute any lane-change maneuver as smoothly as possible. Avoid sudden turns of the steering wheel. The second picture shows the safe path of travel of a car executing a smooth lane change.

Always follow the same procedure for making a lane change, regardless of your reason for making the lane change. Before beginning this maneuver, check to see that the roadway ahead is clear of obstructions.

Follow these steps when making a lane change to the left:
1. Check traffic ahead in both lanes and through both rearview mirrors.
2. Signal and make a blind-spot check over your left shoulder to see if any vehicle is about to pass you.
3. Steer gently into the next lane if it is clear.
4. Cancel your signal and adjust speed.

Follow the same procedure when making a lane change to the right, with one exception. After checking traffic ahead and through both mirrors, check the blind-spot area over your right shoulder. Take only a glance to make this check. Be careful not to pull the steering wheel to the right as you turn to glance over your right shoulder. Keep steering straight as you check your blind spot. If the lane is clear, complete the lane change to the right the same way as to the left.

Review It

1. What is the correct position for steering straight forward and backing straight?
2. What are the three arm and hand signals for turns and stopping?
3. What are the steps for changing lanes?

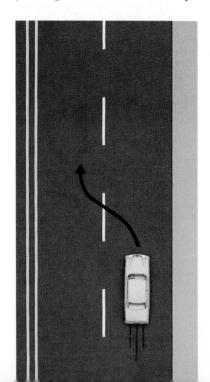
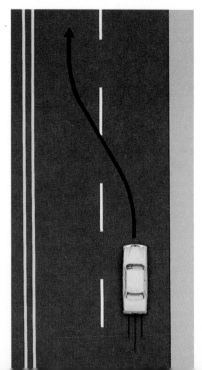

5-2 Turns and Turnabouts

Making turns properly depends on steering control, speed control, and good visual habits. Look far ahead along your planned path of travel to see where your car will go once it has turned. This precaution of looking through a turn helps you know when and how much to turn.

Hand-Over-Hand Steering

You use *hand-over-hand steering* by pulling the steering wheel down with one hand while your other hand crosses over to pull the wheel farther down. The pictures match these steps for correct hand-over-hand steering for a left turn:

1. Begin the turn from a balanced hand position.
2. Place your right hand near the top of the wheel. Start pulling down to the left while releasing your left hand from the wheel.
3. Continue pulling down about a quarter turn with your right hand while crossing your left hand over your right. Grasp the wheel near the top.
4. Pull down with your left hand again as you release your right hand. Continue this action of alternating hands until you have steered enough to complete the turn. As a beginning driver, you might find you need to turn the wheel less than you thought.

Some cars straighten after a turn if you relax your grip and let the wheel unwind through your palms. However, always be ready to unwind the wheel hand-over-hand, especially at lower speeds and with front-wheel drive cars.

Making Left and Right Turns

Make left and right turns cautiously and only after checking the traffic situation around you. Take these precautions:
► Pay special attention to pedestrians, oncoming traffic, and parked cars.

► Obey all traffic signs, signals, and roadway markings. Remember that you must yield to oncoming traffic when preparing to turn left.
► Plan turns well in advance so you are in the correct lane about a block before the turn.

When turning in a stickshift car, you might need to downshift to slow the car before entering a sharp turn. Downshift before the turn so you have both hands free for turning. Be sure to release the clutch before entering the turn.

1.

2.

3.

4.

Procedure for Turning The numbers in the picture match the following steps:

1. Position your car in the correct lane for the turn. For a right turn, be in the far right lane about four feet from the curb if there are no parked cars. For a left turn, be in the lane nearest to the center line. (On a one-way street, be in the far left lane.) Check traffic to the rear. Signal about half a block before the turn.
2. Apply gentle brake pressure to reduce speed.
3. Use your visual search pattern to continue to check traffic all around you. Search for pedestrians and bicyclists.
4. Slow to about 10 mph just before the crosswalk.
5. For a right turn, check to the left again before turning. Then look right, in the direction of the turn. Turn the steering wheel when your car's front wheels are even with the bend of the corner.
6. For a left turn, check traffic to the right and then look left. Turn the steering wheel just before you reach the center of the intersection. Continue looking left into the lane you will enter.

7. As you begin the turn, make a quick blind-spot check through the right side-window. Check that the intersection is still clear. Turn into the nearest lane of traffic going in your direction. Accelerate gently about halfway through the turn. Return the steering wheel to the straight-ahead position.

Backing Left and Right

Use hand-over-hand steering and follow these steps to make sharp turns while backing:

1. Before backing, check for traffic, pedestrians, parked cars, and low stationary objects behind you. Turn your head toward the direction you will back. Look through the rear and side windows in that direction. This driver is in the correct positions for backing left and right.

2. Keep both hands on the steering wheel, ready for hand-over-hand steering. Pull the wheel to the left to back left. Pull the wheel to the right to back right. The back of your car will go in the direction you turn the wheel.

3. Back slowly as you enter the turn. Begin to unwind the steering wheel to finish the turn in a straight position.

When backing left, allow a wide space on the right side. The front wheels will move far to the right of the rear wheels. The front of your car will swing wide to the right.

When backing right, allow a wide space on the left side. This picture shows the space needed and the path your car will follow when you back left and right.

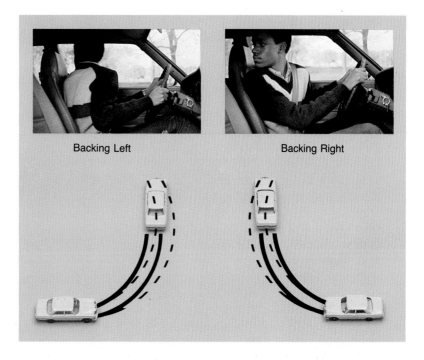

Backing Left   Backing Right

Turning the Car Around

In many cases, the safest and best way to turn your car around is to drive around the block. However, on dead-end streets and in some other locations, you need to use other ways to turn your car around.

A *turnabout* is a maneuver for turning your car around to go in the opposite direction. Turnabouts can be risky since you cross or back into one or more lanes of traffic. Take these precautions when you plan to make a turnabout:

► Do not make a turnabout near hills or curves or within 200 feet of intersections.

► Never attempt a turnabout in heavy traffic.
► Be sure local laws permit the turnabout.
► Select a site with at least 500 feet of clear visibility in each direction.
► Have enough space to complete the maneuver.
► Check continually for traffic and pedestrians.

You must decide which turnabout is best for each situation. Study the five different turnabouts described on pages 84, 85, and 86. The steps for each turnabout match the numbered car positions.

Driveway (Right Side)

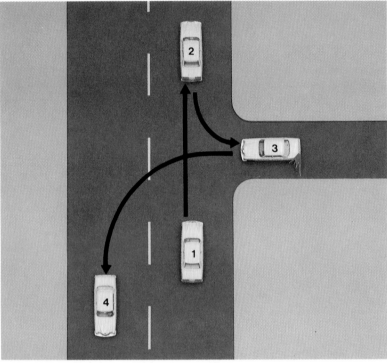

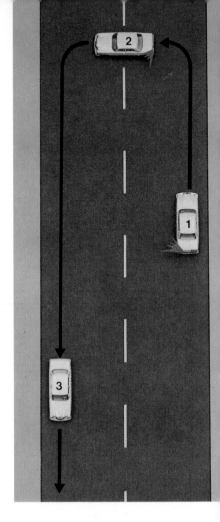

Back into Driveway on Right Side Choose this turnabout if there is a clear driveway on the right and there is no close traffic to the rear in your lane. This turnabout has the advantage of letting you reenter traffic going forward.

1. Check traffic to the rear, and signal a stop. Proceed beyond the driveway.
2. Stop one to three feet from the curb. Check traffic again, and then back slowly to the right to position 3. Stop with the wheels straight.

3. Signal a left turn. Check traffic.
4. Drive forward to position 4.

Mid-Block U-Turn You need a wide space to make a U-turn because no backing is done. In quiet, residential areas, you usually can make a U-turn on a wide street or at an intersection. However, a U-turn at an intersection is illegal in some states. A U-turn is risky because you must cross several lanes of traffic to execute it.

1. Check traffic ahead and to the rear, and signal right. Pull to

the far right and stop. From your stopped position, signal a left turn. Check traffic ahead, to the rear, and in your left blind spot. Turn sharply left while moving slowly to position 2.

2. Check traffic again in both directions. Check the forward space you need to complete the turn. Continue moving slowly toward position 3.
3. Check traffic to the rear. Straighten the wheels while you accelerate gently to proceed in the proper lane.

Driveway (Left Side)

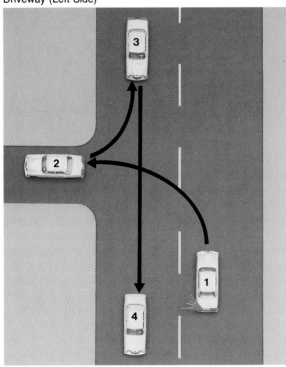

Driveway (Right Side)

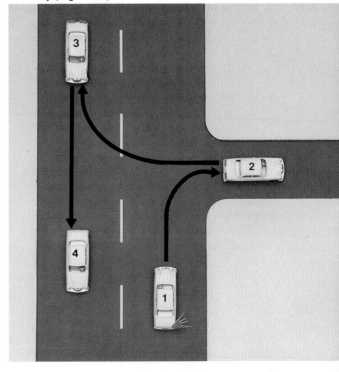

Pull into Driveway on Left Side
You might choose this turnabout if oncoming traffic is light and a driveway on the left is available. A disadvantage of this turnabout is that you must back into the traffic flow before moving forward.

1. Check traffic ahead and to the rear. Signal a left turn and use the left-turn procedure to move to position 2. Stop with the wheels straight.

2. Check traffic again, especially from the right. Back slowly to the right, to position 3. Look to the right rear and side while

backing. Stop with the wheels straight.

3. Accelerate gently, and drive forward to position 4.

Pull into Driveway on Right Side A disadvantage of this turnabout is that you must back across two lanes of traffic before moving forward. Avoid using this turnabout, if possible. It is a high-risk maneuver.

1. Check traffic ahead and to the rear. Signal a right turn and use the right-turn procedure to move to position 2. Stop with the wheels straight.

2. Check traffic again from both directions. Back slowly across the street, turning left toward position 3. Look to the left rear and side when backing. Glance to the front, then continue looking back while stopping with the wheels straight in position 3.

3. Accelerate gently, and drive forward to position 4.

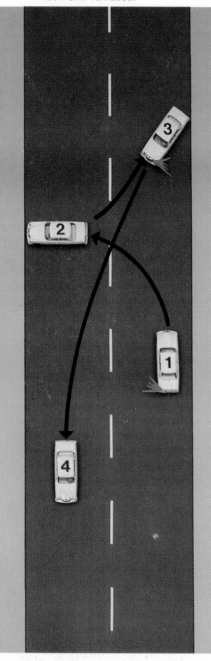

Three-Point Turnabout This turnabout is hazardous to perform. You not only need to cross traffic lanes, but your car is stopped across a traffic lane.

1. Check traffic, and signal right. From a stopped position at the far right, check traffic ahead and to the rear. Signal a left turn. Turn sharply left while moving slowly to position 2. Stop with the wheels straight.

2. Check traffic again. Turn the wheels sharply right while backing slowly to position 3. Back only as far as necessary to complete the maneuver. Stop with the wheels straight.

3. Check traffic again. Move slowly forward while steering left toward position 4.

Deciding Which Turnabout to Use

Consider these factors when deciding which turnabout to use:

► legality of the turnabout
► amount of traffic
► need to enter traffic lanes forward or backward
► ample space and time to enter traffic
► number of traffic lanes to cross.

Backing into a driveway or an alley on the right side is usually the safest type of turnabout to use. You can enter traffic forward from this turnabout. This turnabout makes it easier to choose a safe space in which to enter traffic and to accelerate into that space.

Sometimes you might need to make a turnabout in light traffic. If there are driveways on both the left and the right sides to turn into, choose the left driveway rather than the right. This turnabout lets you back into your own lane rather than back across both lanes. Select a gap in traffic that gives you time and space to complete the maneuver.

There are very few times when you should use a three-point turnabout. Use this turnabout only when you are on a dead-end street or on a rural roadway with no driveways.

Review It

1. What is the procedure for hand-over-hand steering?
2. What are the steps for turning left and right?
3. What space must you consider when backing to the left and to the right?
4. What are five turnabout maneuvers?
5. What are the factors you should consider when planning to execute a turnabout?

Parking your car requires you to use basic maneuvers you have learned. Use *angle parking* to park your car diagonally to the curb. Use *perpendicular parking* to park your car at a right angle to the curb. Use *parallel parking* to park your car parallel to the curb.

Parking is easier and safer if you consider these factors:

► Try to find a parking space with ample room for entering and exiting easily. The size of your car is a factor in determining the space you choose.
► Avoid spaces at the end of parking lanes and near a large vehicle that might block your view.
► Avoid spaces with a poorly parked car on either side.

The following procedures refer to entering a parking space to your right. When parking to your left, adjust your actions and visual checks for the left side. The steps in each procedure match the numbered car positions in the pictures.

Angle Parking

1. Position your car about five feet from the row of parked cars. Signal a right turn, and check traffic to the rear. Begin to brake.
2. Flash your brake lights to warn drivers behind. Continue braking. Check your right blind spot.

3. When you can see down the right line of the parking stall, turn the wheels sharply to the right. Slowly enter the stall.
4. Straighten the wheels when you are centered in the space. Stop before the wheels strike the curb.

Perpendicular Parking

1. Position your car as far to the left of your lane as possible. Signal a right turn, and check your right blind spot. Begin to brake.
2. Flash your brake lights. Check traffic to the rear, and continue to brake.
3. When the front bumper of your car passes the left rear taillight of the car to the right of the empty parking space, turn the wheels sharply right. Slowly enter the stall. Check your right rear fender for clearance.

4. Straighten the wheels when you are centered in the space. Stop before the wheels strike the curb.

Leaving an Angle or a Perpendicular Parking Space Your view often will be blocked as you begin to back into moving traffic. Back cautiously as you look to the rear and sides to search for other roadway users.

1. Creep straight back while you control speed with your foot brake. (Hold the clutch at the friction point in a stickshift car.)
2. When your front bumper is even with the left car's rear bumper, begin to turn right.
3. Back into the nearest lane, and stop with the wheels straight. Shift to a forward gear and proceed.

Angle Parking

Perpendicular Parking

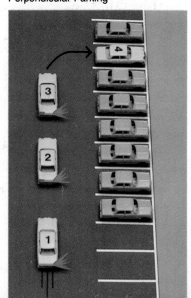

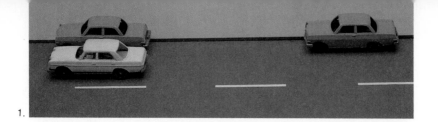

1.

2.

3.

4.

2. When the back of your seat is even with the rear bumper of the front car, straighten wheels. Slowly back straight. Look over your shoulder, through the rear window.

3. When your front bumper is even with the front car's back bumper, turn wheels sharply left. Back slowly and look out the rear window.

4. When your car is parallel to the curb, straighten wheels, and stop before your car touches the car behind. Slowly pull forward to center your car in the space.

Leaving a Parallel Parking Space   You are responsible for avoiding a collision when leaving a parallel parking space. Yield to all approaching traffic.

1. Back straight until your rear bumper almost touches the car behind. Turn wheels sharply left just before you stop.

2. Signal a left turn. Check left blind spot. Move forward slowly.

3. Check right front fender for clearance.

4. Turn wheels slowly to the right when halfway out of parking space. Center car in the lane. Accelerate gently into traffic.

Review It

1. What are the steps for angle parking? perpendicular parking?

2. What are the steps for parallel parking?

Parallel Parking

Successful parallel parking depends on steering and speed control. You must also be able to judge space and distance. Select a space that is about six feet longer than your car. During the maneuver, the front of your car will swing far to the left. Check over your left shoulder to be sure this needed space is clear.

1. Flash brake lights, and signal a right turn. Stop two to three feet away from the front car with the two cars' rear bumpers even. Shift to REVERSE. Check traffic. Look back over your right shoulder. Back slowly as you turn right. Aim toward the right rear corner of the space. Control speed with your foot brake (clutch at friction point in a stickshift car).

5–4 Starting and Parking on Hills

Many times you might find it necessary to stop on a hill such as the one in the picture. You must be able to start moving forward again without rolling back on an uphill grade, and rolling forward on a downhill grade.

Starting on a Hill in a Car with Automatic Transmission

There are two methods for starting on a hill without rolling back. The first method involves the use of the parking brake. The second method uses only the foot brake. Follow these steps when using the parking brake:

1. While holding the foot brake down, set the parking brake firmly.
2. Accelerate until you feel the engine start to pull.
3. Release the parking brake as you continue to accelerate.

    Follow these steps to use only the foot brake:

1. Hold the foot brake down with your *left* foot.
2. While still holding the foot brake with your *left* foot, accelerate gradually until the engine starts to pull.
3. Release the foot brake gently as you increase acceleration to begin moving forward.

Starting on a Hill in a Stickshift Car

Starting in a stickshift car involves the use of the parking brake. Follow these steps in a stickshift car:

1. Be sure the parking brake is set.
2. Shift to FIRST.
3. Use one hand to hold the steering wheel. Hold the parking-brake release with the other hand.
4. Accelerate to a fast idle. Let the clutch out to the friction point.
5. Release the parking brake slowly when you feel the engine begin to pull.
6. Increase pressure on the accelerator, and let the clutch all the way up as your car begins to move forward. Be sure the parking brake is fully released.

    There might be times when you can coordinate the clutch and accelerator to move forward without using the parking brake. Follow these steps:

1. Shift to FIRST while in a stopped position.
2. Keep the foot brake down while releasing the clutch slowly, just to the friction point.
3. Move your right foot quickly from the foot brake to the accelerator. Accelerate gently.
4. Release the clutch smoothly, and increase acceleration.

Parking on Hills

When parking on a hill, you must make sure the car will not roll down into traffic. Take these precautions when you park on a hill:

► Always set the parking brake when parking on a hill.
► Leave the front wheels turned to prevent the car from going into the street if the car should roll. The procedures on page 90 for uphill and downhill parking apply to parking on the right side of the street. Adjust your actions and visual checks when you park on the left side.

Uphill Parking with a Curb

1. Position your car parallel to the street, and stop close to the curb. Just before you stop, turn the steering wheel sharply to the left, as shown in the first picture.
2. Shift to NEUTRAL, and let your car creep back slowly until the back of the right front tire rests gently against the curb.
3. Shift to PARK (FIRST in a stickshift), and set the parking brake.
4. When you leave the parking space, signal, and check traffic before you accelerate gently into traffic.

Uphill Parking with No Curb

1. Pull as far off the pavement as possible. Just before you stop, turn the steering wheel sharply right, as shown in the second picture.
2. Shift to PARK (FIRST in a stickshift), and set the parking brake.
3. When you leave the parking space, allow your car to creep backward while you straighten the wheels. Signal, and check traffic. Shift to DRIVE (FIRST in a stickshift), and accelerate gently into traffic.

Downhill Parking with a Curb

1. Position your car parallel to the street, and stop close to the curb.

2. Let your car creep forward slowly as you turn the steering wheel sharply right, until the right front tire rests gently against the curb, as shown in the third picture.
3. Shift to PARK (REVERSE in a stickshift), and set the parking brake.
4. When you leave the parking space, check traffic and back a short distance while you straighten the wheels. Signal, and check traffic. Shift to DRIVE (FIRST in a stickshift), and accelerate gently into traffic.

Downhill Parking with No Curb

Follow the same procedure as parking downhill with a curb. Turn the wheels sharply right as you creep as near to the shoulder as possible. Note this position in the fourth picture. Use the same steps for parking downhill with a curb to complete your maneuver, and to leave the parking space.

Review It

1. How do you start on a hill without rollback in both an automatic and a stickshift with the use of the parking brake?
2. Which way should the front wheels be turned when parking uphill with a curb? uphill with no curb? downhill with a curb? downhill with no curb?

Uphill Parking with a Curb

Uphill Parking with No Curb

Downhill Parking with a Curb

Downhill Parking with No Curb

Be a Fuel Saver

► When you need to move very slowly, use the idle speed of the engine, not the accelerator. The car can creep without wasting fuel. Hold the clutch at the friction point in a stickshift car.

► Save fuel by slowing early when planning to turn. Accelerate smoothly when coming out of a turn. Sudden acceleration wastes fuel.

► Avoid racing the engine when starting from a stop on an uphill grade. Racing the engine wastes fuel.

► When stopped, turn off the engine if you remain stopped for more than a minute.

Chapter Summary

1. Use a comfortable, balanced hand position for steering straight forward. Make only slight steering corrections. To back straight, turn your body to the right with your right arm over the back of the seat. Look back through the rear window and steer with your left hand. (5–1)

2. Your left arm and hand point up to signal a right turn, extend out to signal a left turn, and downward to signal slow or stop. (5–1)

3. To change lanes, check traffic ahead, through the rearview mirrors, and in blind-spot areas. Signal, and move into the next lane if it is clear. (5–1)

4. To steer hand over hand, pull the wheel down with one hand while your other hand crosses over to grasp the wheel near the top. Your top hand pulls the wheel farther down. (5–2)

5. Be in the correct lane a block before you turn. Signal, and begin to slow while you make traffic checks. Turn into the nearest lane of traffic, and accelerate about halfway through the turn. (5–2)

6. Before backing, check for traffic, pedestrians, and objects behind your car. Turn your head toward the direction you want to back. Look through the rear and side windows. Pull the steering wheel to the left to back left, to the right to back right. Back slowly, and finish in a straight position. (5–2)

7. Execute a turnabout by backing into a driveway on the right, by making a U-turn, by pulling into a driveway on the left or right, or by making a three-point turnabout. (5–2)

8. When deciding which turnabout to use, consider legality, amount of traffic, need to enter traffic forward or backward, space, time, and lanes to cross. (5–2)

9. To angle or perpendicular park, position your car properly, check traffic, and signal. Turn sharply into the space when you can see the right line of the stall for angle parking, or when your front bumper has passed the left taillight of the car to the right of your space for perpendicular parking. (5–3)

10. To parallel park, stop with your rear bumper even and close to the rear bumper of the front parked car. Move slowly while turning the wheel sharply. (5–3)

11. To start on a hill in an automatic-transmission car, set the parking brake, then accelerate and release the parking brake at the same time. Use your left foot on the foot brake, and accelerate with your right foot. In a stickshift car, set the parking brake, shift to FIRST, and hold the clutch at the friction point. Accelerate and release the parking brake. You also can coordinate the clutch and accelerator. (5–4)

12. To park uphill or downhill with a curb, turn the wheels to rest against the curb. If there is no curb, turn the wheels so your car does not roll. (5–4)

Think About It

Imagine that you are on a 2-lane, dead-end, residential street. Driveways are on both sides of the street. Cars are parked almost bumper to bumper along the curbs. Which turnabout would you use and why?

Decision Making

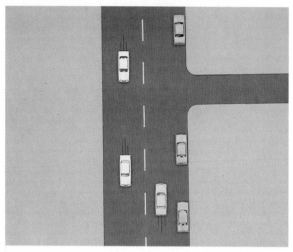

1. You are the driver in this picture and need to make a turnabout. Which type of turnabout would you choose? Why would you choose this type of turnabout?

2. For what reasons should the driver of the car in the picture not choose to park in the open space at the end of the lane?

3. What procedure must the driver of the parked car follow before entering the traffic lane? If there is a collision, who is at fault? Why?

4. In which direction should the wheels be turned for the cars parked uphill? for the cars parked downhill? Why is this important?

Chapter 5 Test

Multiple Choice   Copy the number of each sentence below on a sheet of paper. Choose the letter that best completes the statement or answers the question.

1. To back straight, where should you place your left hand on the steering wheel?
   (a) on the bottom   (b) on the left side   (c) on the right side   (d) on the top   (78)
2. When preparing to change lanes, first
   (a) signal.   (b) check traffic ahead and to the rear.   (c) make a blind-spot check over your left shoulder.   (d) accelerate gently.   (80)
3. When preparing to make a right turn, you should be in the
   (a) left lane.   (b) center lane, if there is one.
   (c) right lane.   (d) special right-turn lane, otherwise you cannot turn right.   (82)
4. When parking uphill on a 2-way street with no curb, turn the front wheels
   (a) to the left.   (b) to the right.   (c) straight.
   (d) either left or right.   (90)
5. The tire that rests against the curb when parked uphill on a 2-way street is the
   (a) right front tire.   (b) left front tire.   (c) right rear tire.   (d) left rear tire.   (90)

Completion   Copy the number of each sentence below. After each number, write the letter of the word or words that complete the sentence correctly.

6. Your car can weave from side to side when you ___.   (78)
7. Holding the clutch at the ___ lets you back your car with controlled speed.   (79)
8. Extend your left arm and hand ___ to indicate a left turn.   (79)
9. Extend your left arm and hand ___ to indicate you will slow or stop.   (79)
10. Pulling the steering wheel down with one hand while the other hand crosses over is called ___.   (81)
11. To slow a stickshift car before turning, ___ to a lower gear.   (81)
12. Turn the steering wheel to the ___ when you want to back to the left.   (83)
13. Turn the steering wheel to the ___ when you want to back to the right.   (83)
14. In many cases, the safest and best way to turn a car around is to ___.   (83)
15. Perform a ___ only when there are no driveways to use for another turnabout.   (86)

   a. back into an alley or a driveway
   b. downshift
   c. drive around the block
   d. friction point
   e. hand-over-hand steering
   f. left
   g. oversteer
   h. right
   i. straight down
   j. straight out
   k. three-point turnabout

Vocabulary   Copy the number of each phrase below. Match the definition in List A with the term it defines in List B.

List A
16. not turn the steering wheel enough   (78)
17. maneuver for turning the car around to go in the opposite direction   (83)
18. parking diagonally to the curb   (87)
19. parking at a right angle to the curb   (87)
20. parking parallel to the curb   (87)

List B
   a. angle parking
   b. oversteer
   c. parallel parking
   d. perpendicular parking
   e. turnabout
   f. understeer

Chapter 6
Intersections

You're the Driver!

Imagine you are driving the car waiting for the children to cross this intersection. The light is about to turn green. You plan to turn left.

Are you stopped in the correct position?

How could the pedestrians affect your left turn?

Where should you be positioned in the intersection while you wait to turn?

Where should you look?

Can you turn left without waiting for oncoming traffic to clear?

Which is the last direction you should look before starting to turn left?

Intersections can be the most dangerous locations on any roadway. Vehicles can create conflicts from several directions. Other roadway users, such as pedestrians and bicyclists, also might be present.

Your decisions require both accurate identifications and predictions.

This chapter tells how to identify each kind of intersection. You also will learn how to interact safely with other roadway users at intersections.

Objectives

The chances of a collision are greater at intersections than at any other point on a roadway. Intersections are dangerous because many drivers' paths cross there. About 40 percent of all collisions and 25 percent of all fatal collisions take place at intersections.

One reason for the large number of collisions at intersections is the driver's failure to identify an intersection. Look for these clues to identify an intersection ahead:

► street signs and street lights
► parked cars on cross streets
► rows of fences and mailboxes
► power lines.

Identifying Uncontrolled Intersections

An *uncontrolled intersection* has no signs or signals to regulate traffic. These intersections usually are found in areas of light traffic, such as residential areas. This picture shows how you would see an uncontrolled intersection to the left, straight ahead, and to the right. Although quiet, these streets can be dangerous because drivers might not be expecting cross traffic or pedestrians. Quick reactions might not protect you at uncontrolled intersections.

Sometimes a driver fails to identify an intersection as uncontrolled. This driver assumes the other driver will stop or, on a quiet street, assumes that no one is there. If you do not see a traffic sign or signal, assume that the intersection is uncontrolled. Be prepared to stop.

Approaching Uncontrolled Intersections

Look left first when you approach an uncontrolled intersection. You cross the path of vehicles from the left first.

Look right first when a building, bushes, or parked cars block your view to the left. Then look left when you reach a position where you have a clear view of the cross street to the left. Drive slowly, as if a vehicle is coming. You can then stop safely if a vehicle appears.

If a vehicle is coming, the driver on the left must yield to the driver on the right. However, predict the worst in each case. Never assume that the other driver will stop. The only safe action is to slow or stop. Treat an uncontrolled intersection as you would a YIELD sign.

Always let a pedestrian go first, no matter where the pedestrian is crossing. As a driver, you must protect pedestrians even if they are breaking a traffic law.

Procedures at Uncontrolled Intersections

To proceed safely through uncontrolled intersections, use the IPDE process at these three locations. The numbers on the cars pictured here refer to the set of steps to be taken in each car location.

IPDE Process at Location 1

1. At mid-block, check roadway condition as you approach the intersection. Check for approaching traffic.
2. Identify whether the intersection is uncontrolled.
3. Identify pedestrians, bicyclists, and motorcyclists in or near the intersection.
4. Check the view to each side. Predict when you can see one-half block to your left and right. That view must be clear for you to go safely.
5. Check the rearview mirror,

then slow. Allow time to use the IPDE process at the other two locations.

IPDE Process at Location 2

1. Look left first. You will cross the path of a vehicle from the left first.
2. Keep your foot over the brake. Be ready to stop if a vehicle is coming from the left.
3. If no vehicle is within one-half block of the intersection, quickly look to the right.

IPDE Process at Location 3

1. Keep looking right. Stop if a vehicle is approaching.
2. If no approaching vehicle is within one-half block of you, glance again in both directions. Then proceed through the intersection.

Review It

1. How should you identify an uncontrolled intersection?
2. What should you do at an uncontrolled intersection?

A *controlled intersection* is one where signals or signs assign the right of way. Obey all STOP signs, YIELD signs, and traffic signals when approaching a controlled intersection. Yield the right of way to through traffic.

Controlled Intersections with Signals

Traffic signals usually have three lights to each cycle—red, yellow, and green. Signals also can have a fourth or fifth light, such as a yellow arrow and a green arrow. Imagine you are stopped at the red light in this picture. Watch the whole cycle closely. Proceed, with caution, when your light turns green.

As you approach an intersection controlled by a traffic signal, check the signal to see if it is about to change. Identify any cars stopped on the cross street. If a car appears to be starting a turn on a red light, predict that the driver might pull in front of you. Move your foot over the brake. Being ready to stop is the only way to achieve a safe path of travel.

Treat each intersection as a separate problem. At mid-block, scan the next intersection to see what color the light is. Look for any traffic moving on the cross street. Before you reach the point where you must brake to stop at an intersection, quickly check left and right. If the light is going to be red or if cross traffic is blocking the way, slow and prepare to stop.

Use the IPDE process when approaching an intersection. Proceed only when you are certain your intended path of travel will be clear. Remember always to yield the right of way to pedestrians.

Stale Green Light   A *stale green light* is a light that has been green for some time. If the light is green and remains green when you first identify it, slow down. Predict that the light will turn yellow soon.

Fresh Green Light   A *fresh green light* has just turned from red to green. A green light does not guarantee that you will have a safe path of travel. Be sure that no driver on the cross street is running the yellow or red light. Look left again before you go.

Yellow Light   When you approach an intersection as the light turns yellow, you must decide whether to stop or proceed. There is a point of no return, where it is no longer safe to stop without entering the intersection. You must proceed. If the light turns yellow before

you reach the point of no return, check traffic to the rear. If it is safe to stop, do so before you enter the intersection. Otherwise, go through the intersection.

Be very careful when completing a left turn on a yellow light. Oncoming traffic might try to hurry through before the light turns red. Wait for all oncoming traffic to stop before starting a turn.

Unprotected Left Turns

An *unprotected left turn* is made at a signal-controlled intersection without a special turn light. When you turn left, you must yield to oncoming traffic. When oncoming vehicles approach the intersection on a green light, they should not have to slow or change position to avoid you.

Use this procedure to make an unprotected left turn:
1. Wait until the light turns green. Move to the center of the intersection, as the yellow car in the picture has done.
2. Keep your wheels straight until you are ready to turn. By doing so, you will not be thrown into oncoming lanes of traffic if you are rear-ended.
3. Stay close to the center line so others can pass on your right.
4. Wait until traffic is clear. Turn left into the lane nearest the center line after making a final check to the right.

Checks to Make on Four-Lane Streets While waiting to turn left in four-lane traffic, make the four checks shown above:
1. **Traffic light** Watch the traffic

light cycle in case the light turns yellow. Thus, you will not miss making your turn when the light changes.
2. **Inside lane** Check speed, distance, and number of oncoming vehicles. Predict possible openings in oncoming traffic.
3. **Outside lane** Check for hard-to-see vehicles that might be hidden by vehicles stopped in the inside lane.
4. **Turn path** Check the exact path your vehicle will take. Look for pedestrians in and near the crosswalk. Begin your turn only when you know you can complete it without stopping. Do not block the outside lane while waiting for pedestrians to clear the crosswalk.

Protected Left Turns

You can make a *protected left turn* when a special left-turn light, green arrow, or delayed green light lets you turn left while oncoming traffic is stopped. Left turns might be prohibited when the protected left-turn cycle ends. If the turn is allowed, respond to it as to an unprotected left turn.

Left-Turn Light   A left-turn light, shown here, provides a protected left turn. The left-turn light can be mounted near the lane with a sign reading, LEFT TURN SIGNAL. However, not all left-turn lanes have left-turn lights.

Green Arrow   A green arrow can appear with the normal red, yellow, and green cycles. The arrow can come on immediately after the red light. In many places the green arrow simply turns off to indicate the protected turn ends soon. Watch the light carefully for the end of the protected turn. Watch for oncoming drivers who might proceed, thinking the green arrow is their green light.

Delayed Green   A *delayed green light* indicates that one side of an intersection has a green light while the light for

the oncoming traffic remains red. This light allows traffic from one side time to turn or go straight before the light for oncoming traffic turns green. Obey your signal only. Do not proceed when oncoming traffic proceeds.

Right-Turn Conflicts

Although a right turn appears to be less dangerous than a left turn, three kinds of conflicts can develop. Be prepared for pedestrian conflicts, conflicts to the rear, and conflicts with oncoming left-turning cars.

Pedestrian Conflicts   As you turn right, pedestrians might step out in front of your car, creating a conflict. Check in and near the crosswalk for pedestrians well before you turn.

Conflicts to the Rear   Signal your right turn one-half block in advance to alert drivers behind you. Tap the brake pedal to flash the brake lights. Brake early, and slow gradually. If you slow or stop suddenly, cars behind you can run into you. Abrupt stops often cause rear-end collisions.

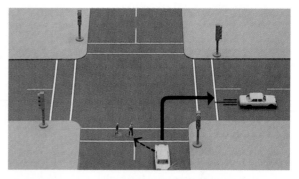

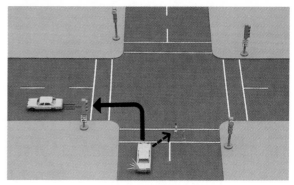

Conflicts with Oncoming Left-Turning Vehicles Study the above left picture to see how conflicts can develop when two cars try to complete turns in the same direction at the same time. Cars turning left often swing wide. Cars turning right might also turn wide. Conflicts can develop if both cars swing wide at the same time. Time your right turn so you complete it just before or after an oncoming driver has completed a left turn. Stay in your lane throughout the turn.

Turns on Red
Check local laws to see if a turn on red is legal. If so, you can turn on red unless a sign posted prohibits this turn.

Right on Red Before turning right on a red light, come to a *full stop* as you would at a STOP sign. After yielding to pedestrians, as the driver in the top right picture has done, move up to a position where you can see clearly to your left. Look left, then right, then

left again. When it is safe to proceed, complete your turn into the nearest right lane.

Left on Red Some states permit a left turn on red if the turn is from a one-way street onto another one-way street. Follow the same procedure as in a right turn on red except that you look for traffic from the right. Then turn into the nearest left lane. The bottom right picture shows this turn.

Controlled Intersections with Signs

Two kinds of signs control intersections. At a STOP sign, come to a *full stop* before entering the intersection. At a YIELD sign, slow and yield the right of way to vehicles on the through street, as shown in the picture to the right.

Signs on two corners of an intersection create a through street. Drivers facing signs at controlled intersections must yield. However, drivers on through streets have no guarantee that drivers on cross streets will stop.

Blocked View

Sometimes parked cars or other objects block your view at intersections. Follow these steps to cross intersections safely and merge with traffic. The numbers on the yellow cars refer to car positions in the pictures.

Crossing Traffic

1. Look through the windows of parked cars. Continue to glance left and right as you creep forward.
2. If the cross street seems clear, move forward to Position 2. Here, you can still stop clear of cars from the left.
3. When the left is clear, glance right. Move to Position 3.

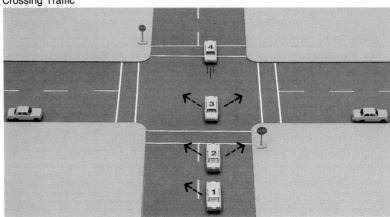

Crossing Traffic

Here, you could stop for a car from the right, if necessary.
4. When clear from the right, go.

Joining Traffic—Right Turn

1. Look in both directions. Then move forward while steering into the right turn.
2. In Position 2, glance left for traffic, then right for turn path. Glance left once more to check for traffic.
3. When clear, go. At Position 3, accelerate to adjust to traffic.

Joining Traffic—Left Turn

1. Glance left and right through windows of parked cars.
2. Stop in Position 2 if traffic is approaching from the left.
3. If the left is clear, move to Position 3. Stop, if necessary, for a car from the right.
4. When clear, go. At Position 4, accelerate properly.

Joining Traffic—Right Turn

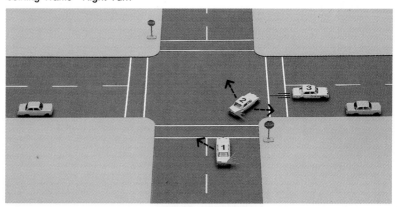

Joining Traffic—Left Turn

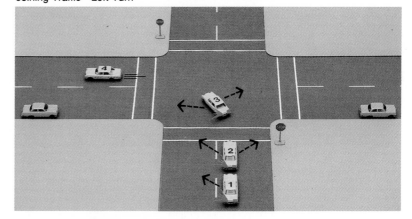

Review It

1. How should you approach an intersection with signals?
2. What checks should you make for an unprotected left turn?
3. How can you prevent each of the three right-turn conflicts?
4. How should you make a right turn at a red light?
5. How should you move from a STOP sign when your view is blocked?

6–3 Judging Time, Space, and Distance

You must be able to judge time and distance accurately at intersections. These judgments are especially important at uncontrolled intersections or intersections that have only YIELD or STOP signs. They are essential for performing two basic intersection skills:
► judging spaces
► knowing how long it takes to pass through or enter intersecting traffic lanes.

Judging the Size of a Gap
A *gap* is the amount of space between vehicles. When you enter a through street from a STOP sign, you must judge the size of the gaps in traffic from the left and right.

You need different size gaps depending on the maneuver you plan to make and the speed of traffic. Crossing a two-lane street takes about 4 to 5 seconds. Turning right and accelerating to 30 mph takes about 6 seconds. Turning left and accelerating to 30 mph takes about 7 seconds. Driver inexperience and reduced traction can increase the time needed to complete a maneuver.

Use these steps to better visualize the size gap you need at an intersection:
1. Stand at a through street, as shown in the picture. Pick a car approaching from the left.
2. Start counting at "one-thousand-one, one-thousand-two," and so on.
3. Continue counting until the car passes the intersection. This process shows you how much time this gap would have given you to cross traffic or to merge safely.

Crossing and Joining Traffic
You need to know how long it takes to turn right, to turn left, and to cross traffic on a typical street. Turning right or left into lanes of other vehicles is called *joining* traffic. You must make time-space judgments to cross or to join traffic.

Estimating Gap Size – 30 mph

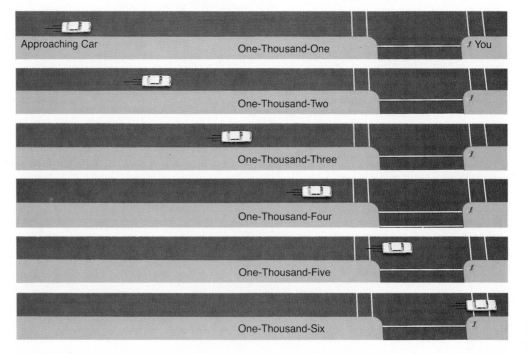

Approaching Car   One-Thousand-One   You

One-Thousand-Two

One-Thousand-Three

One-Thousand-Four

One-Thousand-Five

One-Thousand-Six

Crossing Traffic Crossing an intersection takes about 4 seconds from a stop. If traffic on the through street is traveling 30 mph, you need a gap of about two-thirds of a block in each direction.

Joining Traffic—Right Turn

You need a larger gap to join traffic when turning right than when crossing. You need enough space to reach the speed of through-street traffic without interfering with the flow of traffic.

Imagine you are driving the yellow car in this picture. To join traffic, you must have enough space to turn right and reach 30 mph without forcing the white car to slow. Therefore, the white car must be at least one block away from this intersection.

The faster traffic is moving, the larger the gap must be. At 20 mph, the white car should be more than one-half block away; at 55 mph, more than 3 blocks away.

Joining Traffic—Left Turn

A left turn is more dangerous than a right turn. You cross the paths of traffic from the left before entering traffic from the right. Slowly cross the lane from the left while still gaining speed. The gap to the left should be greater than when you make a right turn. At 20 mph, you need a gap of more than two-thirds of a block in both directions. At 55 mph, you need a gap of more than three and one-half blocks.

Review It

1. How can you estimate the distance a car on a cross street would travel in 6 seconds at 30 mph?
2. Imagine traffic is moving 30 mph on a through street. How large a gap would you need to cross the street?

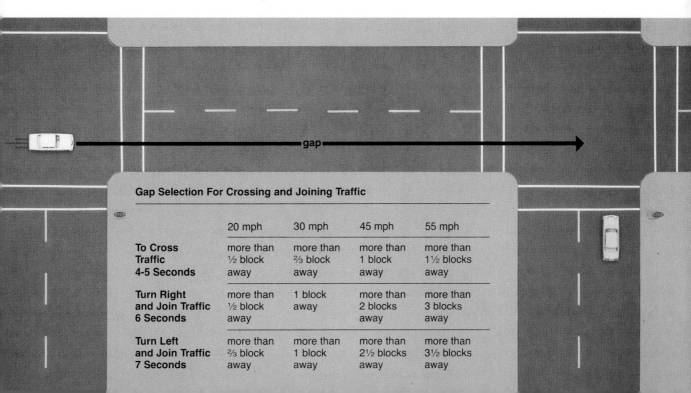

Gap Selection For Crossing and Joining Traffic

	20 mph	30 mph	45 mph	55 mph
To Cross Traffic 4-5 Seconds	more than ½ block away	more than ⅔ block away	more than 1 block away	more than 1½ blocks away
Turn Right and Join Traffic 6 Seconds	more than ½ block away	1 block away	more than 2 blocks away	more than 3 blocks away
Turn Left and Join Traffic 7 Seconds	more than ⅔ block away	more than 1 block away	more than 2½ blocks away	more than 3½ blocks away

6-4 Determining Right of Way

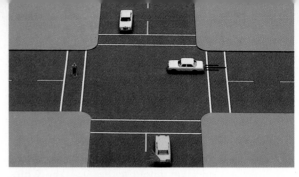

Yield at uncontrolled intersections to
▶ pedestrians in or near the crosswalk.
▶ any vehicle that has entered the intersection.
▶ oncoming traffic when you turn left.
▶ a vehicle from the right if you both arrive at the same time.

A defensive driver knows that conflicts often occur at intersections and is prepared to handle these conflicts. As a defensive driver, allow other traffic to go first rather than create a conflict.

What Is Right of Way?

The term *right of way* describes the privilege of having immediate use of a certain part of a roadway. You have the right of way only when other drivers give it to you.

You will often have to *yield,* let others go first, to be safe. Letting others go first is "yielding the right of way." Sometimes you must yield to prevent a collision. At other times, yielding is an act of courtesy. Most of the time, laws determine the right of way.

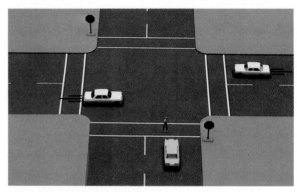

Yield at STOP signs to
▶ pedestrians in or near the crosswalk.
▶ all traffic on the through street.

Situations When You Must Yield

Remember these points in yield situations:
▶ Your action should not cause others who have the right of way to slow or stop.
▶ Traffic signs and signals only show who should yield the right of way. They do not stop traffic for you.
▶ Others can give you the right of way. Never assume others will always yield to you.
▶ A safe action is to yield the right of way even when the law requires the other driver to yield.
▶ Failure to yield the right of way is one of the most frequent violations in fatal collisions.

You must yield the right of way in several situations. Knowing right of way laws will help you make safe decisions. These pictures show the most common situations regarding yielding the right of way. In each situation the yellow car is required to yield.

Yield at fresh green lights to
▶ pedestrians still in the crosswalk.
▶ vehicles still in the intersection.

Review It

1. What is meant by "yielding the right of way"?
2. When should you yield the right of way?

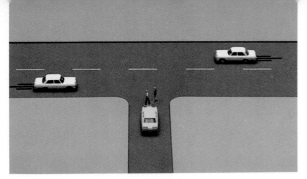

Yield coming from an alley, driveway, or private roadway to
▶ pedestrians before reaching the sidewalk.
▶ all vehicles on the street. (Make two stops.)

Yield when turning left at any intersection to
▶ all pedestrians in your turn path.
▶ all oncoming vehicles that are at all close.

Yield at four-way stops to
▶ all pedestrians in or near crosswalks.
▶ vehicles that arrive first.
▶ a vehicle from the right if you arrive at the same time.

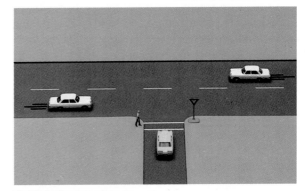

Yield at all YIELD signs to
▶ all pedestrians in or near crosswalks.
▶ all vehicles on the cross street.

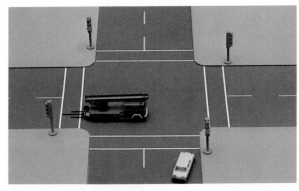

Yield to emergency vehicles
▶ sounding siren or using a flashing light. Stop clear of the intersection close to curb. Wait for emergency vehicles to pass.

Yield to any blind person
▶ carrying a white cane or accompanied by a guide dog.

6-5 Railroad Crossings

More collisions occur at railroad crossings than most drivers realize. Over half of these collisions involve a driver who lives within two miles of the railroad crossing. A driver can become careless after crossing the same tracks day after day and seeing only an occasional train. The driver often forgets that the railroad crossing is a hazard.

Railroad crossings are nearly always marked. In towns and cities, a round, yellow railroad-crossing sign is posted about 250 feet from a crossing. In rural areas this sign is about 750 feet from a crossing. A *crossbuck,* a large white X-shaped sign, often is located beside the crossing. Many times a large white X is painted on the roadway near the crossing.

Controlled Crossings

A *controlled railroad crossing* usually has both red lights and crossing gates. Make a complete stop when the lights are flashing or the gates are down. Remain stopped until the lights stop flashing and the gates are raised. It is illegal to drive around the gates.

Uncontrolled Crossings

An *uncontrolled railroad crossing* does not have red lights or crossing gates. However, most uncontrolled crossings, like controlled crossings, are marked with a round, yellow railroad-crossing sign and the crossbuck seen here. Treat uncontrolled crossings the same as an intersection with a YIELD sign. Slow and be prepared to stop.

Crossing Railroad Tracks

Take these actions when approaching a railroad crossing:

1. Slow down. Check traffic to the sides and to the rear as you approach the round railroad-crossing sign.
2. Turn off the radio, air conditioner, or heater fan to listen for train sounds.
3. Reduce speed to handle a possibly rough road surface safely. Check available sight distance. Reduce speed if the sight distance is short.
4. Stop at a safe distance before the tracks if a train is approaching, if the red lights are flashing, or if the crossing gates are down.
5. Wait for the train to clear. Then check the crossing. Be sure another train is not approaching on another set of tracks.
6. If it is safe to cross, try to keep your speed up to at least 20 mph. Then, your car can roll across the tracks if its engine should stall.
7. If you have a stickshift, shift to a lower gear before crossing to prevent stalling on the tracks.
8. Drive onto the tracks only after you have enough space and speed to clear the tracks. Make sure any vehicles ahead clear the tracks before you start to cross. Never stop on railroad tracks, waiting for traffic ahead to move.
9. When following buses or trucks hauling flammable contents, be prepared for them to stop. Some states require such vehicles to stop at all crossings.

Review It

1. What signs appear at or near both controlled and uncontrolled railroad crossings?
2. What are the procedures to use at a railroad crossing?

Advancements in Traffic Safety

Many collisions occur when an emergency vehicle, proceeding against a red light, is struck broadside by a car proceeding with a green light. A traffic-control system has been developed to help emergency vehicles clear intersections safely. The system holds the green light for an emergency vehicle, but also stops cross traffic with a red light.

The system has three parts: a signal light, a detector, and a phase selector. The signal light is mounted on the emergency vehicle. It works like a strobe light. As the vehicle comes to a signal-controlled intersection, the light shines on a detector near the traffic signal. The detector alerts the phase selector, located in a nearby traffic-control cabinet.

If the emergency vehicle already has a green light, the phase selector keeps the light green. If the light is red, the selector speeds the signal's normal cycle. The light is green when the emergency vehicle arrives. The traffic signal returns to its normal cycle after the emergency vehicle clears the intersection.

Chapter Summary

1. An uncontrolled intersection has no signs or signals to regulate traffic. (6–1)
2. Approach an uncontrolled intersection as you would a YIELD sign: reduce speed and check approaching traffic. (6–1)
3. Identify the color of the light and estimate the traffic flow as you approach an intersection controlled by signals. (6–2)
4. Before making an unprotected left turn, make these four checks: traffic light, inside lane, outside oncoming lane, turn path. Make a protected left turn on a green arrow, a special left-turn light, and a delayed green light. (6–2)
5. Right-turn conflicts can develop with pedestrians, with traffic to the rear, and with oncoming left-turning vehicles. (6–2)
6. Handle turns on red the same as STOP signs. Left turns on red can only be from a one-way street to another one-way street. (6–2)
7. When entering a through street where your view is blocked, look through vehicles or around them, and continue to glance left and right until the view improves. (6–2)
8. You need a gap of 4 to 5 seconds to cross a two-lane street; at least 6 seconds to turn right; at least 7 seconds to turn left. (6–3)
9. Make accurate time-space judgments to cross or join traffic safely. (6–3)
10. Right of way is the privilege of having immediate use of a part of a roadway. (6–4)
11. Yield to traffic in these situations: to enter an uncontrolled intersection from a parked position or an alley; to emergency vehicles; to pedestrians; to vehicles already in the intersection. (6–4)
12. A controlled railroad crossing usually has both red lights and crossing gates. An uncontrolled crossing often has only a crossbuck and a round, yellow railroad-crossing sign. (6–5)
13. When approaching a railroad crossing, reduce speed, listen, look in both directions, and check the tracks. Prepare to stop if a train is coming. Never stop on the tracks, waiting for traffic ahead of you to proceed. (6–5)

Think About It
Two vehicles have collided at an intersection. What factors should be considered to determine which driver should have yielded the right of way?

Decision Making

1. You are driving the yellow car and are approaching an uncontrolled intersection. You and the other car are the same distance from the intersection. What do you predict about the other driver? What should you do?

2. You have just stopped at a red light. You wish to turn left. Is a left turn at this intersection legal on a red light? Where should you check before turning?

3. You are driving the white car, approaching an intersection where several cars are stopped for a traffic light. Note the railroad tracks in front of you. Where should you stop? What could happen in this situation?

4. You are driving the blue car that is stopped at the STOP sign. At what speed would you assume the cars on the through highway would be traveling? How far away would the cars have to be for you to turn left?

Chapter 6 Test

Multiple Choice   Copy the number of each sentence below on a sheet of paper. Choose the letter that best completes each statement or answers each question.

1. An uncontrolled intersection is one in which (a) there is no traffic.   (b) there are no traffic-control signs or signals.   (c) signs assign the right of way.   (d) drivers do not yield the right of way.   (96)
2. Where should the identification process begin at an uncontrolled intersection? (a) at mid-block   (b) 1/4 block from the intersection   (c) just before the crosswalk   (d) just as the front wheels reach the crosswalk   (97)
3. When you are about to cross an uncontrolled two-way street, first look (a) left.   (b) right.   (c) straight ahead.   (d) at the speedometer.   (97)
4. In most states, you can make a right turn during a red light when (a) turning onto a one-way street.   (b) forcing other traffic to slow down.   (c) no sign prohibits it.   (d) pulling out with traffic.   (101)
5. Which action takes the least amount of time at a typical intersection? (a) crossing an intersection   (b) turning left (c) turning right   (d) waiting for a train to pass (104)

Completion   Copy the number of each sentence below. After each number, write the letter of the word or words that complete the sentence correctly.

6. An ____ has no signs or signals to regulate traffic. (96)
7. A traffic light that is green when you first see it, but will soon turn yellow is a ____. (98)
8. Keep your wheels ____ while stopped in an intersection, waiting to turn left. (99)
9. When you have a protected left turn, oncoming drivers face a ____. (100)
10. Crossing an ____ from a stop takes about four seconds. (104)
11. Fitting into a gap in traffic is called ____. (104)
12. You ____ when you allow another driver to proceed first. (106)

13. At an uncontrolled intersection, the driver on the left must yield to the driver on the ____. (106)
14. You must always yield to ____.   (107)
15. It is illegal to drive around ____.   (108)

a. intersection
b. joining
c. pedestrians
d. railroad crossing gates
e. red light
f. right
g. stale green light
h. straight
i. uncontrolled intersection
j. yellow light
k. yield

Vocabulary   Copy the number of each phrase below. Match the definition in List A with the term it defines in List B.

List A
16. intersection regulated by signs or signals (98)
17. light that has just turned from red to green (98)
18. left turn made at an intersection that does not have a special turn light (99)
19. light that remains red while oncoming traffic lanes clear (100)
20. turn made on a left-turn light or arrow while oncoming traffic is stopped (100)
21. distance between approaching cars in which to cross an intersection or join traffic (104)
22. privilege of immediate use of the roadway (106)
23. crossing with crossing gates and signals (108)
24. crossing without crossing gates and signals (108)
25. large, white X-shaped sign (108)

List B
a. controlled intersection
b. controlled railroad crossing
c. crossbuck
d. delayed green light
e. fresh green light
f. gap
g. protected left turn
h. right of way
i. uncontrolled railroad crossing
j. unprotected left turn
k. yield

Chapter 7
Natural Laws and Car Control

You're the Driver!

Think about how you would drive through the situation pictured here. You are going through a sharp curve at a moderate speed.

How will energy of motion affect your car?

What effect does the condition of your tires have as you enter the curve?

If the roadway were slick, how would you react?

How might your safety belt help you maintain control of your car as you drive through this curve?

You need to know how natural laws can affect car control. By knowing these laws, you will be better prepared to avoid trouble by steering, braking, or accelerating.

In this chapter you will learn how and why a car responds as it does under various conditions. Use this knowledge of natural laws to predict how different vehicles will respond in different situations.

Objectives

7–1 Gravity and Energy of Motion

1. Explain how gravity can affect car control. (114)
2. Explain how energy of motion is influenced by the weight and speed of a moving car. (115)

7–2 Friction and Traction

3. Tell how tire traction is used to control a car. (116)
4. List three factors that can reduce traction. (118)

5. List the factors that affect car control in a curve. (119)
6. Explain the importance of knowing the capabilities of other types of vehicles. (120)

7–3 Stopping Distance

7. Define total stopping distance. (122)
8. Explain how to use the 4-second rule. (123)
9. Name four factors that affect braking distance. (123)

7–4 Force of Impact

10. List three factors that can affect a car's force of impact in a collision. (124)
11. List energy-absorbing features built into cars. (125)

7–5 Safety Belts and Other Restraint Devices

12. Explain the correct way to adjust safety belts. (126)
13. Describe passive restraints for adults and safety seats for children. (126)

7-1 Gravity and Energy of Motion

The natural laws of gravity and energy of motion work together to determine how your car will respond. When you ride a bicycle at low speeds, you can easily control the forces involved. When you drive a 3,000 pound car at highway speeds, the forces are much greater. Your control over these forces is much more difficult.

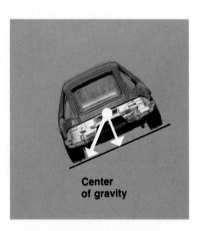

Center of gravity

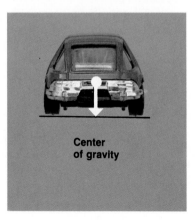

Center of gravity

To maintain control of your car, you must understand the effects of the forces. You must stay alert and be ready to act.

Gravity

The force that pulls all objects toward the center of the earth is called *gravity*. Throw a ball, drop a book, or knock a glass off a shelf; gravity pulls each of these objects back toward the earth. Gravity also pulls vehicles toward the earth.

Uphill and Downhill Effects of Gravity When you drive uphill, your car can lose speed as it works against the force of gravity. You must increase power to maintain speed. You might have to downshift to a lower gear in a stickshift car in order to climb a steep hill.

Before passing on a long uphill grade, make sure you

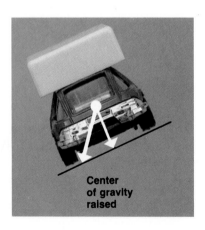

Center of gravity raised

have enough power to both accelerate uphill and pass the car ahead safely. Your car might not have enough power to do both. You can control your car by shifting to a lower gear.

The force of gravity also tends to increase the speed of cars going downhill. You need a longer distance in which to stop. Plan ahead to use a longer distance to stop when going down hills or mountains. Release the accelerator pedal, and use the foot brake to slow your car when driving downhill. By releasing the accelerator, you will also save fuel.

Center of Gravity An object's *center of gravity* is the point around which all of the object's weight is evenly balanced. For example, a circus high-wire performer uses a pole for balance. As the ends of the pole bend down, the pole lowers the performer's center of gravity. This lower center of gravity helps keep the performer from falling.

Most cars have a low center of gravity so they will handle well in turns. These three pictures show how adding weight to a roof-top carrier can raise a car's center of gravity. A car will handle differently when its center of gravity is raised. It will be less stable in curves and during quick maneuvers.

Energy of Motion

The energy an object has as a result of its moving is called *energy of motion* or kinetic energy. The faster a car moves, the more energy of motion it will have. The car will be harder to control.

These pictures show how energy of motion increases dramatically as weight and speed increase. Compare the pictures and note that:

► A vehicle's energy of motion doubles when its weight doubles. When the vehicle's weight doubles, the vehicle needs about twice the distance to stop.

► A vehicle's energy of motion is proportional to the *square* of its increase in speed. When the vehicle's speed doubles, the vehicle needs about four times the distance to stop. When the vehicle's speed triples, the vehicle needs about nine times the distance to stop.

Review It

1. How does the force of gravity affect a car going uphill?
2. How much will a car's energy of motion increase if the car's speed doubles?

Empty truck
25 mph

15 feet

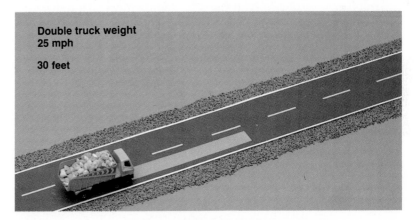

Double truck weight
25 mph

30 feet

Empty truck
50 mph

60 feet

7–2 Friction and Traction

Many drivers think the steering wheel, brake pedal, and accelerator control the car. These are the controls you operate. However, tires actually control the movement of the car. This picture shows the small areas where the tires actually touch the roadway. Each area is about as big as one page in this book.

A gripping action, called *friction*, keeps each tire from slipping when the tires rest or roll on the roadway. You can feel this friction by rubbing your hands together.

The friction created by a tire and the roadway is usually called *traction*. Traction allows a car to grip the roadway so it

can speed up, slow down, and turn. Push the accelerator pedal and the drive wheels turn. The traction the tires provide moves your car forward.

Push the brake pedal, and braking friction slows the wheels. When the wheels slow, traction between the tires and the roadway slows the car. When you turn the steering wheel, the front tires provide traction to turn.

Ice, rain, or even sand on the roadway can reduce the amount of traction between your tires and the roadway. When traction is reduced, your ability to control your car also is reduced.

Tires
Tires can make a difference in the way your car handles. Get the best performance from your tires and your car by knowing about tires and how to care for them.

Tread and Traction The grooved surface of a tire that grips the roadway is called *tread*. When roadways are wet, the tread allows water to flow through the grooves and away from the tire. The tire grips the roadway and does not "float" on the water, giving you better control of your car.

The amount of tread that grips the roadway can increase the traction and control a tire

can produce. A snow tire's large open tread gives extra traction in the same way. By letting snow go through the grooves, more of the tread grips the roadway. Tire size can also change the amount of tread on the roadway. Check the manufacturer's suggested tire sizes for your car before changing tire size.

A bald tire or a tire with little tread does not grip wet or slick roadways well. When the tread is worn down, car control can be reduced to almost nothing. An extremely bald tire might result in a *blowout*, a sudden loss of air pressure in a tire. If you can see wear bars on a tire, or cords coming through the tire tread, replace the tire. See Chapter 17 for information on tire wear and tire maintenance.

Inflation and Traction   A tire works best at a specific pressure. These pictures show how too much or too little air pressure can reduce traction. A tire inflated to the correct pressure grips the roadway evenly. Correct tire pressure also increases fuel economy.

If air leaks out, the tire becomes underinflated. Only the outside edges of the tire grip the roadway well. The outside edges on the tire will wear more quickly.

A tire can be overinflated, have too much air pressure. Only the center of the tire grips the roadway well. The center of the tire wears more quickly.

Temperature also affects tire pressure. If the outside air temperature increases, tire pressure also increases. If the weather turns colder, tire pressure decreases.

Divided Traction   The amount of traction your tires can produce is limited, even under ideal conditions. When you brake, you can use all available traction to stop.

However, tire traction is divided when you slow for a turn. Some traction is used to turn; some traction is used to slow. In this situation, you cannot brake as hard as you would when stopping in a straight line. This limitation also applies when accelerating and turning. If you exceed your traction limit, your car will skid.

Speed also changes your level of car control. At low speeds, you usually can avoid skidding. At higher speeds, you must make adjustments in steering, accelerating, and braking so that you stay within the limits of available traction and avoid skidding.

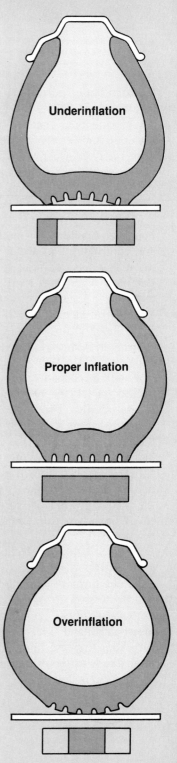

Proper Inflation for Better Grip on Road

Underinflation

Proper Inflation

Overinflation

117

Factors That Reduce Traction

Two elements are needed to maintain high levels of traction. First, your car must be in good condition. Second, the roadway you drive on must be paved, clean, dry, and level.

Poor Car Condition Traction and control are best when your car is new. As your car ages, you must maintain it more often to keep your car's traction and control high. If you allow tires, shock absorbers, or steering system parts to wear excessively, traction and control will be reduced.

Good shock absorbers help create traction. They help keep your tires from bouncing off the roadway as you drive over high and low spots. Worn shock absorbers allow tires to bounce and lose contact with the roadway. Replace worn shock absorbers to maintain traction.

Worn or bald tires do not grip wet roadways well. If you have one or more worn tires and try to stop or turn quickly on a wet roadway, you might lose control and skid. To make sure your tires are safe, check their treads as the driver in the top picture is doing.

Poor Roadway Surface When you drive a car on straight, dry, flat roadways, traction and control are very good. However, traction is reduced if you drive that same car on a wet, snow-covered, or bumpy roadway.

When you leave a paved roadway and then drive on a sandy, muddy, or gravel roadway, traction can be reduced greatly. Slow down when you approach such a roadway. Adjust your speed to conditions before you get to the roadway.

Bad weather can reduce traction on an otherwise good roadway. Snow, ice, and rain can reduce traction. When ice is covered with water from melting snow and ice, traction often is reduced to almost nothing. Watch for wet roadways on bridges or in shaded areas. These areas can freeze *before* other roadway surfaces as the temperature nears the freezing point.

Study the bottom picture. In this situation, you must slow sooner so you have enough traction to stop.

Checking Traction Reduce speed to maintain traction when roadway conditions are poor. Use these steps to check the traction you have:
1. Be sure no traffic is near.
2. Brake *gently* to see how your car responds.
3. If your car does not respond well, reduce speed further.

Curves

Imagine you are driving the car in the top right picture. Note the two forces that act on a car when it rounds a curve or turns a corner. A moving car's energy of motion increases as its speed increases. Energy of motion tries to keep the car going in a straight line. The higher the car's speed, the more the car resists turning.

You must slow down to reduce energy of motion. If you are going too fast, there might not be enough traction to keep you from skidding straight off the curve. Traction from the car's tires and the roadway must be greater than the energy of motion. You can safely steer the car through the curve then.

These factors affect the control you have over your car in a curve:

► **Speed** You have no control over how sharp a curve is, but you can adjust speed. Do not adjust speed in a curve. Instead, slow down ahead of time, before you reach the curve.

Imagine you are driving in the situation pictured at the bottom right. Notice that the driver in front of you is slowing ahead of time before entering a curve.

Now imagine the posted speed around a curve is 20 mph. If you drive through that curve at 40 mph, you might not have the amount of traction you need to stay on the roadway. The amount of traction needed at 40 mph is four times greater than the amount needed at 20 mph.

► **Sharpness of a Curve** The sharper the curve, the more traction the car needs to grip the roadway at a given speed. Use lower speeds for sharp curves. When you approach a sharp curve, slow before entering the curve. Curves on newer roadways, like expressways, are designed to be gradual so you can drive through them at higher speeds.

► **Bank of a Curve** A curve that is higher on the outside than it is on the inside is called a *banked curve*. This type of curve helps to overcome a car's tendency to move to the outside of a curve. This tilt toward the inside improves control by working with the force of gravity.

► **Load** A vehicle's load determines its ability to handle curves. Imagine that a lightly loaded vehicle can barely make a safe turn at 35 mph. That same vehicle, now heavily loaded, must reduce speed to handle the same curve safely.

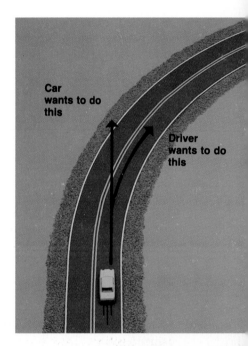

Car wants to do this

Driver wants to do this

Vehicle Capabilities

The number and the variety of vehicles using the HTS are two factors that make the HTS so complex. Think about the last time you were on a highway. More than likely, you met or passed small and large cars, trucks, and even recreational vehicles. To become a safe, fuel-efficient driver, you must know how your car and other vehicles perform under different conditions.

Imagine you are going to drive from your home to a store. Think about what you need to know for this trip. You have just left home and are driving to the store. To complete this trip, you must know how quickly your car can accelerate. When you approach a STOP sign, you must know how much braking power your car has and how to use that power. If a child unexpectedly darts into the street, you might have to swerve. You must know how quickly you can steer into the next lane. Finally, your car will respond differently at higher speeds when you drive on a highway or an expressway. You must modify the way you steer, brake, and accelerate. In short, you must know what to expect in different situations. Your goal is to keep control of your car at all times.

Besides having control of your car, you must know how other vehicles can perform. Being able to judge what others can do will help you to use the IPDE process better. Once

Capability	Small Vehicles	Mid-Size Vehicles	Large Vehicles	Recreational Vehicles
Accelerating	moderate to high depending on engine size	moderate	usually slow	slow in most situations; 4-wheel drive vehicles accelerate well in low-traction situations
Braking	good	ranges from slow to good; heavy loads might reduce vehicle's braking capability	slow, especially when fully loaded	slow
Turning	good for quick turns	good; possibly slower when heavily loaded	poor for quick turns	poor for quick turns; vehicles equipped with special high suspensions can be dangerous in quick turns
Total Control	good response at higher speeds; high winds might make vehicle wander in lane	good response; sluggish response when heavily loaded	slow response, especially when heavily loaded	slow response

you know how vehicles can perform, you will be able to:
► **Identify** vehicles that are, or are about to start, moving.
► **Predict** where another vehicle and your car might conflict.
► **Decide** how to adjust your speed and position to create a space cushion.
► **Execute** a braking, steering, or accelerating action to complete this adjustment.

Think of each vehicle as fitting into one of the four groups in this chart. An example of each type of vehicle is shown on page 120.

Small Vehicles This group includes vehicles such as motorcycles, subcompact cars, and high-powered sports cars.

Mid-Size Vehicles This group includes station wagons, minivans, sedans, and small trucks.

Large Vehicles This group includes trucks, buses, and other large, over-the-road vehicles.

Recreational Vehicles This group includes full-size vans and off-road vehicles.

Grouping vehicles will not improve control of your own car. However, it can give you an idea of how each vehicle performs in various situations.

While driving, you must consider how another vehicle might perform. You also must think ahead to what the other driver is about to do. This

chart shows ways vehicles perform in different situations.

Remember that vehicles will respond differently. If you have any doubts as to how a vehicle will respond, increase your space cushion. Give the vehicle extra room to move.

Review It
1. What is the purpose of grooves on a tire tread?
2. What are three factors that can reduce traction?
3. When should you start to slow for a curve?
4. Why should you know the capabilities of other vehicles?

7-3 Stopping Distance

When you are driving and have to stop, three things must happen. You must:
► identify the situation.
► react.
► slow your car to a stop.

Total Stopping Distance
The distance your vehicle takes to stop is called *total stopping distance*. This distance is measured from the point you first see a problem to the point where your vehicle stops. Study the picture as you read about the three parts of total stopping distance.

Perception Time and Distance
The length of time it takes you to identify a situation is your *perception time*. Perception time can vary greatly depending on visibility, the hazard, and your ability to identify the hazard. The distance a car travels during this time is called *perception distance*.

You cannot estimate perception distance because it varies from person to person. Sometimes it takes longer to perceive a dangerous situation than it does to brake to a stop. You can shorten perception time by using an orderly visual search pattern to get the "big picture."

Reaction Time and Distance
Once you identify a hazard, the length of time you take to act is your *reaction time*. The average driver's reaction time is 3/4 second. Reaction time can be longer if the driver's reactions are somehow impaired. Reaction time also can lengthen if the traffic situation is complex and involves a number of moving or changing hazards. The distance a car travels during this time is called *reaction distance*.

Braking Distance   The distance your car travels from the time you apply the brakes until your car stops is called *braking distance*. A car's energy of motion is proportional to the square of its increase in speed. Braking distance also is proportional to the square of a car's increase in speed. A car going 40 mph has a braking distance four times greater than when it is going 20 mph.

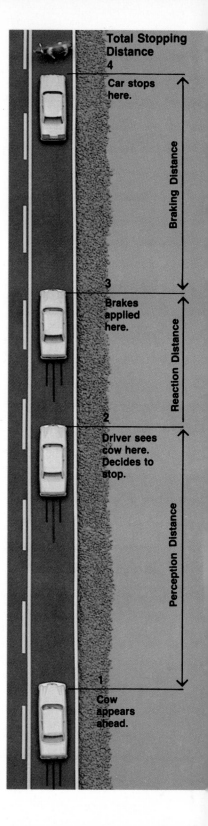

Total Stopping Distance

4 Car stops here.

Braking Distance

3 Brakes applied here.

Reaction Distance

2 Driver sees cow here. Decides to stop.

Perception Distance

1 Cow appears ahead.

Estimating Your Stopping Distance

This chart shows approximately how far a car travels at various speeds while the driver reacts and brakes the car to a stop. Change the driver, car, or driving surface, and these distances can vary.

Judging distances can be difficult. Use the 4-second rule to estimate your stopping distance under ideal conditions. Four seconds is the approximate time you need to react and bring your car to a stop.

Use these steps to estimate stopping distance:

1. Pick a fixed check point (a shadow or set mark on the roadway) ahead of your car.
2. Count off 4 seconds: "one-thousand-one, one-thousand-two, one-thousand-three, one-thousand-four."
3. Check your car's position. Have you just reached the fixed check point? If so, you can assume the distance you picked in Step 1 was the approximate distance it would have taken you to stop.

Factors That Affect Braking Distance

Although the laws of nature affect all vehicles in the same way, never assume you can stop in the same distance as the vehicle ahead. The factors listed here can increase braking distance:

► **Speed** The higher the speed, the longer the braking distance. At high speeds, you might have a harder time controlling your car.
► **Car Condition** A car with worn tires, shock absorbers, or brakes needs a longer braking distance. If the brakes are worn on only one side of the car, the car might pull to one side in a stop. It will take longer to stop.
► **Roadway Surface** Rain, snow, ice, dirt, sand, and gravel on the roadway increase braking distance.
► **Driver Reaction** A driver who panics and slams on the brakes might lose control in an emergency situation.
► **Hills** Braking distance increases when driving downhill.
► **Load** A heavy load can increase braking distance.

Review It

1. What are the three parts that add up to make a total stopping distance?
2. How can you estimate stopping distance?
3. What factors could affect braking distance?

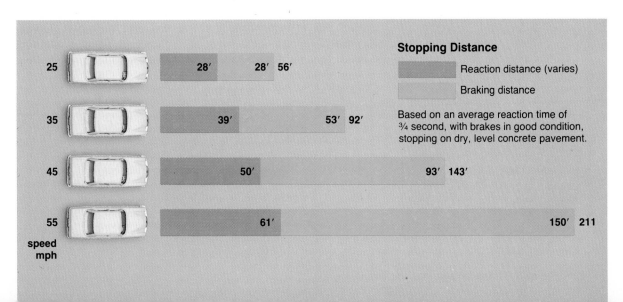

Stopping Distance

☐ Reaction distance (varies)
☐ Braking distance

Based on an average reaction time of ¾ second, with brakes in good condition, stopping on dry, level concrete pavement.

speed mph	Reaction	Braking	Total
25	28'	28'	56'
35	39'	53'	92'
45	50'	93'	143'
55	61'	150'	211'

7-4 Force of Impact

10 mph

20 mph

40 mph

The force with which one moving object hits another object is called *force of impact*. Study these pictures as you read about force of impact.

Factors Affecting Impact

Three factors determine how hard the force of impact will be when a car hits another object. These factors are:

► **Speed** When a moving object hits something, the object's speed is the most important factor in determining how hard it hits. The force of impact is proportional to the square of the speed.

A car moving at 20 mph hits a tree four times as hard as it would have if it were moving at 10 mph. At 40 mph, the car hits sixteen times as hard as at 10 mph. Car occupants will be seriously injured or killed if they are not wearing safety belts and then are thrown against the instrument panel at 40 mph. Compare the damage done at these different speeds.

Any reduction in speed can greatly reduce the damage in a collision. This fact explains why it is so important to reduce speed before a collision.

► **Weight** The heavier a vehicle is, the harder it will hit. A car weighing twice as much will hit a solid object twice as hard. However, this does not mean a smaller car better protects its occupants in a collision. In most cases, a larger car can better absorb the impact and protect its occupants.

► **Distance Between Impact and Stop** The distance a car covers between the time it first hits an object and its stopping point can vary greatly. Imagine hitting something solid, such as a large tree. Your car will stop very quickly because the tree will not give.

The force of impact in this type of collision is very damaging. However, the damage will be less if you can hit something softer, such as a fence or hedge. The softer object cushions the impact. It helps slow your car gradually and reduce the force of impact. Given a choice of hitting something hard or soft, try to hit the soft object.

Energy-Absorbing Features

Automobile manufacturers have designed many energy-absorbing features to protect car occupants. Two of these features, a padded dash and head restraints, are pictured here.

► **Front and Rear Crush Areas** Newer cars have areas that crush upon impact. Crush areas protect occupants by absorbing some of the force of impact. For example, when a car hits a solid object head-on, the car's front end crushes. As the front end crushes, the force of impact lessens.

► **Energy-Absorbing Bumpers** Most bumpers are designed to absorb low levels of impact. They protect the front and rear of the car.

► **Side Door Beams** Steel beams are inside each door. The beams help protect occupants from side impacts.

► **Reinforced Windshield** Plastic sheeting is used to reinforce windshield glass. This feature helps protect occupants against broken glass.

► **Energy-Absorbing Steering Wheel and Column** These features absorb some of the force of impact in a collision.

► **Padded Dash** Metal areas are covered. Knobs are recessed.

► **Head Restraints** The padded areas are located on the backs of the seats. Head restraints help protect against whiplash in rear-end collisions.

Review It

1. What are three factors that can affect the force of impact?
2. What are four energy-absorbing features and how do they work?

7–5 Safety Belts and Other Restraint Devices

Two collisions occur when a car with unrestrained occupants smashes into a solid object. The first collision occurs when the car hits the object and stops. The second collision occurs when the occupants hit the inside of the car.

A *restraint device* is any device that is used to hold car occupants in their seats during a collision. Restraint devices are designed to hold and protect a car's occupants during both the first and the second collision.

Safety Belts

A safety belt that you must buckle is an *active restraint*. This belt must be adjusted properly to give maximum protection. The lap belt should fit snugly across the hips. The shoulder belt should fit comfortably across the chest with a minimum of slack. You should be able to slip only your closed fist between the belt and your chest. The picture shows how a fastened safety belt works to protect the wearer.

Safety belts have been proven effective in reducing collision-related injuries and deaths. Many states have passed, or are considering, laws that require the use of safety belts and child seats. In areas where safety-belt use is required, collision-related deaths and injuries have been dramatically reduced.

A safety belt also can help you in other emergencies. The belt holds you in place so you can better control the steering wheel.

Other Restraint Devices

Other types of restraint devices have been developed to protect car occupants, particularly children. These devices include passive restraints and child seats.

Passive Restraints A *passive restraint* is a device that performs a function similar to an active restraint. However, you do not need to fasten a passive restraint. An air bag and an automatic safety belt are two examples of passive restraints.

An air bag provides protection primarily in front-end collisions. It inflates automatically the instant a car hits an object. The bag deflates immediately after the collision.

An automatic safety belt fastens after a front-seat occupant sits down and closes the door. This safety belt protects in much the same way as a regular safety belt protects.

Child Seats A regular safety belt is too large to be used on a young child. A properly installed child safety seat protects a young child in the same way a regular safety belt protects an adult. All states now require that every child ride in a child seat until the child is a certain age. Older children usually must be buckled in with a regular safety belt.

Review It

1. How should you adjust a safety belt?
2. What is the difference between an active restraint and a passive restraint? Give an example of each.

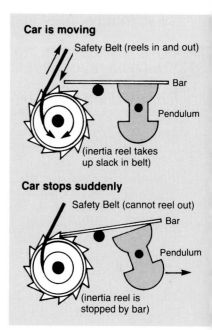

Car is moving

Safety Belt (reels in and out)

Bar

Pendulum

(inertia reel takes up slack in belt)

Car stops suddenly

Safety Belt (cannot reel out)

Bar

Pendulum

(inertia reel is stopped by bar)

Be a Fuel Saver

► Inflate your tires to the right pressure to save fuel and maintain traction.
► Place loads in the trunk of your car rather than on a roof-top carrier. You will cut wind resistance and increase gas mileage.
► Accelerate slightly before going up a hill. You can use the car's energy of motion, instead of more fuel, to start up the hill.

► When preparing to turn, save fuel by letting up on the accelerator.
► Accelerate and brake gradually. You will have better control of your car, save fuel, and increase tire life.

Chapter Summary

1. Gravity slows a car going uphill and speeds it up going downhill. When a car's center of gravity is raised, the car is harder to control. (7–1)
2. The faster a car moves, the more energy of motion the car has. A car's energy of motion also increases as the car's weight increases. (7–1)
3. You use the traction created by your car's tires and the roadway surface when you steer, brake, and accelerate. (7–2)
4. Worn shock absorbers, bald or under-inflated tires, and rough and slippery roadway surfaces can reduce traction. (7–2)
5. A car's speed and weight and the sharpness and bank of a curve are factors which affect car control when driving through a curve. (7–2)
6. You can make better judgments by knowing about the capabilities of different vehicles. (7–2)
7. Perception distance, reaction distance, and braking distance add up to total stopping distance. (7–3)
8. Use the 4-second rule to estimate your stopping distance while driving. (7–3)
9. Speed, car condition, roadway surfaces, driver ability, hills, and load can affect braking distance. (7–3)
10. Increasing speed, adding weight, or shortening the distance between impact and the point where your car would stop in a collision can increase the force of impact. (7–4)
11. Energy-absorbing features such as crush areas, bumpers, side door beams, steering columns, and head restraints absorb some of a collision's force of impact. (7–4)
12. When fastening a safety belt, the lap belt should fit snugly across your hips. Slack in the shoulder belt should only allow you to slip your closed fist between the belt and your chest. (7–5)
13. Other restraint devices include air bags, automatic safety belts, and child seats. (7–5)

Think About It

1. Since safety belts have been proven effective, why do you think some people still choose not to use them?
2. A driver who is about to collide with another car might decide to "give up." Why is "giving up" a poor decision?

Decision Making

1. The car ahead is blocking your lane. You cannot stop. How can you reduce the force of impact?

2. You are driving the yellow car and have slammed on your brakes to avoid a head-on collision. Your wheels are sliding. You want to head for the shoulder to avoid trouble. What should you do?

3. You are approaching this curve at 40 mph. To maintain control, when should you adjust your speed?

4. The driver ahead is braking to maintain control. What two factors might increase the stopping distance in this situation?

Chapter 7 Test

Multiple Choice Copy the number of each sentence below on a sheet of paper. Choose the letter that best completes each statement.

1. The large open tread of a snow tire gives extra
   (a) grooves. (b) traction. (c) tire pressure.
   (d) strength. (117)
2. To estimate stopping distance, use
   (a) the 4-second rule. (b) reaction distance.
   (c) braking distance. (d) traction. (123)
3. A car's speed, its weight, and the distance between impact and stop determine the
   (a) center of gravity. (b) energy of motion.
   (c) perception time. (d) force of impact. (124)
4. A restraint device that you must fasten is
   (a) an air bag. (b) an active restraint. (c) a
   passive restraint. (d) a seat lever. (126)
5. An air bag is a type of
   (a) active restraint. (b) brake. (c) passive
   restraint. (d) indicator. (126)

Completion Copy the number of each sentence below. After each number, write the letter of the word or words that complete the sentence correctly.

6. Adjust power when driving on hills to overcome the effects of ____. (114)
7. Using a roof-top carrier might raise your car's ____. (114)
8. If you increase your car's speed, its ____ will be proportional to the square of its increase in speed. (115)
9. A ____ is a sudden loss of air pressure in a tire. (117)
10. Your available ____ for braking is divided when you slow for a turn. (117)
11. Worn shock absorbers can ____ traction on a rough roadway. (118)
12. When preparing to drive through a curve, adjust your ____ ahead of time. (119)
13. By knowing how your car and other vehicles might react in different situations, you will be better able to use the ____. (120)
14. Your perception time will ____ in a complex traffic situation. (122)

15. All states require the use of ____. (126)
   a. blowout
   b. center of gravity
   c. child seats
   d. decrease
   e. energy of motion
   f. gravity
   g. increase
   h. IPDE process
   i. overinflated
   j. speed
   k. traction

Vocabulary Copy the number of each phrase below. Match the definition in List A with the term it defines in List B.

List A
16. force that prevents slipping (116)
17. grooved surface of a tire (116)
18. curve where the outside of the roadway is higher than the inside of the roadway (119)
19. distance it takes your car to stop from the instant you see a hazard (122)
20. time you need to identify a situation (122)
21. distance a car travels during the time you perceive a situation (122)
22. time it takes you to act after perceiving a situation (122)
23. distance a car travels while you act (122)
24. distance a car travels from the time the brakes are applied until the car stops (122)
25. device designed to hold car occupants in their seats during a collision (126)

List B
   a. banked curve
   b. braking distance
   c. force of impact
   d. friction
   e. perception distance
   f. perception time
   g. reaction distance
   h. reaction time
   i. restraint device
   j. total stopping distance
   k. tread

Chapter 8
Interacting with Cyclists

You're the Driver!

The wide variety of vehicles you will interact with as a driver includes motorcycles and bicycles. The small size and lower stability of motorcycles and bicycles present special problems for other drivers.

What problem might this motorcyclist encounter when the light changes to green?

Should the car driver predict that there is a motorcycle behind the approaching van?

What conflict might occur due to the open car door on the right?

How might the bicyclist cause a conflict?

You must know what to expect from cyclists to prevent possible conflicts. People in cars are somewhat protected in a collision. Cyclists have very

little protection and are more likely to be injured or killed in a collision.

As a car driver, you have a special responsibility to protect cyclists as much as possible. This chapter discusses the special problems cyclists can cause, your responsibilities, and ways cyclists can help car drivers.

Objectives

8–1 Interacting with Motorcyclists

8–2 Motorcyclist Actions that Can Affect You

8–3 Interacting with Bicyclists

8–1 Interacting with Motorcyclists

You might never ride a motorcycle. However, you will be a safer driver if you understand some of the special problems involved with motorcycles and motorcyclists.

The number of motorcycle registrations has increased greatly during recent years. Motorcycle-related injuries and deaths have also increased.

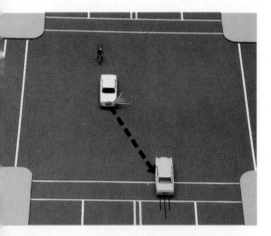

These injuries and deaths result primarily from the exposed position of the motorcyclist. Unlike a driver who is protected by a car, a motorcyclist has little or no protection. The motorcycle's small size, instability, and handling characteristics add to potential problems in traffic. As a car driver, you must accept a major share of responsibility for protecting motorcyclists as they interact within the HTS.

Using the IPDE Process to Protect Motorcyclists

Most drivers tend to be alert for other cars and larger vehicles that might cause conflicts. Motorcycles are smaller than cars and can be driven in several different positions within a traffic lane. Therefore, other roadway users must make extra efforts to be aware of motorcyclists. Other roadway users can use the IPDE process to help prevent conflicts.

The identify step is crucial for drivers because motorcyclists are more difficult to see than larger vehicles, particularly in rush-hour traffic. The size and location of motorcycle taillights, brake lights, and turn signals also makes motorcycles less noticeable. The small size of motorcycles makes it difficult for car drivers to judge motorcycle speed and distance in traffic.

Identify places where motorcycles might be hidden from view. Scanning the roadway ahead and behind for motorcyclists requires an understanding of where they might be and what they might do. The driver of the yellow car in the top picture should be scanning through the windows of the other car looking for motorcyclists.

Predict the possible actions of motorcyclists by remembering the instability factor and the handling characteristics of motorcycles. Base your decisions on the problems and conditions confronting the motorcyclist. In short, think like the motorcyclist.

Execute your actions smoothly, and avoid sudden actions that can surprise the motorcyclist. The driver in the bottom picture has caused a possible conflict by opening the car door before checking to see if a motorcyclist is there.

Where to Look for Motorcyclists

Most car-motorcycle conflicts occur at intersections. Look for motorcyclists in the following situations.

Vehicle Turning Left in Front of Motorcyclist   Before turning left in front of the oncoming motorcyclist, the car driver in the top picture must be sure of the motorcyclist's intended path. Even though the motorcyclist is signaling a left turn, the driver should predict that the motorcyclist will continue straight.

Vehicle Turning Right at Intersection or Driveway   Many car drivers do not check their rear-view mirrors and blind spots frequently enough to be aware of traffic to the rear. Therefore, they might turn right, directly in front of a motorcyclist. In the middle picture, the driver could have identified the motorcyclist by checking the mirrors frequently and by glancing over the shoulder. The motorcyclist could have reduced the possible conflict by keeping a greater following distance and by staying out of the blind spot of the car driver.

Motorcyclist Turning Left   In the bottom picture, the driver of the yellow car might not see the oncoming motorcyclist signaling a left turn. When you cannot see the entire intersection clearly, expect smaller vehicles to appear in your path. Be prepared to act to avoid a conflict.

Motorcyclist Passing Car on Right or Left Check your rearview mirrors and blind spots frequently anticipating that motorcyclists will pass you. Be especially aware of being passed on either the right or left at an intersection where there is more space. Even though motorcyclists should not pass at intersections, always watch for them so you can avoid conflict.

Motorcyclist Meeting an Oncoming Car You are more likely to see an oncoming motorcyclist in the daytime if the motorcycle's headlight is on, as in the top picture. Many states require that the motorcycle's headlight be on at all times. Whenever you see an oncoming motorcyclist, stay on your side of the roadway until the motorcyclist has passed.

Tailgating Motorcyclist Braking distance is about the same for cars as for many motorcycles under ideal conditions and with skillful use of brakes. However, if the driver of the yellow car in the middle picture braked suddenly to let the car on the shoulder in, the tailgating motorcyclist could lose control. The motorcyclist does not have enough following distance to stop in time. When following another vehicle, check your rearview mirrors and increase your following distance to 3 seconds or more if a motorcyclist is tailgating you.

Motorcyclist Riding in Driver's Blind Spot The roof support columns on your car can block your view of a motorcyclist. The bottom picture shows how these support columns could hide a motorcyclist in your blind spot. Always check the blind-spot areas before turning or changing lanes.

Protecting Motorcyclists

Unlike a driver protected inside a car, a motorcyclist is fully exposed to dangers causing possible injury or death. For this reason, you must accept an extra share of responsibility for avoiding conflicts with motorcyclists. The following qualities of motorcyclists and motorcycles can cause special problems.

Motorcyclists Can Lack Experience and Skill

Some motorcyclists ride rented or borrowed motorcycles and have not had enough practice to develop sound judgment and good control. Others, who own their own motorcycles, might not have received proper riding instruction. Be alert when approaching a motorcyclist. Predict judgment and control errors due to inexperience and lack of skill.

Handling Traits of Motorcycles

Help protect motorcyclists from conflicts by being aware of the handling traits of motorcycles and how they operate. Notice in the left picture that the motorcyclist leans to the side when making a turn. The motorcyclist can have difficulty handling a motorcycle in a turn on windy days or on rough roadways, as the right picture shows.

Increase Your Following Distance

Most motorcycles have only two wheels in contact with the ground and are less stable than cars. A motorcyclist's balance and stability depend on the two small areas of tires gripping the roadway. Water, sand, oil slicks, or loose gravel reduce traction and can make motorcycle control even more unstable.

Watch for a motorcyclist's balance and stability problems. Predict that the motorcyclist might maneuver unexpectedly or even fall. Give the motorcyclist extra space by increasing your following distance to at least 3 seconds. By doing so, you give yourself an extra margin of safety should the motorcyclist fall.

Make Sure the Motorcyclist Knows You Are There

When following a motorcyclist, assume the motorcyclist is not aware of your presence. Traffic noise and motorcycle noise make it more difficult for the motorcyclist to hear. The small size of the mirrors on the handlebars and the vibration of the motorcycle can restrict the motorcyclist's view to the rear. Tap your horn well behind the motorcyclist before passing to remind the motorcyclist that you are there.

Review It

1. Why should you accept an extra share of responsibility for protecting motorcyclists?
2. How can you use the IPDE process to help protect motorcyclists while driving?
3. What are five places where you should look for motorcyclists while driving?
4. What can you do to avoid a conflict when following a motorcyclist?

Although you share the responsibility for protecting motorcyclists, the motorcyclists have the primary responsibility for avoiding collisions. How motorcyclists ride, the protective equipment they use, and the special riding problems they have affect other roadway users.

How Motorcyclists Ride

Receiving proper instruction when learning any skill usually ensures better performance when using that skill. This point is true in all types of sports, as well as in driving a car and riding a motorcycle.

Since motorcyclists share the roadways with others and present special problems for them, motorcyclists should make every effort to develop safe riding skills.

The best way to learn the skills needed to ride safely is to take a motorcycle-riding course taught by a certified instructor. The students in this picture are receiving proper instruction. Many high schools, colleges, and some safety councils offer such instruction.

The basic procedures for operating a motorcycle safely are even more critical than those

procedures for a car. A beginning motorcyclist must learn to start, stop, balance, and control a motorcycle safely before riding in traffic. Using proper riding techniques results in fewer conflicts between motorcyclists and other roadway users.

Braking and Accelerating A car driver needs only to step on the foot-brake pedal to stop a car. However, a motorcyclist must operate separate brakes for front and rear wheels. A lever on the right handlebar operates the *front brake*. This brake supplies up to 70 percent

of the motorcycle's braking power. A foot pedal controls the *rear brake*. A motorcyclist must coordinate both foot and hand brakes carefully for maximum braking effort. If the front brake is applied too hard, it can lock the front wheel and cause loss of control. This action often causes collisions with other roadway users.

A motorcyclist must coordinate the hand throttle, hand clutch, and foot-gearshift lever to accelerate smoothly. Balance problems can occur if the motorcyclist does not coordinate the throttle and clutch properly.

Loss of Balance Unlike a four-wheeled vehicle, a motorcycle might have difficulty remaining upright while in motion. Be alert and anticipate that motorcyclists can lose balance due to:

► **Surface Conditions** Sand, mud, gravel, oil drippings, water, and objects on the roadway can cause balance and control problems for motorcyclists.

► **Following Distance** Motorcyclists can increase following distance to reduce risk of collisions. They should use a 3-second following distance, as seen here, since they might not be stable in a sudden stop.

Motorcyclists also must maintain a safe following distance to avoid being struck by small pebbles or dirt thrown back by the vehicle ahead. Trying to avoid the dirt or pebbles can cause motorcyclists to lose balance. As a driver, check your rearview mirrors often, be aware of following motorcyclists, and avoid making sudden stops.

Use of Protective Equipment

Since cars can injure motorcyclists severely in a collision, it is the responsibility of motorcyclists to protect themselves as much as possible. Motorcyclists can reduce or prevent injuries by using *protective equipment*. A motorcyclist's protective equipment includes:

► *helmet*—headgear worn to reduce or prevent head injuries
► eye protection—goggles or a *face shield,* a plastic device attached to the helmet
► heavy shoes or boots
► pants and jacket made of heavy material
► gloves.

Helmets are important in saving motorcyclists' lives. Motorcyclists who do not wear helmets are three times more likely to suffer fatal head and neck injuries than riders who wear helmets.

Special Riding Problems

Weather and roadway conditions have a greater adverse effect on motorcyclists than on cars. Allow extra time and space for motorcyclists in all types of adverse conditions. Practice caution when following motorcyclists who are crossing railroad tracks or carrying passengers. Railroad tracks and passengers can each cause balance and control problems.

Adverse Weather Conditions

A motorcyclist cannot cope with adverse weather conditions as well as you. A puddle that hides a pothole can jolt your car; the same hidden hole could throw a motorcycle out of control. Just as for car drivers, the worst time for motorcyclists is immediately after rain starts. As rain mixes with dirt and oil on the roadway, traction is greatly reduced. Since balance is important for motorcycle control, reduced traction is far more critical to motorcyclists.

You can turn on your windshield wipers when it rains. When dirt splashes on the windshield, you can use the windshield washers. A motorcyclist has neither device. Therefore, the motorcyclist's vision is greatly reduced and can be distorted under these conditions.

Motorcyclists should use extreme care crossing railroad tracks and painted lines on roadways as they can be extremely slippery when wet. Motorcyclists can gain extra traction by riding in a vehicle's wheel tracks, as shown here. This practice can help prevent a collision if the car driver brakes suddenly.

As a car driver, remember that bad weather makes it harder to see a motorcyclist who might be hurrying to find protection from the weather. Be extra alert and allow a greatly increased space cushion under adverse conditions.

How Motorcyclists Can Help Car Drivers

Motorcyclists can use special techniques and strategies to reduce conflicts with car drivers. The safe-riding strategies of motorcyclists, though, will not diminish the alertness and caution you must practice when motorcyclists are present.

Motorcyclists Crossing Railroad Tracks Railroad tracks are a special problem for motorcyclists. Motorcycle tires can get caught in the grooves of the tracks, causing the motorcyclist to lose balance. A motorcyclist should cross railroad tracks as close to a right angle as possible, as above. Predict that the motorcyclist might lose balance.

Motorcyclists Carrying Passengers A motorcycle carrying two people calls for double caution from car drivers. Be alert for a difference in acceleration, braking, and turning when a motorcyclist is carrying a passenger.

A passenger can create balance and control problems for a motorcyclist. The passenger might lean the wrong way on curves and turns, or might bump the motorcyclist when brakes are applied suddenly. Motorcyclists should not carry passengers until they have mastered a variety of traffic situations alone.

Be Visible in Traffic Motorcyclists should position themselves in traffic so they will be seen easily. Riding in the left wheel track of the car ahead makes a motorcyclist most visible to other roadway users. The motorcyclist in the top picture is in the correct position and is thus more visible to oncoming drivers.

In addition to greater visibility, riding on the left side of the lane forces other drivers to use the other lane to pass. This motorcycle position adds a margin of safety to the passing maneuver. It also reduces the chance that the motorcyclist will be forced off the roadway.

Motorcyclists should not ride between lines of moving vehicles. This practice is both illegal and dangerous for both drivers and motorcyclists. Be especially alert for this practice on busy expressways and city roadways during rush hours.

Riding in Groups When motorcyclists are traveling together, they should ride in groups of two so they are more visible to other roadway users. Riding side by side in the same traffic lane can be hazardous if either motorcyclist should lose balance or control. Motorcyclists' positions should be staggered so the motorcyclist on the left is ahead of the motorcyclist on the right, as in the top left picture.

Motorcyclists should make turns at corners in single file and turn in the correct lane, as in the top right picture. Give motorcyclists extra space as they turn in front of you.

Riding at Night Night riding further increases possible conflicts between motorcyclists and car drivers. It is far more difficult for car drivers to judge the speed and the position of a motorcycle at night.

Motorcyclists should take added precautions when riding at night. They can make themselves more visible by putting reflective tape on helmets and wearing reflective clothing. Equipping the motorcycle with reflectors helps make the motorcycle more visible to others, as seen in the bottom picture.

Review It

1. How do a motorcycle's braking and acceleration differ from those of a car?
2. What protective equipment should a motorcyclist use?
3. Why do adverse weather conditions affect motorcyclists more than car drivers?
4. How can motorcyclists make themselves more visible to others?

8–3 Interacting with Bicyclists

During recent years, many people have become bicyclists. People are riding bicycles for fun, exercise, and transportation. This increase in bicycle use has increased the number of bicycle-related injuries and deaths.

Bicyclists and car drivers use many of the same roadways together. By cooperating, they can avoid conflicts. Car drivers, though, should accept a greater share of responsibility for avoiding conflict since bicyclists have no protection.

Protecting Bicyclists

Many conflicts with bicyclists could be avoided if all roadway users accepted the bicycle as a vehicle. Both car drivers and bicyclists are required to obey traffic laws.

As a car driver, give bicyclists extra space whenever possible. Some bicyclists might not be able to control their bicycles well and might suddenly get in your path. When following a bicyclist, be aware of the possible pathways the bicyclist can take. Predicting a possible change of direction usually enables you to stop in time to avoid a collision.

Use the IPDE process constantly as you encounter bicyclists in the traffic scene. Scan wide enough to include the sides of the roadways, as well as sidewalks. Whenever you identify a bicyclist in a traffic situation, predict every possible action the bicyclist might take. You then are better prepared to decide on the correct action to execute, if an action is needed.

Preventing Conflicts with Bicyclists
Passing bicyclists on a two-lane roadway presents a problem for both drivers and riders. Consider the position of the bicyclist in traffic when you plan to pass.

Always start your passing maneuver well behind the bicyclist. You must have at least one half of a lane between your car and the bicyclist in order to pass safely, as shown here. If the bicyclist's position does not provide this space, wait for a gap in oncoming traffic and then pass.

Other techniques that will help prevent conflicts with bicyclists are:

► Warn a bicyclist of your presence with a tap on the horn well before you move to pass the bicyclist.
► Signal your intentions early when you plan to turn or stop.
► Help others identify a bicyclist by adjusting your position. At night, use low-beam headlights or a brief flick of high-beam headlights so that others can see the bicyclist. Try to avoid shining your high-beam headlights into a bicyclist's eyes. The glare could temporarily blind the bicyclist.
► Reduce speed when a bicyclist presents a problem.
► Look for bicyclists before opening the street-side door. Blocking a bicyclist's path by opening a door causes many collisions.

Bicyclists' Responsibilities

As bicyclists share the roadways with others, they also
must share the responsibility
for avoiding conflicts. Because
of their small size and maneu-
verability, bicyclists can turn
their bicycles so quickly that
they can surprise you and
cause a collision.

Causes of Bicycle-Car Collisions

Bicycle collisions often involve
a motor vehicle. The bicyclist
is at fault in most cases. The
tremendous difference in
weight and speed between car
and bicycle places the bicyclist
at a major disadvantage in any
collision.

The following factors contribute to bicycle collisions
with motor vehicles:

- ▶ bicyclists' inexperience and
  lack of skill
- ▶ bicyclists' disregard for, or
  ignorance of, traffic laws
- ▶ bicyclists' unsafe or defiant
  attitudes toward other roadway
  users
- ▶ low visibility of bicyclists,
  especially at night
- ▶ roadway hazards, such as oil
  slicks, loose gravel, potholes,
  railroad tracks, water, and
  gratings.

Safe-Riding Practices Bicyclists should follow these safe-
riding practices:

- ▶ Ride on the right-hand side of
  the roadway.
- ▶ Obey all signs, signals, and
  traffic laws.
- ▶ Walk bicycles across busy
  intersections.
- ▶ Wear light-colored clothing and
  have reflectors on bicycles
  when riding at night, as in this
  picture.
- ▶ Do not listen to music through
  earphones while bicycling.
  Wearing earphones while bicycling or driving a motor vehicle
  is illegal in many states.
- ▶ Keep bicycles in safe operating
  condition.

Safety groups recommend
increased bicycle-safety programs in elementary and junior
high schools and increased
police enforcement of bicycle-
riding violations. These
recommendations, along with
greater driver awareness of bicyclists, can help reduce the
potential conflict between drivers and bicyclists.

Review It

1. In what ways can you help
   protect bicyclists?
2. What five factors can contribute to bicycle-car collisions?
3. What safe-riding practices
   should bicyclists follow?

Safe Driving Tips

Mopeds and motor scooters are small, low-powered, two-wheeled vehicles. Their size and affordable prices have made mopeds and motor scooters very popular with roadway users. Keep these points in mind when interacting with mopeds and motor scooters:

► *Mopeds and motor-scooter engines are smaller than motorcycle engines. Be aware that mopeds' and motor scooters' speed and acceleration are less than those of a motorcycle. Increase your following distance when approaching a moped or motor scooter.*

► *Mopeds and motor scooters weigh less than motorcycles, making them easier to maneuver.*

However, moped and motor-scooter tires are narrower than motorcycle tires. These tires give less contact with the roadway than motorcycle tires. Watch for loss of control of mopeds and motor scooters in adverse conditions.

► *Mopeds and motor scooters are smaller, quieter, and less noticeable than motorcycles. Always check your blind spots before maneuvering.*

► *Many moped and motor-scooter riders are untrained and inexperienced. Some moped riders might even be underage. Be especially alert when driving near a moped or motor scooter.*

Chapter Summary

1. As a car driver, you have a responsibility for protecting motorcyclists. Your car can protect you, but a motorcycle provides little protection to a motorcyclist on a roadway. (8–1)

2. Use the IPDE process to identify where motorcyclists might be and predict their actions. Base your decisions on what you identify and predict. (8–1)

3. Look for motorcyclists at intersections and driveways, when passing and meeting, and in your blind spots. (8–1)

4. Protect motorcyclists by giving extra space, knowing how motorcycles handle, increasing following distance, and tapping your horn to signal your presence to motorcyclists. (8–1)

5. Motorcyclists use a hand brake and a foot brake, car drivers use only one foot brake. Motorcyclists must coordinate use of the throttle with the clutch. (8–2)

6. Protective equipment for motorcyclists includes helmet, eye protection, heavy shoes, pants, jacket, and gloves. (8–2)

7. Special problems for motorcyclists are adverse weather, railroad tracks, and passengers. (8–2)

8. Motorcyclists can reduce conflicts by being visible, riding in groups, making turns properly, and wearing reflective materials at night. (8–2)

9. Prevent conflicts with bicyclists by using the IPDE process, passing correctly, signaling intentions, reducing speed, and looking for bicyclists before opening car doors. (8–3)

10. The major causes of bicycle-car collisions are bicyclist inexperience, disregard for laws, defiant attitudes toward others, roadway hazards, and drivers' difficulty in seeing bicyclists. (8–3)

11. Bicyclists should ride on the right side of the roadway, obey laws, walk bicycles across busy intersections, wear light-colored clothing at night, and keep bicycles in safe operating condition. (8–3)

Think About It

Why would stopping a motorcycle on a wet roadway be even more difficult than stopping a car?

Decision Making

1. What is the car driver's responsibility in avoiding a collision? How could the car driver above have avoided this possible conflict?

2. What action must the car driver take before turning right? Why is it difficult to see the motorcyclist? How could the motorcyclist have avoided this situation?

3. What protective equipment should this motorcyclist wear?

4. You are driving the car above. What do you predict the bicyclist will do? What actions will you take?

Chapter 8 Test

Multiple Choice Copy the number of each question below on a sheet of paper. Choose the letter that best answers each question.

1. What makes motorcycles hard to see in traffic?
   (a) lack of turn signals (b) their small size
   (c) lack of reflective tape (d) their ability to maneuver in traffic (132)
2. Where in traffic is a car driver most likely to have a conflict with a motorcyclist?
   (a) parking lots (b) driveways (c) express lanes (d) intersections (133)
3. Which piece of equipment best protects a motorcyclist from head and neck injuries?
   (a) helmet (b) face shield (c) leather jacket
   (d) heavy boots or shoes (138)
4. What position in a lane should two motorcyclists take when riding together?
   (a) single file (b) parallel (c) staggered, one behind the other, left motorcyclist ahead
   (d) staggered, one behind the other, right motorcyclist ahead (140)
5. How much space should a car driver have when passing a bicyclist?
   (a) half a lane (b) full lane (c) half a block
   (d) fifteen inches (141)

Completion Copy the number of each sentence below. After each number, write the letter of the word or words that complete the sentence correctly.

6. Because of the size and location of motorcycle lights, it is more difficult for car drivers to judge speed and ____ of motorcycles. (132)
7. Use a 3-second following distance when a motorcyclist is ____ you. (134)
8. Always check your ____ before changing lanes to know if motorcyclists are beside you. (134)
9. Extra ____ must be taken by car drivers in order to protect motorcyclists. (135)
10. Braking and ____ require hand and foot coordination when riding a motorcycle. (137)
11. Motorcyclists should cross railroad tracks as close to a ____ as possible. (139)

12. Motorcyclists wearing ____ are more visible at night. (140)
13. Bicyclists should ride on the ____ side of the roadway. (142)
14. Inexperience and lack of skill contribute to ____ collisions. (142)
15. Bicycle collisions often involve a ____. (142)

   a. accelerating
   b. bicycle-car
   c. blind spot
   d. distance
   e. left-hand
   f. motor vehicle
   g. reflective material
   h. responsibility
   i. right-hand
   j. right angle
   k. tailgating

Vocabulary Copy the number of each phrase below. Match the definition in List A with the term it defines in List B.

List A
16. operated by hand lever on a motorcycle (136)
17. operated by a foot pedal on a motorcycle (137)
18. worn to prevent injury to the head (138)
19. plastic device attached to the helmet (138)
20. helmet, face shield, heavy clothing, heavy shoes or boots, and gloves (138)

List B
   a. face shield
   b. front brake
   c. goggles
   d. helmet
   e. protective equipment
   f. rear brake

Unit 3
Driving in Different Environments and Conditions

Chapter 9
Driving in Towns and Cities

Chapter 10
Highway Driving

Chapter 11
Expressway Driving

Chapter 12
Adverse Conditions

Chapter 13
Emergencies

The highway transportation system is composed of people, vehicles, and roadways. During your life, you will drive on a variety of roadways. These roadways will vary from the street on which you live to the multilane expressway pictured here. Highways such as these did not exist fifty or sixty years ago. Today, these multilane highways are relatively common and much more complex.

In this unit you will learn how to drive safely in various environments and conditions. You will learn how to drive in towns and cities, as well as on highways and expressways. Since conditions will not always be ideal, you also will learn how to drive safely during adverse conditions and how to handle emergencies.

Chapter 9
Driving in Towns and Cities

You're the Driver!

You are approaching the crowded city intersection pictured here and want to make a right turn. Other vehicles and pedestrians are blocking the intersection.

Where should you be predicting points of conflict?

How should you respond if the light changes?

How far ahead must you look for hazards?

Why might you cover the brake?

How might pedestrians create conflict?

How slow should you go through this intersection?

Have you signaled your intention to turn?

When you drive on town and city streets, you share a limited amount of space with many roadway users. This chapter discusses how to use special skills when driving in these situations. By keeping a positive attitude toward other drivers and pedestrians, driving in towns and cities will be easier for you.

Objectives

9–1 Characteristics of Town and City Traffic

1. Name two factors that can make town and city driving difficult. (150)
2. Explain how to use the IPDE process for city driving. (151)

9–2 Following and Meeting Traffic

3. Tell how to use a 2-second following distance. (152)
4. List the actions to use to manage a tailgater. (154)

9–3 Using Basic Skills in Traffic

5. Explain how far ahead to look in city traffic. (156)
6. Describe what to avoid when covering the brake. (158)
7. Describe what lane you should drive in on a two-way street. (160)

9–4 Adjusting to Traffic Patterns

8. Tell how to identify a one-way street. (162)

9. Describe the proper lanes for turning left and right from a one-way street. (163)

9–5 Pedestrians and Other Roadway Users

10. Name three areas where you should predict pedestrian traffic. (166)
11. Explain how to yield to emergency vehicles. (166)
12. List precautions to take with buses and parking lots. (167)

9-1 Characteristics of Town and City Traffic

Once you can maneuver your car, you are ready to learn how to drive in towns and cities. As you drive in these places, you will notice that some situations are harder to manage than others.

Complex Traffic Situations
If you drive on a highway in good weather with little traffic, you might encounter few hazards. Your driving task should be relatively easy. The same would be true if you drive at low speeds on a suburban street with many hazards.

Two factors can make driving in towns and cities difficult:
► the number of hazards you meet
► the rate at which you meet the hazards.

In the two situations just described, you were driving at highway speed with few hazards, and at a slower speed with a number of hazards. You could adjust your driving for both situations. However, if you had to react to several hazards while traveling at a higher speed, the difficulty of the situation would increase.

Number of Hazards Mile for mile, town and city roadways have the highest number of hazards. Cars, trucks, pedestrians, bicycles, and other hazards all demand your attention. Compare the two situations pictured here and decide which situation has more hazards.

Time, Distance, and Speed As you drive, remember that it takes time to use the IPDE process. If a hazard, such as a car, is at a given distance, slowing is the only way you can gain more time to think and react. When the number of hazards increases, you must decrease speed.

Using the IPDE Process

Driving in heavy city traffic will test your driving skills. You can best avoid conflicts by focusing your attention on your driving task. Avoid such distracting activities as drinking a soft drink or coffee, listening to very loud music, or being irritated by other roadway users. You do your best when your attitude is upbeat and you pay attention to the driving scene.

As you study this picture, think of the IPDE process skills you would need to drive down this street. When driving in the city, focus on the IPDE process in these ways:

▶ **Identify** Be more aggressive in using visual skills.
▶ **Predict** Since there are more hazards, be prepared to predict possible points of conflict earlier.

▶ **Decide** With little space to the sides, always be ready to reduce speed and change vehicle position.
▶ **Execute** Be prepared to use car controls in an instant.

Review It

1. What are two factors that can make driving in cities difficult?
2. How should you focus on the IPDE process for city driving?

To be a safe driver in towns and cities, maintain a space cushion between yourself and possible hazards. Managing the distance between your car and those ahead is the first step.

Following Others

Three advantages to maintaining a good following distance are:

► You are better able to see farther down the roadway.
► You have more time to use the IPDE process and adjust to traffic.
► You avoid the vehicle ahead if it stops suddenly.

2-Second Following Distance

Using a following-distance procedure is the best way to measure your following distance.

A 2-second following distance is considered safe for normal driving conditions. Use these steps to measure a 2-second following distance:

1. Pick a fixed checkpoint down the roadway. Roadway markings or shadows make good checkpoints.
2. When the vehicle ahead passes the checkpoint, count to yourself: "one-thousand-one, one-thousand-two," and so on.

If your car is just short of the checkpoint after your 2-second count, your following distance is safe for normal conditions. The driver in these pictures has just completed checking a 2-second following distance.

If you passed your chosen checkpoint before completing your 2-second count, you are too close. Slow and check your following distance again.

This 2-second technique works well at all speeds for measuring a normal following distance. As your speed increases, so does the distance your car travels during your 2-second count. Thus, when you count off 2 seconds, your following distance will be greater at higher speeds than at lower speeds.

This 2-second distance is not the total stopping distance you need to avoid hitting a stationary object. A 2-second following distance only protects you from moving vehicles ahead.

Increase your following distance to 3 or more seconds under adverse conditions or if you need more time to complete the IPDE process. Maintain extra distance when:

► You are first learning to drive. Your reaction time might be slower in complex situations.
► You are following a tailgater or are being tailgated.
► Traction is poor.
► You are pulling a heavy load or trailer.
► You are driving downhill.
► The driver ahead seems unsure of the next action to take.

Looking Ahead of the Car Ahead The 2-second rule is only one technique you can use when following other cars in traffic. When following another car, look over, through, and around the car ahead. Be alert for brake lights and for anything that might cause the car ahead to stop. The driver in this picture has identified the pedestrian and is ready for the car ahead to stop.

Areas for Sudden Stops Knowing where sudden stops might occur can alert you to high-risk areas. Three common high-risk areas are:
► intersections with signal lights
► lanes next to parked cars
► parking lot entrances and exits.

Looking Away Safely Imagine you are checking your mirrors or looking for a house number. Suddenly, the driver you are following slams on the brakes while you are looking away.

By the time your eyes return to the roadway, it might be too late to stop. Take these precautions to prevent this type of collision:
► Be sure the situation ahead has no hazards before you look away.
► Take several split-second glances rather than one long look.
► Ask a passenger to help look for a street name, house number, or other navigation needs.

Being Followed

You are in a high-risk situation when someone is *tailgating,* or following you too closely. However, you can take several actions to lower your risk of being tailgated.

Why Tailgaters Are a Hazard

A tailgater is a hazard because if you brake suddenly, the tailgater might hit you from the rear. Imagine you are driving the yellow car in the first picture. Your following distance is 2 seconds. However, car B is tailgating you. Suddenly, the driver in car A brakes hard for

an emergency stop. You brake hard to keep from hitting car A. However, car B hits you in the rear.

Managing Tailgaters

If you are being tailgated, take these actions to avoid being hit from behind:

▶ Increase your following distance to 3 or more seconds.

▶ Move slightly to the right to give the tailgater a better view ahead. The second picture shows how a driver who is being tailgated can improve the view ahead for the tailgating driver.

▶ Signal early for turns, stops, or lane changes.

▶ Flash your brake lights ahead of time to warn a tailgater that you plan to slow or stop.

Responding to Oncoming Traffic

If a driver crosses the center line toward you, you must react instantly. Knowing how to respond to this situation might give you just enough time to avoid a collision.

Reasons for Crossing the Center Line A driver might cross into the path of oncoming traffic for these reasons:

► **Driver impairment** A driver might be sleepy, distracted, confused, or intoxicated.

► **Poor judgment** A driver might misjudge speed or distance.

► **Poor visibility** Direct sunlight, blinding headlights, or bad weather can reduce a driver's ability to see.

► **Reduced space** A snowbank, narrow bridge, or an object in or near the roadway might force a driver across the center line.

► **Sudden moves by others** Children, cyclists, or pedestrians might make a last-second move in front of a car.

► **Loss of traction** Snow, ice, or even a strong cross-wind might cause a driver to cross the center line.

Avoiding Conflicts If a car comes toward you, take these actions to avoid a collision:

► Slow so the other driver can return to the normal lane. You also can slow so that you meet at a point where there is more room. Stop if necessary.

► Turn on or flash headlights.

► Move to the right to give the oncoming driver more room, as this driver has done. Swerve sharply to the right in an emergency situation.

Review It

1. How many seconds should you use for a normal following distance?
2. What can you do to help yourself if someone tailgates you?

9–3 Using Basic Skills in Traffic

When you drive in a town or city, you must respond to a wide variety of traffic situations. Unfamiliar streets, signs, vehicles, and pedestrians add to the complexity of your driving task. Use your best driving skills and maintain a positive attitude toward others to drive safely.

Looking Ahead While Staying Back

How far ahead should you look while driving in a town or city? In addition to looking around your car, look regularly at the traffic scene a block or more ahead. By looking around and looking ahead, you are better able to spot trouble and adjust in advance.

To look ahead this far, you must maintain a safe following distance. Look at the different sight distances in these pictures. By keeping a 2-second following distance, as shown in the top picture, you can see farther down the roadway and will have more time to react.

Approaching Traffic Signals

Check traffic signals down the roadway by looking at least a block ahead. By doing so, you will have more time to react.

If the light is red, slow and prepare to stop. If the signals

on your street are coordinated and the light turns green, you can drive for several blocks without stopping.

If the light is green when you first notice it, predict it will change soon. A traffic light that has been green and soon will turn yellow is called a *stale green light*. The DON'T WALK pedestrian signal shown in the top picture is on and has started to flash. This signal warns that the light is about to turn yellow. If the pedestrian signal is flashing, you must decide if you have enough time to safely drive through the intersection. Your decision will depend on your distance to the intersection, speed, and the closeness of traffic behind.

Never speed up to get through a green light before it changes. At any speed, there is a *point of no return,* a place beyond which you can no longer stop safely without entering the intersection. The driver in the bottom picture is slowing to stop because the light is going to change to red. The yellow light usually lasts about four seconds. Be alert for drivers on side streets who might see the light changing and enter the intersection the instant the light turns green.

Be alert for a door opening suddenly
as you approach parked cars.

Covering the Brake

If the traffic scene ahead is stable and free from hazards, you can maintain speed and continue on. However, when a quick stop might be needed, such as in the first picture, be ready to stop by *covering the brake*. To cover the brake, take your foot off the accelerator and hold it over the brake pedal so that you are ready to stop quickly.

Take these actions to identify and react to the hazard of parked cars:
► Glance through rear windows of parked cars to look for drivers.
► Look for parked car's brake lights, exhaust, or wheels turned out.
► Cover your brake.
► Tap your horn, if necessary.
► Be ready to stop or swerve.

While driving past parked cars, also watch for a car door that might open unexpectedly, as shown in the second picture. Drive at least one car door's width away from parked cars if your lane is wide enough to do so.

When you cover the brake, do not rest your foot on the brake pedal. This action is called *riding the brake*. When you ride the brake, your brakes wear faster and your brake lights stay on. Drivers behind you might assume you are going to slow or stop when your brake lights are always on. If you do not slow or stop, these drivers might become confused or angry. Only flash brake lights to warn drivers behind that you plan to slow or stop.

Adjusting Speed

Imagine you have been driving for an hour in the country. You are just coming into the town shown in the picture. The speed limit is 25 mph. However, traffic conditions should tell you to adjust your speed, to drive even slower.

Use these techniques to select the best driving speed:
► Try to flow with traffic.
► Stay within the speed limit.
► Adjust for other drivers who might block your way.

Many drivers do not realize they will save only a second or two in a block by driving 5 mph faster. This chart shows how little time is saved by driving at faster speeds.

Speed (mph)	Minutes needed to go 10 miles	Minutes saved over next lower speed
25	24	—
30	20	4
35	17	3
40	15	2

159

Selecting the Best Lane

When two or more lanes of traffic are going in the same direction, select the best lane for your purpose. You will use different lanes at different times.

The left lane is for faster traffic. However, sometimes traffic can be held up by cars waiting to turn left. This backup is especially troublesome when there are only two lanes going in the same direction.

If the street has three lanes going in one direction, choose the lane where traffic flows the smoothest. The center lane, as shown below, is usually best.

Lane Positioning The three situations described here show the importance of proper lane positioning in multilane traffic:

▶ If you are driving on a multilane street and find you are caught in heavy traffic, increase your following distance to more than 2 seconds. Slow slightly to stay away from bunches of traffic.

▶ Each area to the immediate right and left behind your car is a *blind spot*. These areas are not seen in your mirrors and might be blocked by the corner posts of your car. When possible, adjust your speed to stay out of other drivers' blind spots.

▶ You might encounter a single hazard such as a car pulling out from a side street. In this situation, move in the opposite direction to create a greater space cushion.

If several hazards appear from different directions, position your car in the center of your lane. Cover the brake, slow, and be prepared to stop.

Changing Lanes Once you start driving in a lane, try to stay in that lane. Follow the steps below when you must change lanes. Make only one lane change at a time.

1. Check traffic in both lanes and in your mirrors.
2. Signal your lane change early. Look over your shoulder to check your blind spot.
3. Change lanes without slowing the flow of traffic.
4. Cancel your signal and adjust speed.

Overtaking and Passing

On a multilane street, you might want to *overtake,* or drive faster than, the vehicle ahead. To overtake a vehicle, simply change lanes and drive past the vehicle.

Passing in a town or city can be very dangerous because of heavy roadway use. You must be alert for pedestrians, cross traffic, traffic signals, and on-coming traffic.

Sometimes you might have to pass another vehicle on a two-lane, two-way street, a risky maneuver. Pass only if it is legal. It is illegal to pass at intersections or over double yellow center lines. Follow these steps to lessen your risk:

1. To be sure you can see ahead clearly, start your pass when you have a safe following distance.
2. Signal for a lane change.
3. Check your mirrors for following traffic.
4. Look over your shoulder to check your blind spot.
5. Check traffic once more as you accelerate to pass. If you have any doubt, do not pass.
6. Signal briefly and return to your lane when the front of the car you have passed appears in your inside rearview mirror.

To improve rush-hour travel, many city streets now have special lanes for bus traffic, as shown here. Many cities also have carpool lanes. Drivers who travel alone must use other, slower lanes. With these special lanes, people can ride together to save time and fuel, reduce pollution, and avoid parking problems.

Review It

1. How far ahead should you look when driving in the city?
2. What should you avoid doing when you cover the brake?
3. What must you consider when selecting the best lane while driving on a multilane street?

9-4 Adjusting to Traffic Patterns

As you drive in towns and cities, you will encounter a wide variety of situations. You must be ready to adjust to each situation.

Driving on Two-Way Streets
Most city streets are two-way streets with one lane going in each direction. Other streets are multilane and have two or more lanes going in the same direction.

Many town and city intersections do not have traffic controls. You cannot be sure what other drivers will do as you approach an uncontrolled intersection. Therefore, slow and be prepared to yield or stop when you approach an intersection.

Some intersections have special left-turn lanes. If you turn left at an uncontrolled intersection, you must yield to oncoming traffic.

Angle or parallel parking often is allowed along two-way streets. When driving close to parked cars, be alert for possible conflicts. At the first sign of movement from a car or pedestrian, slow, stop, or move to another lane.

Driving on One-Way Streets
One-way streets can move a greater volume of traffic with less congestion. Less congestion often results in greater safety.

Identifying One-Way Streets
When you come to an unfamiliar street, determine if it is a

one-way street and the direction it is going. These clues can help you identify a one-way street:
► At most one-way street intersections, ONE WAY signs are posted on a STOP sign, YIELD sign, or traffic-light post.
► Moving traffic and parked cars all point the same way.
► Lane lines are broken white lines.
► All traffic signs face the same direction. If you are driving on a street and all signs are facing the other direction, you probably are going the wrong way on a one-way street.

Imagine you are approaching the situation pictured here. Even if you did not see the DO NOT ENTER sign, you should still be able to identify this as a one-way street. All the cars face you.

Wrong-Way Drivers If you encounter a car headed the wrong way on a one-way street, slow, steer right, and sound your horn. If there is time, flash your headlights to alert the other driver.

Entering One-Way Streets
Imagine you are driving the yellow car in the first picture. To enter the one-way street going right, turn from the right lane into the first available right lane. To enter a one-way street going left, make a sharp left turn into the first available left lane. Signs are used to alert you when a street is about to become a one-way street.

Lane Choice on One-Way Streets If you plan to drive on a one-way street for a distance, avoid any lane that is next to parked cars. If a clear center lane is available, use it to reduce possible conflicts.

When you plan to turn, position your car ahead of time. Move into the right or left lane one or two blocks before your turn.

Leaving One-Way Streets
When making a left turn, leave a one-way street from the far left lane, as the yellow car in the second picture is doing. Turn from the far right lane for right turns. If the outer lane is used for parking, start your turn in the next available lane near the parked cars.

On some one-way streets, the outside lanes might be for turns only. On other one-way streets, you can turn onto a multi-lane street from more than one lane. Roadway markings or overhead signs will direct you.

You might be forced to leave a one-way street when it turns into a two-way street. Signs warn you when a one-way street is about to become a two-way street.

Handling Detours, Blocked Lanes, and Narrow Streets

Slow and be ready to yield the instant you see your path of travel will be changed by a detour, blocked lane, or narrow street. If the lane of traffic next to you is moving around a detour or blocked lane, move into that lane ahead of time to smooth the flow of traffic. If you must stop, wait for following or oncoming traffic to clear the available lane before going ahead. Obey any worker who is directing traffic.

The top picture shows that if your lane is blocked, you cannot swing out to pass before oncoming traffic has cleared the other lane. You must wait until the way is clear.

The bottom picture shows that parked cars have created a difficult situation. If there is not enough space ahead for your car and the oncoming car, slow or stop between parked cars so the oncoming car can go past. Move ahead when the lane is clear.

Responding to Stopped Vehicles

Always be alert for pedestrians who might step from behind a vehicle at an intersection or from between parked cars. Note in the first picture that the stopped car partially hides the child who is crossing the street.

Imagine you are driving in an outside lane of a four-lane, two-way street. Traffic is stopped in the left lane. In this situation, be alert for a driver to swerve out from the left lane into your lane. Be prepared by slowing.

When visibility is limited, be prepared for the unexpected. If a large vehicle is waiting at an intersection as you approach, your view might be blocked. An oncoming turning vehicle might move in front of you. As you approach, cover the brake and be ready to stop.

Imagine you are the driver in the second picture. You are traveling at 25 mph and the car on the right is about to pull out. To protect yourself, first slow, then tap your horn, and be ready to stop.

Review It

1. What can you do if another driver approaches you from the wrong direction on a one-way street?
2. What are the proper lanes for turning left and right from a one-way street?

9-5 Pedestrians and Other Roadway Users

As a driver, you have a special responsibility to watch for pedestrians and other roadway users. Many times, they will not know about some of the problems drivers must manage.

Pedestrians

Your car gives you some protection in a collision. However, pedestrians have no such protection. As a responsible driver, always stay alert for pedestrians.

Most pedestrians killed are under 15 or over 45 years old. Children can act impulsively; older pedestrians might not see you. Make every effort to let them know you are there. Many times, a simple wave of the hand or tap of the horn will do. Be ready to stop in every situation. Some areas where you should predict pedestrian traffic are discussed below.

Crosswalks and Intersections
When pedestrians use crosswalks, they might assume all drivers will stop. When crossing at an intersection with a green light, pedestrians might not even look for you. Always yield in these situations. Be prepared to stop if necessary.

Alleys and Driveways When leaving an alley or driveway, always stop before crossing the sidewalk, and look for pedestrians. Tap your horn as a warning. Once across a sidewalk, be prepared to stop again if traffic is coming.

Jogging Areas Although a jogger is safer using a sidewalk or jogging path, you will encounter joggers on the street. If a jogger is coming toward you, the jogger should see you. The jogger might be using a portable stereo radio with earphones and might not hear you. In any event, be ready to slow, steer around the jogger, or stop.

Emergency Vehicles

Looking in your mirrors and seeing an emergency vehicle approaching with siren wailing and lights flashing can be a frightening experience. Some drivers simply freeze at the wheel as in the situation pictured here.

Your quick response to emergency vehicles might save a life. Take these steps to clear the way for an emergency vehicle:
1. Always be alert for emergency vehicles. The instant you identify one, find a place to safely pull out of the way and stop.
2. If you are in heavy traffic, move in the direction other drivers are moving to clear the way.
3. Once you have pulled out, stay there until the emergency vehicle passes. Be sure another emergency vehicle is not following the first. Check traffic, and proceed when your path of travel is clear.

Buses

Imagine you are the driver in the picture below. The child has just left the bus and is darting across the street. Children leaving a school bus or adults leaving a regular bus might run in front of the stopped bus. Always be ready to stop near a bus that is stopped.

Most states require traffic going *both* ways on a two-way street to stop when a school bus stops to load or unload passengers. In most states, if a median strip divides the roadway, the vehicles approaching the bus on the other side of the median need not stop.

A school bus has flashing red lights and, in some states, a STOP sign that swings out from the side of the bus. Do not proceed until the lights stop flashing and the STOP sign is withdrawn.

Use these techniques to be ready for sudden pedestrian actions around buses:

► **Look Carefully** The "big picture" extends beyond the curb to sidewalks, driveways, and cross streets. Standing cars might hide pedestrians, especially children, approaching or leaving a bus.

► **Position Car** Sometimes you might approach a place where a pedestrian is getting off a bus or running to catch a bus. If so, slow down and move over to increase the distance between you and the pedestrian. Both you and the pedestrian will have more time to see and respond to each other.

► **Communicate** Tap your horn early to make eye contact with the pedestrian.

► **Control Speed** Reduce speed and cover the brake, if needed, to give yourself more time to respond.

Parking Lots

Pedestrians and other vehicles can create problems in parking lots. In tight spaces, a car, bicycle, or pedestrian can block your path in an instant.

Use these guidelines to lower your risk in parking lots:
- Drive no faster than 15 mph.
- Follow pavement markings. If you cut across an open lot, other drivers will not be able to predict your actions.
- Search for pedestrians.
- Avoid tight parking spaces.
- Do not back into a parking space. You might be headed in the wrong direction.
- Position your car in the center of your parking space.
- Do not swing your door into another parked vehicle.
- Back slowly and look in all directions when leaving a parking space. The driver backing out of the parking space in this picture cannot see the approaching pedestrians because the van blocks the driver's view.

Review It
1. Where must you be particularly careful of pedestrians?
2. What steps should you follow to clear the way for an emergency vehicle?
3. What precautions can you take regarding buses and parking lots?

Be a Fuel Saver

► Try to use the least crowded route to save fuel when commuting.
► Look ahead and adjust to traffic in advance. You can smooth the traffic flow and save fuel.
► Reduce fuel consumption by combining short trips into one trip.
► Use public transportation or a non-motorized means of transportation such as a bicycle.

Chapter Summary

1. The difficulty of driving in the city increases by the number of hazards you meet and the rate at which you meet them. (9–1)

2. Look aggressively, predict possible conflicts earlier, decide to reduce speed and change position if necessary, and be prepared to use car controls in an instant when using the IPDE process in city driving. (9–1)

3. Find a 2-second following distance by first picking a fixed checkpoint. Then, start a 2-second count as the vehicle ahead passes the fixed checkpoint. If you pass the checkpoint before completing the 2-second count, increase your following distance. (9–2)

4. Manage a tailgater by increasing your following distance, and moving slightly to the right. Signal early for turns, and flash your brake lights before coming to a stop. (9–2)

5. Look at least one block ahead to identify hazards when driving in a town or city. (9–3)

6. Avoid riding the brake when covering the brake in a tight driving situation. (9–3)

7. On a two-way city street, slower-moving traffic should stay in the right lane. Faster-moving traffic should stay in the left lane. If there are three lanes going in the same direction, the center lane usually provides the smoothest traffic flow. (9–3)

8. Use these clues to identify a one-way street: ONE WAY signs posted at intersections; cars and signs all face the same direction; lane lines are white. (9–4)

9. When turning from a one-way street, use the farthest available lane on the right for right turns. Use the farthest available lane on the left for left turns. (9–4)

10. Expect pedestrian traffic in crosswalks and intersections, exits of alleys and driveways, and jogging areas. (9–5)

11. Yield to emergency vehicles by starting early to look for a place to pull over and stop. Follow other traffic to clear the way for the emergency vehicle. Wait until all emergency vehicles have passed. (9–5)

12. Look carefully, slow down, and communicate to protect passengers boarding or leaving a bus. Drive slowly, and obey pavement markings to lower your risk in parking lots. (9–5)

Think About It

When a fire truck is enroute to a fire, it is not uncommon for car drivers to block the way. Why do you think this happens?

Decision Making

1. You are about to drive around the car ahead. What other hazard should you have identified? How will you respond?

2. You are driving the red car at 25 mph. The car on the right wants to turn left at the intersection one block ahead. What should you do?

3. You have been driving for two blocks where parking has been prohibited on the right. How could you have improved your lane position?

4. You are driving the red car on this narrow street. How can you reduce the conflict between the yellow van and you?

Chapter 9 Test

Multiple Choice Copy the number of each question below on a sheet of paper. Choose the letter that best answers each question.

1. What is the point beyond which you can no longer stop without entering an intersection?
   (a) fixed checkpoint   (b) point of no return
   (c) stopping point   (d) braking point   (157)
2. Where is it illegal to pass in city traffic?
   (a) at intersections   (b) a two-way street with one lane in each direction   (c) in alleys   (d) on one-way streets   (161)
3. What color are lane lines on a one-way street?
   (a) red   (b) blue   (c) white   (d) orange   (162)
4. What should you do if you encounter a car headed the wrong way on a one-way street?
   (a) Call the police.   (b) Slow, steer right, and sound your horn.   (c) Park and flash your headlights.   (d) Make a sharp left turn into the first available left lane.   (163)
5. What should you do when your path of travel is blocked by roadway work?
   (a) Squeeze into the next lane at the last minute.
   (b) Swing out to pass before oncoming traffic takes your space.   (c) Drive on the shoulder, if possible.   (d) Obey any worker who is directing traffic.   (164)

Completion Copy the number of each sentence below. After each number, write the letter of the word or words that complete the sentence correctly.

6. An increased number of ____ can make town and city driving more difficult.   (150)
7. Always try to maintain a ____ second following distance.   (152)
8. If another driver is tailgating you, move slightly to the ____.   (154)
9. When driving in a town or city, look ____ blocks ahead.   (156)
10. The ____ of traffic often flows the smoothest on a street with three lanes going in one direction.   (160)
11. Look over your right shoulder to check your right ____.   (160)
12. A street might have a ____ for use by bus and carpool traffic.   (161)

13. Stop before crossing the ____ when coming out of an alley.   (166)
14. If a ____ divides a roadway, vehicles approaching a school bus from the opposite direction usually need not stop.   (167)
15. Back slowly and look in all directions when leaving a ____.   (168)

   a. blind spot
   b. center lane
   c. hazards
   d. left
   e. median strip
   f. one or more
   g. parking space
   h. right
   i. sidewalk
   j. special lane
   k. two

Vocabulary Copy the number of each phrase below. Match the definition in List A with the term it defines in List B.

List A
16. following a vehicle too closely   (154)
17. traffic signal that is green and is about to turn yellow   (157)
18. holding your foot above the brake pedal   (158)
19. driving with your foot resting on the brake pedal   (158)
20. approach and pass a slower-moving vehicle ahead in your lane   (161)

List B
   a. adjusting speed
   b. covering the brake
   c. overtake
   d. riding the brake
   e. stale green light
   f. tailgating

Chapter 10
Highway Driving

You're the Driver!

On most trips, much of your driving will be on highways. Some highways are two lane; some are multilane. Highway conditions vary.

How do the roadways in this picture differ from those in towns and cities? Are there any traffic controls at the intersection directly ahead?

If you were driving this close behind the slow-moving vehi-cle, why would you have difficulty seeing ahead? At what speed should you be traveling?

How might you pass this slow-moving vehicle safely?

How might the truck on the side roadway present a problem to you?

Driving on highways presents a variety of problems. Driving at higher speeds and at night can increase these problems.

This chapter discusses how to use the IPDE process during highway driving. You also can learn how to handle highway hazards safely.

Objectives

Wide open spaces make driving on rural highways look safer than driving in towns and cities. However, statistics prove otherwise. Almost twice as many traffic deaths occur on rural highways than on urban roadways. Higher speeds on the highways result in more serious injuries. When a collision does occur, medical aid might not be able to reach the scene quickly.

Roadways

Highway road surfaces range from pavement to dirt. Lane widths can be wide or narrow. Roadway shoulders can be wide, narrow, or almost nonexistent. Roadways might be in poor condition with many potholes. Lighting might be inadequate for night driving. Traction on rural highways varies from excellent on dry pavement to poor on wet, muddy roadways.

Roadway conditions can change greatly within short distances. You must be alert to identify problems sooner and make adjustments to changing roadway conditions. Study the highway pictured here. What are its good features? Which features could be improved to make this highway safer?

Speed

No single decision is more important in highway driving than determining safe speed. Speed affects:

► how far ahead you must look.
► vehicle control.
► the distance you need to stop.
► the extent of damage and injury, as well as the survival rate, in a collision.

A 55 mph speed limit applies to most highways. Speed limits will be lower where traffic or other conditions make it necessary. Rain, snow, curves, hills, and narrow lanes require reduced speed. Always observe this basic speed rule: *Do not drive faster than roadway conditions permit.*

Consider other traffic when choosing your speed. Rural highways often have lighter traffic loads than urban roadways. Therefore, rural speed limits usually are higher than urban speed limits.

Traffic Controls

Traffic controls help you travel safely. Signs, signals, and roadway markings provide advance information and warnings in these situations:

► locations of hazards you cannot yet see
► areas of high-speed cross traffic

► unusual and unexpected highway features, such as sharp curves
► channeling of traffic into less space, such as the detour around a construction zone or a lane ending.

An example of the value of warning signs is shown in the left picture above. The sign informs you that a STOP sign, not yet visible, is just beyond the hill. The stop might be so close that, without the warning, you might have difficulty stopping.

Traffic controls can become quite complex if they control many lanes of traffic. The right picture above shows a major highway intersection. The arrows allow two or three lanes of traffic to move at the same time or to cross several lanes safely. Roadway markings can specify certain turns also.

Roadside Hazards

Highways, especially older roads, can have many hazards. Signposts situated on roadway shoulders might be near the paved roadway. They can block use of the shoulder in an emergency. Guardrails, bridge railings, bushes, and trees also might be near the road's edge. Roadway shoulders might be rough and narrow. Ditches might be deep. Consider these hazards when deciding on a safe speed.

Roadside service stations, stores, and restaurants can create hazardous situations. Vehicles slowing down to pull off or attempting to reenter the highway can be hazards to other drivers. A driver who makes a last-second decision to stop along a roadside is especially hazardous.

Review It

1. Why is speed the most important decision in highway driving?
2. What roadside hazards do highway drivers face?

Collision-free driving comes from thinking ahead in a constantly changing traffic scene. After driving long distances on highways with little traffic, you might feel that no conflicts can develop. Without continuous planning, you might encounter problems without warning.

Applying the IPDE Process

Traveling at higher speeds increases your chances of a collision. The faster you go, the less time you have to complete the IPDE process. Use the IPDE process at higher speeds:

► **Identify** hazards much farther ahead than at low speeds because you reach the hazard more quickly. Keep your eyes moving. The number of eye movements decreases as you concentrate on seeing far ahead. The sooner you identify a hazard, the more time you will have to decide and execute a safe maneuver.

► **Predict** conflicts. You might not have as much time to make predictions. You must predict much farther ahead and determine what to do before you arrive. Early predictions give you more time to make safe decisions.

► **Decide** what you must do while you still have ample time. Decide before a situation becomes critical.

► **Execute** your decision. Give yourself ample time to act.

Controlling your car is more difficult at higher speeds. You might not be able to stop or swerve in time to avoid a collision. At higher speeds you can more easily lose control of your car. Hard braking or sharp turns can cause skidding and total loss of control.

Drive at a speed from which you can stop or swerve in time to avoid a collision. A proper, safe speed is an important protection in all traffic situations.

Study this highway traffic scene. Note how each step of the IPDE process is important for each driver.

Visual Search Pattern

The process of searching or scanning critical areas is an *orderly visual search pattern*. Use an orderly visual search pattern, such as the one below, to help you adjust for any unusual event:

► Look to the sides of the roadway as well as ahead of your car. This wide field of view

brings into your line of sight
hazards alongside the roadway
and at intersections.

► Check for such safety features
as wide shoulders, shallow
ditches with gentle slopes, and
traffic controls. Anticipate how
the lack of these features will
affect your decisions.

► Check the roadway surface.
Such surfaces as gravel or mud
can cause loss of traction.
Potholes and ruts can also affect car control.

► Glance in the rearview mirror
every 4 to 7 seconds. See if a
following driver is tailgating or
is starting to pass you.

► Check your speed as well as
dashboard warning lights after
you make all visual checks.
Determine that there are no
immediate problems.

► After looking away briefly, return your attention to the roadway ahead. Take quick glances
away from the traffic scene
only when you have deter-
mined the situation is not
changing.

Two-Lane Highway Driving

Much of your highway driving
will be on two-lane roadways
with 55 mph speed limits.
Know the characteristics of
two-lane highways and the
techniques to drive safely on
them.

Curves A warning sign usually marks a sharp curve on a
two-lane highway. If a curve is
very sharp, an *advisory speed
sign* often will appear below
the warning sign. This square
yellow sign informs you of the
maximum safe speed for that
curve under ideal conditions.
Both signs are especially important in the situation pictured here. The driver is
coming to the top of a hill and
cannot see the curve ahead.

When you approach a curve,
take the following steps:

1. Take quick glances across the
curve to identify oncoming
traffic. Be alert for any driver
who might enter the curve at
high speed and cross the center line into your lane. You
could be forced toward the
edge of the roadway.

2. Maintain proper lane position
by glancing ahead at your intended path of travel.

3. Evaluate the sharpness of the
curve. Slow down to a suitable
speed before entering the
curve. The advisory speed sign
tells the maximum speed you
should travel.

4. After entering the curve, accelerate gently.

5. Once around the curve, re-
sume a safe speed.

Hills Unlike a curve, a hill is not marked with warning signs unless it is unusually steep or long. On two-lane highways, the uphill portion is usually a no-passing zone. You cannot see far enough ahead to pass safely. Your *sight distance,* or how far you can see ahead, becomes shorter as you near the hilltop. Slow to a speed that allows you to check for traffic coming over the hill. Keep to the right side of the roadway.

Intersections Highway intersections can vary greatly. Traffic signals probably will control busy intersections for two-lane highways. Identify traffic signals at a distance so you can predict what color the light will be when you arrive. If the light is green when you first see it from a distance, predict that it probably will be red by the time you arrive. If the light is red, adjust your speed so you might arrive when the light is green.

The most common intersection is one in which a side roadway crosses a highway. The side roadway usually will have a STOP sign. Traffic on the side roadway might have difficulty entering the main roadway if the main roadway has a hill or a curve. Trees and bushes can obscure the view at the intersection.

Imagine you are the driver of the yellow car in this picture. Predict that the driver of the white car might pull out in front of you. The driver might misjudge the time and distance needed to enter and accelerate to highway speed.

Following Traffic Use the 2-second rule when following a vehicle on the highway. At highway speeds, the actual distance between vehicles is greater on the highway than in the city.

Vehicles cover distances in a short time at highway speeds. Hazards can quickly develop into conflicts. A 2-second following distance provides you the distance and time to prevent conflicts under normal conditions.

Sometimes a tailgater might be so close behind you that your braking could cause the tailgater to hit you. Always have an *escape path* ready, an opening into which you can move to avoid colliding with another vehicle. Sometimes a maneuver to the left or right, such as onto the shoulder, is a usable escape path.

Longer following distances are necessary when you are:
► being tailgated.
► on a steep downhill slope.
► following a motorcyclist.
► pulling a trailer.

Adjust your speed and position to keep a space cushion around your car. If a vehicle cuts into your 2-second following distance, drop back gradually. Reestablish a 2-second following distance between you and that vehicle.

Slow-Moving Vehicles The driver of a *slow-moving vehicle* might be unable to gain highway speed quickly or at all. For example, farm tractors cannot reach highway speed. These large machines usually move at 15 to 25 mph.

If you see a slow-moving vehicle on the highway, identify it as early as possible. The orange triangular sign at the rear of the vehicle, such as on this tractor, helps identify the vehicle as slow-moving. Because your car will approach a slow-moving vehicle rapidly, be ready to change lanes to pass if there is no oncoming traffic. Decide quickly when and

where to pass after you have checked traffic and roadway conditions. Your lane might be narrowed because the slow-moving vehicle takes more than half the roadway. Slow down before passing it.

Animals Wild and tame animals are often a problem on highways. They are unpredictable and can easily become frightened and run into your path.

When a dog, cat, or small wild animal dashes onto the highway, you might be tempted to brake hard or to swerve

sharply. You might forget the traffic situation momentarily. Before you brake or swerve, be sure that another more serious collision will not occur as a result of your action.

Large animals are a different problem. Hitting a cow or horse can cause injury to you and your passengers as well as to the animal. Watch especially for people riding horses, as in the right picture above. Slow down and steer around large animals to prevent a collision. Watch for a pet on a leash, a blind person with a seeing-eye dog, and livestock being herded across or alongside a roadway.

In areas with such large wild animals as deer, scan a wider area than usual. If you see one deer, expect others. Reduce speed in animal-crossing areas.

179

Meeting Traffic Meeting oncoming traffic can be dangerous. Often only a few feet separate you from oncoming vehicles. On highways with 55-mph speed limits, head-on collisions can cause serious injury or death.

Watch for the problems of an oncoming driver, as well as your own, when meeting. Choose where to meet, especially on older, narrower roadways. Use these guidelines for selecting a place to meet:

► Use the technique of separating hazards whenever possible. Slow down or speed up to control where you will meet another hazard. In the top picture, a parked car is on your side of the roadway. The oncoming driver might not identify the parked car and might maintain speed. In this situation, slow down to meet the oncoming car before passing the parked car. In the bottom picture, slow to let the other vehicle cross the bridge first.

► Meet where the most space is available. If you are on a narrow roadway, meet where you will have enough swerve space. Avoid places with bad pavement edges. If the roadway is not wide enough for two cars to meet, pull off the roadway and stop. Proceed when the other car has passed.

Be alert for an oncoming driver who may want to pass.

► If you are meeting a line of cars, drive near the right edge of the roadway. Notice how the driver of the oncoming car has moved to the right edge. By doing so, your car will be visible to more drivers. Some drivers might be anxious to get ahead in the line. Watch for drivers who might pull out to pass without checking for oncoming traffic.

► Meeting vehicles at the top of a hill can be dangerous. As your car nears the hilltop, your sight distance becomes shorter. An oncoming driver might be passing a vehicle and will be in your lane as you top the hill.

Oncoming drivers might cross the center line into your lane for other reasons:

► a blowout, a pothole, rocks on the roadway, or a strong cross wind

► unexpected loss of traction due to rain, snow, mud, or ice

► driver impairment due to fatigue, distractions, intoxication, or illness.

Meeting Slow-Moving Vehicles Watch carefully when meeting a slow-moving or a standing vehicle with an oncoming car close behind it. The driver of the following car might not see you coming and might swerve around the slow-moving vehicle into your lane. If the following driver sees you but is unable to stop in time, that driver might hit the slow-moving vehicle. The wreckage from that collision could slide into your path before you could react.

Meeting at Night A defensive driver knows that some drivers might have poor night vision. At night, headlights shining over a hill can warn you of an approaching vehicle. If you are using high-beam headlights, dim them early. Do not look directly into an oncoming car's headlights. Instead, glance to the right edge of the roadway. Even if both of you are using low-beam headlights, you both might be momentarily blinded as the cars reach the hilltop. Be prepared to take evasive action to avoid a collision.

Railroad Crossings About three of every four railroad crossings lack complete controls, such as flashing lights and gates. Many crossings are in rural areas where trains often travel at high speeds. See Chapter 6 for how to cross a railroad crossing safely.

Multilane Highways

Some rural highways can have four or more lanes. These highways have many of the features of rural two-lane highways, such as higher speeds and intersections. Some intersections are large and have major highways crossing them; others are small and are crossed by country roadways.

Multilane Highways with Center Lines   Highways with two or more lanes in each direction often have only a double solid yellow center line to separate high-speed traffic. It is illegal to cross double yellow lines, except to turn left. Passing is legal only in the lanes on your side of the center line.

Divided Highways   A guardrail or a *median strip,* an area of ground, separates two-way traffic on divided multilane highways. Some median strips are only a few feet wide; others are much wider, as seen in the picture.

Cross each half of a multilane highway as though it were a one-way street. Turn left or right onto a multilane highway as though you were entering a high-speed, one-way street.

Lane Choice   In most instances, stay away from the lane nearest the center. This lane usually is for passing or for turning left. In some states, the law requires that you stay in the right-hand lane for normal driving.

Turning at Intersections   When leaving a multilane highway, turn right from the right lane. Make left turns from the lane next to the center line or median strip.

Some intersections have special turn lanes for right and left turns. However, if these lanes

are not present, watch for vehicles in your rearview mirror while waiting to turn. A vehicle could hit you from the rear before you turn. If you see such a vehicle approaching at high speed, accelerate rapidly across the intersection. Continue straight ahead.

Entering a Multilane Highway
Use these procedures to enter a multilane highway, such as the one pictured, from a side roadway:
► For a right turn, first look for a large gap in traffic. Then enter the nearest lane that is going in your direction. Accelerate

promptly to move out of the intersection. Change lanes only after clearing the intersection.
► For a left turn, first cross the lanes on the near side of the highway. Turn into the lane just across the center line. Choose a time when no traffic is approaching in this lane. Accelerate more promptly to highway speed than you do for a right turn. Left turns require almost twice as much roadway space and acceleration as right turns.

Entering the highway from a private driveway presents the same problems as entering from a side roadway. Other

drivers might not know you are there. Warning signs do not alert drivers to possible conflicts at driveways as they do for side roadways. Therefore, look for a larger gap than when entering from a side roadway.

Review It
1. How is the IPDE process used during highway driving?
2. What checks should you make in a visual search pattern?
3. Why is meeting other vehicles on two-lane highways dangerous?
4. How can you make turns from and onto a multilane highway?

Passing another car on a two-lane highway is a potentially dangerous maneuver. In order to pass safely, you must know the proper procedures. You also must make critical decisions quickly.

Decision to Pass

Before deciding to pass, you must be able to answer "yes" to these questions: Is it legal? Is it safe? Is it worthwhile? The major responsibility for passing safely belongs to the driver who is passing.

Preparing to Pass

Take these actions when preparing to pass:

► Determine when you are rapidly closing the distance between you and the car ahead. Also determine if the car ahead is going at least 10 mph slower than you. If so, you might decide that passing would be to your advantage.

► Check the highway and signs ahead. Make sure that passing is legal in this area.

► Check for any other reason why you should not pass, such as poor sight distance ahead.

► Check the traction on the roadway ahead. You need a longer distance to pass safely when traction is not ideal. Under such conditions, accelerate gradually while changing lanes and keep a firm grip on the steering wheel.

Passing on Two-Lane Highways

Use these steps to pass on a two-lane highway:

1. When it is safe and clear to pass, tap the horn to warn the driver ahead that you are going to pass. When you pass at night, quickly change the headlight beam from low to high and back to low.
2. Signal for a lane change to the left. Check the blind spot over your left shoulder.
3. Change lanes smoothly.
4. Cancel the signal.
5. Pass at a speed at least 10 mph faster than the car you are passing. *Passing must be done within the speed limit.*

► Check ahead of the car you will pass. Make sure there is room for you to return to your lane after passing.
► Check the right roadway shoulder ahead. Make sure there are no hazards that might cause the driver ahead to swerve to the left.
► Check the rearview mirrors for possible fast-approaching vehicles. Delay passing if another car is about to pass you.

► Glance over your left shoulder. Make sure no vehicle is in your blind spot. If you have been checking the rearview mirror regularly, you probably already know. Check again to be sure.
► Check the oncoming traffic lane. Make sure you have plenty of space to pass safely. *If in doubt, do not pass.*
► Check driveways and intersections ahead. Make sure that

no one will be entering the highway.

You now have made all necessary checks. If all is clear, you are ready to pass. If not, slow down and follow the car ahead. Use the 2-second following distance rule. Then start over; repeat all of the checks. With practice, you can make these checks in just a few seconds.

6. At this point, you can still drop back and return to the right lane if any unexpected problem occurs ahead. If all is clear, continue to accelerate to the proper speed.
7. Maintain speed. Remain in the left lane until you can see both headlights of the car you are passing in your inside mirror.
8. Signal for a lane change to the right. Check the inside mirror again. Check over your right shoulder.
9. Return smoothly to the right lane. Be careful not to slow down during the return.
10. Cancel the signal and adjust your speed.

Being Passed

The driver who is passing has the major responsibility for passing safely. However, you, the driver being passed, have certain responsibilities as well.

You should be aware that another car is passing, even without a warning horn or flashing headlights. Glance in the rearview mirror regularly to see if cars are approaching. Stay to the right side of your lane to give the other driver a better view ahead and more room to pass.

Determine if the passing driver is having difficulty completing the pass. If so, help the other driver by slowing down. *It is illegal to speed up while being passed.*

Sometimes the passing driver decides not to pass and drops back. If so, accelerate slightly to open up space behind you.

No-Passing Situations

No-passing areas are marked by solid yellow lines. Signs often are also used to indicate no-passing areas. Passing is illegal and unsafe when:

► sight distance ahead is limited.
► space is narrow.
► cross-traffic is a hazard.

In these situations, passing is unsafe even if no warning signs or lines are there.

► **No Passing Going Uphill**
Passing is not allowed in the last 700 to 1,000 feet before the crest of a hill. The picture at the right shows that the driver of the yellow car cannot see oncoming traffic in time to pass safely.

Some states with steep hills and mountains have special uphill-passing lanes. Passing is legal downhill where visibility is good and there is no solid yellow line.

► **No Passing at Intersections or Railroad Crossings** Passing is illegal within the last 100 feet before an intersection or a railroad crossing. Slow down when approaching an intersection. The picture below shows why passing at an intersection is dangerous. Note how a driver turning from the crossroad might enter your lane.

No-Passing Conditions

Do not attempt to pass in these conditions:

► The car ahead is going at or near the speed limit.
► Fog, snow, or rain limit sight distance.
► Roadway surface is slick.
► Several vehicles are ahead of you.
► You cannot complete the pass before a no-passing zone starts.
► Oncoming traffic is too close.
► You will stop or turn soon.

Passing on Multilane Highways

Oncoming vehicles present little danger for passing on multilane highways. However, check all lanes going in your direction before you pass. If you are in a center lane, check both right and left lanes. Finally, check all lanes on the passing side. Be sure no one is about to enter your passing lane from a far lane. The car you are about to pass should be traveling several mph slower than you.

Review It

1. What checks do you need to make before deciding to pass?
2. What are the steps for passing safely on highways?
3. What must you do when you are being passed?
4. What are six conditions and situations for no passing?

► **No Passing on Bridges or Underpasses** Passing is illegal within the last 100 feet before a bridge or underpass. An underpass or a bridge can cut off the shoulder, as in the picture above. You or the car you passed might need to use the shoulder in an emergency.

► **No Passing on Curves** Passing is illegal on curves. You do not have enough sight distance to see around curves. The driver of the yellow car in the picture above cannot see the oncoming car ahead. Stay in your own lane on any curve, out of the way of oncoming traffic.

Driving through mountains and deserts can offer many challenges to your patience and skill. Pay special attention to speed-limit and warning signs in these areas.

Mountain Driving

Mountain driving presents more special problems and situations than driving in flat areas. You must consider the effects of gravity constantly. Gravity tends to pull down on a car going downhill. Gravity also slows a car's forward motion when going uphill.

Mountain roadways have many curves. They often zig-zag with a series of sharp turns called a *switchback*. The sign in the above left picture warns that a switchback is ahead.

Up the Mountain Steady acceleration is necessary to maintain speed while driving uphill. If the slope is very steep, downshift in a car with manual transmission. With an automatic transmission, the car will downshift by itself.

Stay to the right and tap your horn as a warning when you cannot see oncoming traffic around mountain curves. An oncoming vehicle can cross into your lane because the driver is going too fast for the curve. Driving too fast on curves is a major cause of collisions in the mountains.

Loaded trucks, recreational vehicles, and cars pulling trailers move slowly up mountain roadways. You have no choice but to follow at their speed and at a safe following distance. The picture above shows a *pull-out area,* a place where slow-moving vehicles can pull over and stop. The faster traffic following behind can then proceed.

Down the Mountain Gravity pulls you faster and faster downhill unless you resist it. Shift to a lower gear before starting downhill. Downshift an automatic transmission manually to drive down a mountain safely. Never coast downhill in NEUTRAL or with the clutch disengaged.

With either transmission, adjust speed with occasional use of the brakes. Do not apply the brakes steadily; brake fade can

result. If you are braking often, slow the car and downshift to the next lower gear. Keep your speed low enough so that you can stay in your lane. Keep your car under control at all times.

Be aware of the possible speed control problems of large trucks going downhill. Some mountain roadways have runaway vehicle ramps for trucks that develop braking problems down long, steep grades. The picture shows such a ramp.

Sometimes two vehicles will meet on a narrow mountain roadway. Neither vehicle can pass safely. The vehicle heading downhill must back up until the vehicle going uphill can pass since it is more dangerous to back a vehicle downhill.

Weather in the Mountains

Early morning fog, snow, and ice can make mountain driving difficult. Many mountain highways become snowbound in winter. Call the local police or state highway department for roadway conditions during adverse weather.

Altitude Affects the Driver

High altitude can cause shortness of breath, faster heartbeat, and headaches. The reduced supply of oxygen in mountain air can also lessen concentration and cause drowsiness. The effects are worse for tired drivers. Do not drive if you are affected. If you are traveling with others, take turns driving.

Altitude Affects the Car

Thin mountain air also affects car engines. Acceleration is sluggish. Climbing power is lessened. Liquids boil and change to vapor more quickly. If the temperature light comes on or the gauge registers hot, stop and let the engine cool. You also can cool the engine somewhat by turning on the heater to draw off some engine heat.

A vehicle's engine gets hot during mountain driving. When you turn off the engine, gasoline can vaporize in the fuel line near the hot engine. This condition is *vapor lock*. Fuel cannot be pumped into the engine in a gaseous state. Therefore, the engine will not start. Allow the engine to cool, then restart it.

If you do much mountain driving, you can prevent most of these problems. A mechanic can adjust the engine for better performance at higher altitudes.

Desert Driving

Desert areas are bigger and hotter than most drivers realize. Driving in a desert area is hard on the driver, the car, and the roadway.

The Driver The intense heat of daytime driving creates maximum stress on you. You experience a sameness of scenery that can lull you into a false sense of security. Sun glare can reduce your visibility seriously. Wear good quality sunglasses. Change drivers often. If you are driving alone, stop every hour or so at a rest area. Carry a water supply for both the passengers and the car. The desert is harsh if something goes wrong.

The Car The car needs more service for desert driving than for other environments. If you drive several hours daily, check the radiator fluid level at every fuel stop. Check the battery fluid level daily unless it is a sealed battery.

Caution: Never remove the cap from a hot radiator. Hot fluid and steam can burn you. Check the fluid level in the coolant recovery tank. Otherwise, wait for the radiator to cool.

Check tire pressure before you begin the day's drive. Tire pressure will build up during the day's drive, but do not reduce the pressure. Any reduction in tire pressure when tires are hot will cause the tires to become even hotter. A blowout could occur.

The Roadway Well-paved highways with gentle curves and hills invite higher speeds. However, roadway shoulders that look firm are often sandy. Wheels sink into sand quickly. If you need to park off the roadway, choose an area that looks firm. Car tracks show that the area has been packed down.

Sandstorms and Dust Storms Do not drive during a sandstorm or dust storm if you can avoid it. If caught in a sandstorm or dust storm as shown here, slow down immediately. Drive carefully off the traveled portion of the highway, onto the shoulder. Turn off your vehicle's lights. Wait until the storm has passed.

If you must drive, go slowly enough to see ahead clearly. Use low-beam headlights both to help you better see and be seen. As soon as possible after the storm, change the oil, oil filter, and air filter.

Flash Floods A *flash flood* is a sudden rush of water from heavy rains. Flash floods can happen suddenly and unexpectedly. They are especially dangerous in the desert where the ground washes away easily. If a flash flood occurs, go to higher ground and wait for the water to subside. Stay away from creeks or drainage areas.

Review It

1. How does gravity and altitude affect the car when driving in the mountains?
2. How should you service the car during desert driving?

Besides cars, many other kinds of vehicles, such as trucks and trailers, use the highways. These vehicles differ in size, speed, and performance.

Semi-Trailer Trucks

Trucks occupy a lot of roadway space. The 2-second interval is enough to prevent a collision. However, 2 seconds does not allow enough clear sight distance ahead. You might not be able to identify potential problems clearly.

Do not follow too closely, as the driver in the left picture has done. You will not be able to see clearly. You will be able to see farther ahead by maintaining a greater following distance. Increase your following distance, as the driver in the right picture has done.

Drive nearer the left edge of your lane when following a truck. Your car will then be visible to oncoming drivers. Move back to the center of the lane while meeting oncoming vehicles.

Speed of Trucks   Large trucks can travel as fast as cars, but trucks do not reach highway speed as quickly. Trucks are designed to carry heavy loads, not to accelerate quickly. Plan to pass a truck when the truck driver has to shift several gears to gain speed. Such places are just over the crest of a hill or when leaving a STOP sign or a traffic light after a stop. First, be sure you are both clear of the intersection.

Meeting Trucks   You do not have much room when meeting large trucks on narrow two-lane highways. Move slightly to the right in your lane. Check the position of the truck in its lane. Look well ahead and drive in a straight line. If possible, choose a meeting point where the shoulder offers a good escape path. When meeting trucks, you might feel your car being moved sideways by a wind gust. Be especially alert for wind gusts when driving a small car, a panel truck, or a car with a top carrier. Hold the steering wheel firmly to stay on course.

Special-Purpose Vehicles

Campers and cars towing trailers need more time and space to reach highway speed. The "Wide Load" sign in the top picture warns that this load might be wider than a traffic lane.

Other special-purpose vehicles use highways during certain times of the year. Roadway maintenance crews make many repairs during the summer. After a snowfall, expect to see snowplows like the one pictured. Expect slow-moving vehicles, like this farm vehicle, in farm areas during harvest time.

School Bus

You must stop for a school bus that is loading or unloading students. You do not have to stop if the bus is on the other side of a divided highway.

Remember that you are traveling at highway speed. Be prepared to make a smooth stop when the bus driver indicates a stop. Look for a STOP sign and flashing lights in front and to the rear of the bus.

Review It

1. What makes trucks and special-purpose vehicles hazardous on the highway?
2. What are the precautions to take when stopping for a school bus?

Be a Fuel Saver

► Drive at steady speeds on the highway. Over-acceleration and frequent braking use more fuel.
► If possible, approach highway traffic signals so that you will arrive when the light is green.
► Pass where you can safely do so at a steady speed. Pass so you do not have to slow and follow and then accelerate again.
► When driving up mountains, use a lower gear so the engine does not have to work so hard. Climb hills at a steady speed.

► Immediately ease off the accelerator pedal when the brake lights of the car ahead of you come on. You might not have to brake at all, thus saving both fuel and wear on the brakes. In addition, you will not waste fuel by having to accelerate to highway speed again.

Chapter Summary

1. Adjust speed to highway conditions. (10–1)
2. Be alert for signs, guardrails, bridge railings, bushes, and trees near the edge of a highway. Other hazards include rough, narrow roadway shoulders and roadside facilities. (10–1)
3. Use the IPDE process to determine a safe highway speed. Identify hazards, predict what might occur, decide on an action to avoid a conflict, and then execute the decision if necessary. (10–2)
4. Use an orderly visual search pattern to identify potential highway hazards. (10–2)
5. While driving on a two-lane highway, be alert for curves, hills, intersections, and slow-moving vehicles. (10–2)
6. Turn right from the right lane to leave a multilane highway. Make left turns from the lane closest to the center line or median strip. (10–2)
7. Check these factors when deciding to pass: legality, visibility, roadway surface, hazards, oncoming traffic, and fast-approaching traffic from the rear. (10–3)
8. A safe passing procedure includes these points: selection of a safe passing location, consideration of oncoming vehicles, signaling to drivers ahead and behind, proper lane change procedure, and adequate acceleration. (10–3)
9. If you are being passed, move to the right side of your lane. Let the passing driver complete the pass. (10–3)
10. Do not pass when visibility and space are reduced, when roadway or weather conditions are poor, or when other vehicles might interfere with a safe pass. (10–3)
11. Varying weather conditions, altitude, and related effects of gravity make mountain driving more challenging than regular highway driving. (10–4)
12. Different weather conditions and roadway surfaces make desert driving harder on both the car and the driver. (10–4)
13. Trucks and other special-purpose vehicles can be a hazard due to their size, speed, and capabilities. Adjust your own speed and following distance as needed. (10–5)
14. Stop for a school bus that is loading or unloading passengers. You do not have to stop if the bus is on the other side of a divided highway. (10–5)

Think About It

You are following a large truck on a flat, two-lane highway. The truck is traveling twenty miles below the posted speed limit. The shoulder of the roadway is narrow, and there is a deep ditch along the roadway. You want to pass the truck. What should you do?

Decision Making

1. What hazards do you see? How can you avoid these possible hazards?

2. You are driving the yellow car. You are being passed by another car. You see the oncoming car getting close. What should you do to help the passing driver?

3. You are approaching a curve where your view of the roadway ahead is reduced. What procedures do you follow? What do you identify and predict?

4. You are driving the yellow car. You and the oncoming truck are going to meet on the bridge. The wide truck takes up part of your lane. What should you do?

Chapter 10 Test

Multiple Choice Copy the number of each sentence below on a sheet of paper. Choose the letter that best completes each statement or answers each question.

1. The single most important decision in highway driving is
   (a) the roadway surface. (b) weather. (c) speed. (d) roadside hazards. (174)

2. Your sight distance as you approach a hill
   (a) becomes shorter. (b) becomes longer. (c) stays the same. (d) is only affected by curves. (178)

3. When meeting a line of cars, you should
   (a) drive near the center line. (b) drive near the right edge of the roadway. (c) drive on the shoulder of the roadway. (d) accelerate. (181)

4. Which action is illegal when being passed?
   (a) speeding up (b) maintaining your speed (c) slowing down (d) staying in your lane (186)

5. What does a solid yellow line on your side of the center line indicate?
   (a) do not pass (b) passing permitted (c) do not drive over 45 mph (d) do not stop (186)

Completion Copy the number of each sentence below. After each number, write the letter of the word or words that completes the sentence correctly.

6. Use the ____ technique to handle one hazard at a time when two or more hazards are present. (180)

7. On a multilane highway, make left turns from the ____. (182)

8. Many states require that on multilane highways, drivers stay in the ____ for normal driving. (182)

9. Passing is illegal within the last 100 feet before an ____. (186)

10. To drive down a mountain safely, shift to a ____ gear before starting downhill. (188)

a. center lane
b. intersection
c. lane next to the center line or median strip
d. lower
e. right-hand lane
f. separating

Vocabulary Copy the number of each phrase below. Match the definition in List A with the term it defines in List B.

List A
11. a process of scanning critical areas in a regular sequence (176)
12. a sign giving the maximum safe speed on a curve (177)
13. how far you can see ahead (178)
14. an opening to move your car into as to avoid a collision (178)
15. a vehicle usually identified by an orange, triangular sign at the rear of the vehicle (179)
16. an area that separates two-way traffic on a divided, multilane highway (182)
17. series of extremely sharp turns on a mountain roadway (188)
18. a safe stopping area on a mountain roadway (188)
19. condition in which fuel in gaseous form prevents the engine from starting (189)
20. a sudden rush of water, from heavy rain, that can wash out roadways (190)

List B
a. advisory speed sign
b. escape path
c. flash flood
d. median strip
e. multilane highway
f. pull-out area
g. sight distance
h. slow-moving vehicle
i. switchback
j. vapor lock
k. orderly visual search pattern

Chapter 11
Expressway Driving

You're the Driver!

Imagine you are driving the middle car on the entrance ramp to this expressway. Traffic is heavy and is moving very fast.

What do you predict that the driver in front of you might do?

What actions should you take as you approach the acceleration lane?

How can you communicate with the driver behind you?

What should the drivers on the expressway do as they approach acceleration lanes and merging traffic?

What traffic signal might you find on some expressway entrance ramps?

In this chapter, you will learn how to use expressways safely and efficiently. You also will learn how to handle special problems in expressway traffic.

Objectives

11–1 Characteristics of Expressway Traffic

Driving on expressways is one of the most common and efficient ways to travel. Expressways include interstate highways, freeways, and toll-roads. An expressway is a limited access or *controlled-access highway*. Vehicles can enter or leave an expressway only at interchanges.

Advantages of Expressways
Expressways give you the best protection for driving at higher speeds. Expressways carry more traffic and are safer than other highways. Collisions and fatality rates are far lower on expressways than on other roadways.

Five reasons why expressways have fewer collisions are:
► Cross traffic is eliminated since there are no intersections.
► Expressways have a median strip or barrier between opposing lanes of traffic.
► Pedestrians, animals, and slow-moving vehicles are not permitted on most expressways.
► The design of expressways helps keep vehicles from hitting fixed objects.
► Expressways are designed to help drivers anticipate conditions ahead.

Expressway Interchanges
These pictures show the most common types of expressway interchanges. These interchanges have two features:
► Vehicles can cross over an expressway or under it.
► Vehicles can enter and leave an expressway without interfering with the flow of traffic.

Strategies for Safe Driving on Expressways
Although expressways have advantages over other types of roadways, collisions are often more serious. Use the strategies discussed on page 200 to help you become a safe expressway driver.

Cloverleaf Interchange
Eliminates left turn
and cross-traffic conflicts
for all movements.

Diamond Interchange

A diamond interchange is used when a busy expressway is crossed by a street that has much less traffic. A complete cloverleaf is not needed because left turns can be made easily on the less busy street.

Trumpet Interchange

A trumpet interchange is used where a side road forms a T-intersection with an expressway. The trumpet enables traffic to enter and leave the expressway without crossing traffic.

Directional Interchange

A directional interchange is used in complicated intersections to channel traffic in several different directions.

Prepare Yourself and Your Car
The constant higher speed of expressway driving strains both you and your car. You must stay alert and keep your car in top condition when driving on an expressway.

Have a travel plan before driving on any expressway, regardless of trip length. For a short trip, know the name, route, or number for both the entrance and exit you will use. For a long-distance trip, such as through another state, plan stops for food, fuel, and rest.

Once on an expressway, concentrate fully on the driving task. Boredom and fatigue can occur easily when driving on an expressway. You cannot make the decisions and actions necessary for safe expressway driving when you are tired. Always be alert for the actions of other drivers.

Mechanical failure can occur even during a short trip on an expressway. Check your car's gauges frequently. Many expressway service calls are for cars that have run out of fuel or radiator coolant, as this picture shows.

Build Experience Gradually
When you first drive alone on an expressway, choose a time when traffic is light. Practice entering and exiting several

times before driving in heavier traffic. Practice lane changes too, even if there are no vehicles to pass. Once you have developed confidence in light traffic, you will be better prepared to drive in heavier traffic.

Concentrate on the Driving Task   Traffic conflicts can develop more rapidly at higher speed, especially in multilane expressways. Give your full attention to the driving task. Try not to think about other matters. Concentrate strictly on the changing scene to be a safe expressway driver.

Cooperate with Other Drivers
You must be willing to cooperate with others on an expressway. Cooperating might be difficult when someone cuts you off or moves into the space cushion ahead of your car. Resist the urge to challenge other drivers for any reason. The mature, responsible driver cooperates with others rather than competes.

Review It
1. Why do fewer collisions occur on expressways than on other roadways?
2. What strategies can you use to help you become a safe expressway driver?

Before entering an expressway, make sure you are using the correct entrance ramp. Guide signs mark most entrances and give the route number, direction, and name of a city located in that direction. Many drivers have mistakenly tried to enter an expressway by using an exit ramp. To prevent this error, most states post signs saying WRONG WAY or DO NOT ENTER.

Most expressway entrances have the three parts shown here:

► The *entrance ramp* gives you time to evaluate traffic as you prepare to merge onto the expressway.

► The *acceleration lane* is usually long enough so you can accelerate to the speed of traffic on the expressway.

► The *merging area* is the third part of an expressway entrance. Try to enter the expressway from the merging area at about the same speed as the cars in the first lane. Once on the expressway, adjust your speed to the flow of traffic as soon as possible.

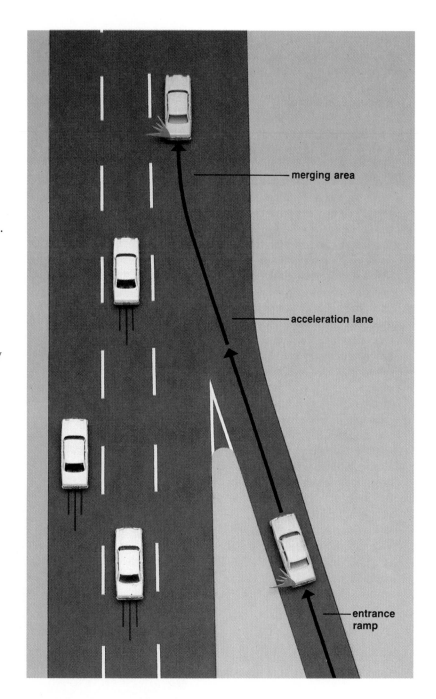

merging area

acceleration lane

entrance ramp

Steps for Entering

Follow these steps to enter an expressway smoothly and safely:

1. Be sure the entrance is the one you want and that the ramp is an entrance ramp. Look for a WRONG WAY or DO NOT ENTER sign.

2. Once on the entrance ramp, be alert for vehicles ahead and behind, as shown in the top picture. Look for a gap in traffic that your car will fit into safely by taking quick glances through your left outside rearview mirror and over your left shoulder. Signal your intention to merge well in advance.

3. Once on the acceleration lane, adjust your speed to the flow of the traffic. Continue to glance quickly in the mirror and over your shoulder to decide the time and place to enter the gap, as shown in the middle picture.

4. Before entering the merging area, decide which vehicle to follow in the traffic flow. As you enter the merge area, adjust your speed to match the traffic flow. Position your car at a safe interval behind the car you plan to follow. Merge smoothly, as shown in the bottom picture.

5. Once in traffic, cancel your turn signal and adjust to the speed of traffic. Keep a safe space cushion around your car.

Possible Entrance Problems

Entrance mistakes cause many conflicts and collisions on expressways. Heavy traffic, short entrance ramps, short acceleration lanes, and high dividing walls also can cause entrance problems.

Use the IPDE process on expressway entrances:
▶ Make all visual checks quickly. Identify possible problems on each part of the expressway entrance.
▶ Predict possible actions of other drivers. Then, you can decide how to adjust and execute your entrance actions without difficulty.

Entrance Ramp Know which expressway entrance you want to use. Sometimes you might begin to drive onto an entrance ramp that you do not want. If so, continue on the entrance ramp and get on the expressway. Exit at the first opportunity and drive to the entrance you want. *Never back up on an entrance ramp or on an expressway.*

When you are on an entrance ramp, look for other traffic on the ramp. If traffic is on the ramp, adjust your speed immediately to avoid conflicts. Some ramps, particularly ramps with sharp curves, have signs posting a speed limit.

Check your speed and stay within the speed limit. Exceeding the speed limit makes it difficult to control your car, especially in a curve.

Begin looking immediately for a gap in traffic if the entrance ramp is short or there is no acceleration lane. Watch cars ahead of you and behind you. Maintain a safe space cushion.

Gaps are difficult to find in heavy traffic. If no gap is acceptable, you must slow or even stop before entering the acceleration lane or the expressway. Flash your brake lights to warn the driver behind you in such cases. Avoid stopping whenever possible. If there is no acceleration lane, adjust your speed on the entrance ramp so your entrance onto the expressway matches your chosen gap.

The vehicle ahead of you on an entrance ramp can present a problem if it slows or comes to a full stop, as shown here. Give the other driver time to find a gap. Make sure the driver merges safely before you accelerate. Try to adjust your speed so you can continue moving rather than stopping. Stopping could cause a rear-end collision. Also, if you stop, you will have to use a slower speed for your entry.

Some entrance ramps have high walls that divide expressway traffic and entering traffic. In this case, you will be far along the entrance ramp before you can see the traffic. Begin checking your left rearview mirror and looking over your shoulder as soon as you can see traffic on the expressway.

Entrance Ramp Signal Lights

Sometimes signal lights regulate traffic entering an expressway. Signal lights often are used during rush hours to space the vehicles entering the expressway.

The timed signal lights shown here provide intervals at which vehicles enter the expressway. The lights are red and green in most cases. You must wait for a green light before entering the expressway.

Acceleration Lane

Once on an acceleration lane, try to adjust your speed to that of the expressway traffic. The amount of traffic both on the expressway and in the acceleration lane determines your safe speed in the acceleration lane. During rush hours, entering traffic and expressway traffic can make it impossible to accelerate to expressway speed.

Some entrances have short acceleration lanes. In such cases, you usually do not have the space to accelerate to the speed of expressway traffic. You need a longer gap to enter traffic and accelerate to the traffic speed.

Make every effort to enter an expressway without stopping. Time your entrance and adjust your speed properly. Stopping is extremely hazardous. A driver who is behind you might be looking for a gap, and not realize that you have stopped. If you must stop:

1. Flash your brake lights to warn drivers behind you. Drive the entire length of the acceleration lane.
2. Pull onto the shoulder at the end of the acceleration lane or merge area.
3. You are now in an emergency situation. Wait for a safe gap, and accelerate quickly as you join traffic.

Sometimes you might follow a driver who seems unsure about joining traffic. If so, slow down and leave more space between your car and the vehicle in front of you. Be prepared for the driver to stop suddenly.

Merging Area

Time your entrance in order to blend smoothly and safely into expressway traffic. Adjusting your speed is critical as you enter expressway traffic. Accelerate as you enter the moving traffic. The drivers ahead of you might cause you to adjust your speed and to even select a new gap. Once you are on the expressway, accelerate to expressway speed when traffic permits. Stay in your lane until you are adjusted and accustomed to the expressway speed.

Review It

1. What are the steps for entering an expressway?
2. What problems might make entering an expressway difficult?

Wait until light turns green to enter the expressway.

Once on an expressway, stay alert and be prepared to adjust to the changing traffic scene. Vehicles are moving at high speeds; be ready to use all of your driving skills and knowledge. You must know what to look for, where to look, and how to interpret the information you receive. Use this information to predict and decide accurately.

Applying the IPDE Process

Using the IPDE process on an expressway can help you maintain a safe path of travel. However, higher speeds, multiple lanes to watch, and heavier volume of traffic make the identify step more difficult.

Higher speeds increase the distance that you need to look ahead to identify and predict possible conflicts. While expressways are designed to give drivers a long sight distance, multiple lanes increase the amount of visual information you must gather.

Keep these points in mind:
▶ Identify the volume of traffic in different lanes. Watch for brake lights on vehicles in all lanes.
▶ Note signs, signals, and roadway markings.
▶ Be aware of roadway conditions. Stopping distances increase for all vehicles under adverse conditions.

A predictable traffic flow is one safety feature of an expressway. However, always watch closely for drivers who make sudden stops or attempt to back up. At a distance, a car backing up might still look like a car going forward. Continually predict the actions of others around you. Be especially alert for sudden lane change maneuvers.

Execute your decisions smoothly. Avoid making sudden, unexpected decisions or changes in direction. Signal your maneuvers early. Maintain a safe space cushion.

Lane Choice

You can help the flow of expressway traffic by staying in the right-hand lane. Leave the center and left-hand lanes for drivers who are passing and for faster-moving traffic.

Sometimes the far right lane has frequent possible conflicts from vehicles entering the expressway. During rush hours, consider using the center or left lane to avoid conflicts in the far right lane. Both the drivers entering and the drivers on the expressway share the responsibility for protecting each other from conflicts.

Trucks, buses, and vehicles towing trailers are required to use only the right lanes on many expressways. Sometimes you will be using these same lanes. If so, make every effort to avoid driving between two large vehicles. The driver of this car has a short sight distance and limited side vision because of the large vehicles surrounding the car. When you are in such a situation, slow down and make a lane change as soon as possible.

Avoid straddling lane lines. This action prevents other drivers from passing and maintaining their lane positions.

Signs, Signals, and Roadway Markings Part of your decision on lane choice is based on information from expressway signs, signals, and roadway markings. You are better able to maintain a safe path of travel and avoid making sudden last-second decisions if you:

► know your destination.
► read signs and roadway markings.
► always think ahead.

Sometimes several overhead signs are posted above the roadway at the same place. One sign might say EXIT, another might warn of the NEXT EXIT, and yet another might show route numbers and names of distant cities. In some states, an overhead sign with a yellow panel indicates the exit lane, as in the top left picture. If you are in the exit lane, you must exit or move out of the lane safely.

Overhead signals tell you if lanes are open or closed to traffic. A yellow X gives an early warning that the lane will be closed farther ahead. A red X appears farther down that lane to alert you to a closed lane. If you have not changed lanes by the time you reach the red X, you might become trapped in that closed lane. A green arrow means the lane is open for traffic.

Many expressways into and out of cities have express lanes. In most cases, these lanes have only one entrance; traffic moves without conflict from merging vehicles. Express lanes have few exits. The exits are near the city or in the city. The same lanes are used for morning rush hours into the city and for evening rush hours leaving the city. Traffic direction is reversed. Notice in the top right picture that you may not enter the express lanes, but the green arrows indicate open lanes.

The right edge of the expressway should be marked with a white line. The left edge should show a yellow line. These lines help you position your car especially at night or during limited visibility.

Driving too slowly can be dangerous and is a potential cause of rear-end collisions. Other drivers might not realize how slowly you are driving until they are too close to you. Use the far right lane if you are driving at the minimum speed limit.

Common Speed If you drive at the *common speed*, the speed used by most drivers, you can better blend with expressway traffic. Sometimes the common speed is above the maximum speed limit. Resist the temptation to increase your speed to keep up with the faster vehicles. Drivers who exceed the speed limit are likely to weave in and out of traffic to pass other vehicles. This practice is dangerous not only to the driver exceeding the maximum speed limit, but also to other drivers on the expressway.

Wolf Packs An experienced, responsible driver avoids a group or bunch of vehicles known as a *wolf pack*. Reduce your chances of being involved in a conflict by being a "loner" on the expressway. A driver traveling in the middle of a wolf pack is more likely to

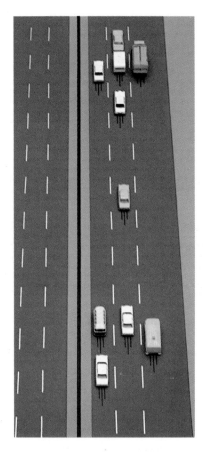

Speed Limits The maximum speed limit on most expressways is 55 mph. Some states have a lower speed limit for trucks and other large vehicles. Most vehicles travel at the speed limit in good conditions. A *minimum speed limit* is posted on many expressways to keep traffic from moving too slowly. The minimum speed limit is the slowest legal speed you can drive. The minimum speed limit is seldom below 40 mph. If driving conditions are poor, you might have to drive below the minimum speed limit. The sign in the picture above shows the maximum speed limit of 55 mph and a minimum speed limit of 45 mph.

have trouble with lane changes than a loner. Reduce your speed temporarily to get out of a wolf pack or to let a wolf pack pass.

Two wolf packs are shown in the picture above. The driver of the yellow car in the center lane wisely decided to be a loner by driving between the packs.

Following

One of the most important requirements for driving on an expressway is keeping a safe following distance. Following too closely reduces your sight distance, leaves you little room to maneuver, and is the major cause of expressway collisions.

Apply the 2-second following distance rule when driving on the expressway. The white car in the center lane in the top picture has established a safe following distance. However, the white van is following too closely.

Maintaining at least a 2-second following distance is your best protection to keep a safe path of travel and to avoid a rear-end collision. If a driver cuts into the space ahead of your car, slow down to reestablish a safe following distance.

When the roadway is wet or slippery, reduce your speed and increase your following distance to 3 or 4 seconds. Increasing your following distance is especially important when you are:

► following a truck or bus that is blocking your vision.
► following a motorcyclist.
► driving in bad weather.
► driving in heavy traffic.
► being tailgated.

► driving a heavy vehicle or pulling a trailer.
► operating a motorcycle.
► entering or exiting an expressway.

Blind Spots Remember that you have a blind spot in back of each rear corner of your car. Check your blind spots often to be alert for other drivers.

If you are following in a driver's blind spot, keep far enough behind so that you are not in the driver's blind spot. Reduce speed, or accelerate and pass to stay out of the other driver's blind spot. The driver in the right lane in the bottom picture is entering the truck driver's blind spot.

Being Followed

Many drivers think that they have no control over the space cushion to the rear. The best action to take to get rid of tailgaters is to reduce speed slightly. This action might encourage the tailgater to pass. If a driver continues to tailgate, change lanes if it is safe to do so. Frequently check traffic behind to stay aware of tailgaters.

Lane Changing

Avoid changing lanes too often. Any change from the regular traffic pattern can cause conflicts. Unnecessary weaving from one lane to another can lead to a collision. Take these steps to change lanes:

1. Change lanes one at a time. Signal *every* lane change, regardless of whether or not other vehicles are present. Do not expect signals to clear the way. Signals only alert drivers of your intention to move.
2. Check traffic in both rearview mirrors. Check the blind-spot area in the direction you want to move.
3. If the way is clear, move to the next lane.
4. Cancel the signal after you have changed lanes.

Changing lanes on an expressway is more complicated when three or more lanes are moving in the same direction. Many times a problem occurs

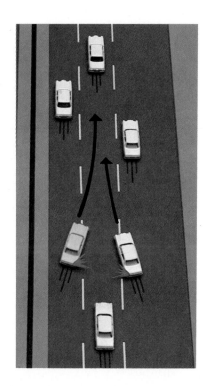

when two drivers want to use the same space at the same time, as shown in the first picture. A quick glance over the shoulder would let you check the lane to see if it is open. If you are not sure of another driver's intentions, make this additional check: See if another driver opposite you is speeding up or signaling to move into the gap you have chosen. If so, delay your lane change until it is safe to make your move.

Sometimes you will change lanes so entering traffic can merge safely. Remember that

some expressways have entrance ramps on the left as well as on the right. If you are driving in the left lane and see a driver entering from the left, change lanes just as you would for traffic entering from the right. If you cannot change lanes, as shown in the second picture, slow down or accelerate to open a gap.

Lanes often are closed for repair work. When a lane is closed, use only the lanes open to traffic. It is both illegal and hazardous to use the shoulder or median as an "extra" lane when traffic is backed up.

Passing and Being Passed

Passing other vehicles on an expressway usually is safer than passing on a two-lane highway. Since you do not encounter oncoming traffic on an expressway, a head-on collision is not a threat. However, expressway speeds and a higher traffic volume demand caution, concentration, and constant use of the IPDE process when passing.

Passing on the left is usual on expressways. However, passing on the right usually is permitted if a slower driver is in the left lane. Choose a lane that allows others to pass you on the left. If you are continually being passed on the right, take the tip and move to the lane on your right.

When passing another vehicle, follow the procedure for making a lane change to the left, as the yellow car in the picture is doing. Identify any other users in a lane who might conflict with your passing maneuver. Make sure the driver you will pass knows that you are passing. Tap the horn to alert the other driver of your intention to pass. After passing, return to your original lane by making a lane change. Throughout your maneuver, keep an adequate space cushion between you and the vehicle you are passing.

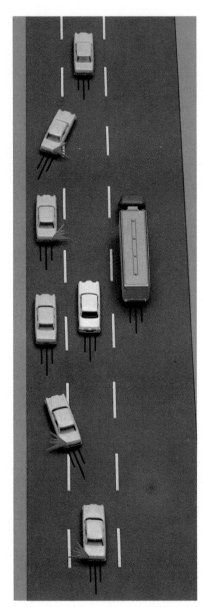

Make these two actions automatic when you pass:
► Use lane-change signals.
► Check traffic behind with rearview mirrors and traffic to the sides with one or more quick glances to the left or right, as necessary.

When you are being passed, note the position of the vehicle passing you. If you do not have enough space cushion to the side, move away from the passing vehicle. Continue to check the vehicle that is passing you. Keep your speed steady and do not accelerate. Blending into the flow of traffic is just as important during passing as it is when entering or exiting an expressway.

Review It

1. How can using the IPDE process help you maintain a safe path of travel on expressways?
2. Why should you read signs ahead of time on expressways?
3. Why is a safe following distance especially important on expressways?
4. What two actions should be automatic when changing lanes to pass on an expressway?

11–4 Exiting Expressways

Leaving an expressway can be a smooth procedure when you know in advance which exit to take. Most expressway exits provide a *deceleration lane,* an added lane in which to slow down without blocking vehicles behind. Note the deceleration lane in this picture. The deceleration lane leads into the *exit ramp,* the ramp leading off the expressway. If you do not slow down enough in the deceleration lane, you might enter the exit ramp at too high a speed. Identify the regulatory sign that shows the exit ramp speed limit. Check that your speed does not exceed the posted limit.

Sometimes you might need to exit an expressway from the left lane. Follow the same procedure as when you exit from the right lane.

If you miss the exit you want, go on to the next exit. *Never stop or back up if you go past your exit.* If you have selected the wrong exit, do not cross the V-shaped lines on the roadway. Continue to exit, and then enter the expressway again at the first opportunity.

Applying the IPDE Process
Use the IPDE process and plan well ahead to exit an expressway:
1. Identify the expressway signs stating the distance to your exit. Determine whether the exit is on the right or left side. Plan lane changes early. Change only one lane at a time.
2. Predict actions of other drivers who might change lanes suddenly to use the same exit.
3. Decide on the proper speed for control of your car as you exit.
4. Execute your maneuver smoothly as you prepare to blend with slower traffic off the expressway.

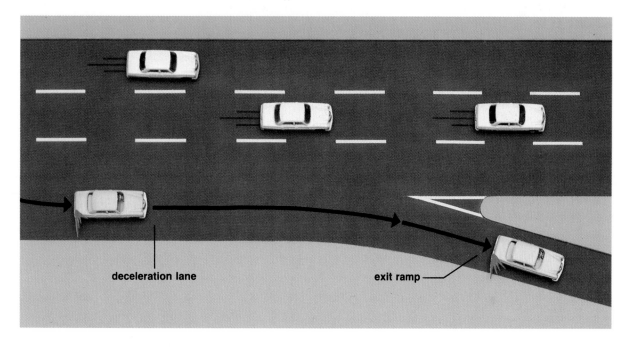

deceleration lane

exit ramp

Steps for Exiting

Follow these steps to exit an expressway:

1. About one-half mile before the exit, signal and move into the lane that leads into the deceleration lane, as shown in the top picture. Avoid last-second decisions and sudden moves.
2. Move into the deceleration lane, as shown in the middle picture. Do not slow down until your car is out of the expressway traffic flow.
3. Cancel your signal. Flash your brake lights to warn drivers behind that you are slowing down.
4. Check rearview mirrors so that you know the speed of following traffic. Slow down gradually to keep a space cushion ahead and behind you.
5. Identify the exit-ramp speed sign, as shown in the bottom picture. Check your own speed, and adjust to the exit-ramp speed limit.

Be alert when entering traffic on a local highway or street after leaving the expressway. Anticipate lower speed limits, two-way traffic, intersections, and pedestrians.

Possible Exiting Problems

Leaving an expressway should be a smooth operation. However, problems such as those discussed below can occur.

Crossing Paths The picture above shows that the same lane is used as both an entrance and an exit on some expressways. In this situation, one driver might accelerate to enter the expressway while another might decelerate to exit at the same time. Both drivers must watch out for the other to avoid conflicts. In this case, it usually is safer to let the entering driver go first.

Ramp Overflow Traffic can back up from an exit ramp into the expressway, as the picture to the right shows. Rather than joining the overflow and risking a rear-end collision, go past the exit and use the next exit. Start slowing early if you must use a backed-up exit. When you see vehicles backed up near the exit ramp, flash your brake lights to warn traffic behind you. Check traffic to the rear to see if it is slowing. If it is not slowing, try to pass the exit area smoothly, and drive to the next exit.

Short Deceleration Lane Slow more quickly if a deceleration lane is short. Being aware of traffic behind you is extremely critical in such situations. As you enter a deceleration lane:
▶ judge the lane's length.
▶ identify the exit ramp speed.
▶ check speed while braking.
▶ watch traffic to the rear.

Review It

1. What steps should you follow when exiting an expressway?
2. What are three possible exiting problems?

11-5 Special Situations on Expressways

Expressways can provide the safest type of driving. However, certain conditions can create hazards.

Expressways Through Cities

Although expressways move traffic efficiently through cities, such expressways have many more entrance and exit ramps than rural expressways. More ramps increase merging traffic conflicts and, also, give late decision-makers opportunities to make sudden moves.

Remember these points when driving through a city, especially during rush hours:

▶ In most cases, drive in the center or left lane to avoid merging vehicles.

▶ Know well in advance where you want to exit. Get in the correct lane early. A high volume of fast-moving traffic can make lane changing difficult and dangerous.

▶ Look constantly for signs, signals, and roadway markings.

▶ Predict that other drivers might be less aware and less alert than you are. Try to predict other drivers' sudden actions and driving errors. Be prepared to react correctly to avoid conflicts.

Disabled Vehicle

Take these steps at the first sign of trouble with your car:

1. Signal and pull as far as possible onto a safe place on the shoulder or median.

2. Turn on your emergency flasher lights. Get everyone out of the car and away from traffic.

3. When safe to do so, raise the hood and tie a white cloth to the antenna or door handle, as shown in the left picture.

4. Set out *emergency flares* or reflectors if you have them. Place them at least 500 feet behind your disabled car. Both devices warn approaching drivers of your disabled car.

Roadway Repair

Be alert for roadway repair zones, as seen in the right picture. Watch for orange construction signs as you begin to slow early. Slow to the posted speed limit in the repair zone.

Rural Interstate Highways

Driving long distances on interstate highways can become monotonous. Check your speed frequently, and look as far ahead as possible. Use hillcrests and curves to scan far ahead to determine your safe path of travel.

Some drivers tend to drive faster on rural interstates. Do not increase your speed even though you are passed. Larger vehicles and tractor-trailer trucks on rural interstates might pass you. Wind gusts from these vehicles can make car control more difficult. As such a vehicle starts to pass you, reduce your speed a little. Grip your steering wheel firmly.

Remember that larger vehicles cannot stop as quickly as you can. Try not to let these vehicles tailgate you. Pass a larger, slower-moving vehicle only when it is safe to do so.

Tollbooths Tollbooth areas are located along some expressways. You stop at a tollbooth and pay a fee, or toll, for driving on the expressway.

Tollbooth areas can create special problems. Some drivers make last-second lane changes and quick stops as they approach a tollbooth. Rough sections of roadway, called *rumble strips,* are built into the approach lanes of many tollbooth areas. Rumble strips warn

drivers of the tollbooth area ahead.

When approaching a tollbooth area, look for a green light above a tollbooth, as shown here. A green light indicates that the tollbooth is open for traffic. Do not enter a booth with a red light overhead; that booth is closed.

Most toll areas have two types of tollbooths. One type is machine-operated or automatic. A second type is operated by an attendant. Traffic usually moves more quickly through automatic tollbooths. If you select an automatic tollbooth, make sure you have the exact change ready before you enter the tollbooth. In most cases, attendant-operated tollbooths collect tolls from drivers without exact change, drivers of large vehicles, and drivers of vehicles towing trailers.

As you leave a tollbooth, watch the vehicles leaving the booths on both sides of you. Other drivers might want to enter the same lane as you. If you are in doubt as to who goes first, yield to the other drivers.

Highway Hypnosis   Staying alert can be a problem when driving long distances on expressways or interstates. You drive mile after mile at steady speeds with few hills, curves, or interchanges. You can be lulled into an inattentive, drowsy state called *highway hypnosis*. Some drivers have actually fallen asleep while driving because of highway hypnosis. Other drivers might sit back in a less-than-alert state, becoming spectators rather than attentive drivers.

Take these actions when you notice you are becoming drowsy or inattentive:
► Sit up straighter, open a window, or change a radio station.

► Stop at the next rest area, and stretch or take a walk as these people are doing. Get a drink of water.
► If you need more rest, stop at a safe place and get some sleep.

These steps can help you avoid highway hypnosis:
► Avoid eating heavy meals.
► Wear comfortable clothes.
► Sing or talk with passengers.
► Avoid driving for very long periods of time.
► If you are using cruise control, turn it off for a time so you must pay more attention to your speed.
► Keep your eyes moving, scanning the roadway ahead.
► Check your mirrors regularly.

► Note all traffic signs, signals, roadway markings, and changing traffic conditions.
► Let someone else drive.

Velocitation   Hours of driving can fool you into thinking your car is traveling slower than it really is. You might then unconsciously drive too fast. This condition, called *velocitation,* can be especially hazardous when you exit an expressway.

The roadways you drive on after exiting usually have a lower speed limit. If you are "velocitized," you might continue to drive at expressway speeds after making your exit. To correct this condition, check your speed often when exiting and after joining other traffic off the expressway. Take time to adjust to lower speeds.

Keep alert during all expressway driving. Use the IPDE process continually, and cooperate with other drivers. The expressway environment can afford you many years of safe and enjoyable driving.

Review It
1. What are the special problems of driving on an expressway through a city?
2. What should you do if your car becomes disabled?
3. How can you prevent highway hypnosis or velocitation?

Be a Fuel Saver

► Accelerate moderately and steadily to the speed of expressway traffic as soon as possible.
► Try to maintain a steady speed in expressway traffic. Frequent accelerating and braking wastes fuel.
► Try to pass slower vehicles as soon as you encounter them. Do not slow to their pace, and then speed up.

► Anticipate changing traffic conditions well ahead of time. Adjust your speed gradually as you approach traffic congestion.
► Listen to the radio for traffic reports during rush hours.

Chapter Summary

1. Expressways have a lower collision rate due to their design. Cross traffic is eliminated, opposing traffic lanes are divided, and slower-moving vehicles and pedestrians are not permitted. (11–1)
2. Become a safe expressway driver by building experience gradually. Concentrate on your driving task, and cooperate with other drivers. (11–1)
3. To enter an expressway, use the correct entrance, check traffic, look for a gap, signal, adjust your speed to expressway traffic, and merge smoothly. (11–2)
4. Possible entrance problems are short entrance ramps, no acceleration lane, no gap in traffic, a vehicle ahead stopping, and a wall dividing the ramp and the traffic. (11–2)
5. When driving on an expressway, use the IPDE process to identify signs, signals, and the volume of traffic, predict sudden actions of others, avoid last-second decisions, and execute all actions smoothly. (11–3)
6. Read signs ahead of time to note exits, lane closures, route numbers and names, and to avoid last-second decisions. (11–3)
7. A safe following distance helps prevent rear-end collisions. (11–3)
8. Always use lane-change signals when changing lanes to pass another vehicle. Use rearview mirrors and blind-spot checks to check traffic behind and to the sides. (11–3)
9. To exit an expressway, move into the lane that leads to the deceleration lane, signal, and warn drivers behind you in the deceleration lane. Check rear traffic, and continue to slow down. Adjust to exit ramp speed. (11–4)
10. Possible exiting problems are vehicles crossing paths to exit and enter, ramp overflow, and short deceleration lanes. (11–4)
11. Expressways through cities have many entrance and exit ramps that cause merging conflicts and sudden moves. Fast-moving traffic can make lane-changing difficult. (11–5)
12. If your car is disabled, pull as far as possible off the roadway, and turn on your emergency flasher lights. Get passengers away from your car. Tie a white cloth to the antenna or door handle. Set out flares or reflectors. (11–5)
13. Prevent highway hypnosis by keeping yourself comfortable and alert. Check your speed often to prevent velocitation. (11–5)

Think About It
Under what conditions might you legally drive slower than a posted minimum speed limit?

Decision Making

1. The yellow car is about to enter the merge area. What should Car 1 do? How can Car 2 help? What should Car 3 predict?

2. What problems does a lane straddler cause on an expressway? What can you do to reduce the hazard of this situation?

3. What should the approaching driver already have identified in this situation? What should the driver predict and decide? What actions should the driver take?

4. The driver of the yellow car plans to exit the expressway. The same lane is used for exiting and entering. What should the driver of the yellow car do? Why is this decision wise?

Chapter 11 Test

Multiple Choice Copy the number of each sentence below on a sheet of paper. Choose the letter that best completes each statement or answers each question.

1. The major cause of expressway collisions is
   (a) construction. (b) following too closely.
   (c) passing. (d) exiting. (208)
2. If you are being passed continually on the right, you should
   (a) stop. (b) speed up. (c) move to the lane to your right. (d) move to the left lane. (210)
3. Where should you begin to slow down when exiting an expressway?
   (a) in the merge area (b) in the deceleration lane (c) on the ramp (d) in the acceleration lane (211)
4. At the first sign of car trouble, you should
   (a) signal and get off the roadway. (b) flash the brake lights. (c) blow the horn. (d) signal and stop in the right lane. (214)
5. When can velocitation be especially hazardous?
   (a) when driving on an expressway (b) when passing (c) when changing lanes (d) when exiting an expressway (216)

Completion Copy the number of each sentence below. After each number, write the letter of the word or words that complete the sentence correctly.

6. A ramp leading into an expressway is an
   ____ . (201)
7. The left edge of an expressway's traffic lanes should be marked with a ____ . (206)
8. A group of vehicles traveling in a bunch is called a ____ . (207)
9. To avoid a conflict, ____ to other drivers moving into the same lane as you after leaving a tollbooth. (215)
10. Rough areas built into a roadway are ____ . (215)

a. entrance ramp
b. rumble strips
c. white line
d. wolf pack
e. yellow line
f. yield

Vocabulary Copy the number of each phrase below. Match the definition in List A with the term it defines in List B.

List A
11. permits traffic to enter expressway only from interchanges (198)
12. area where you join expressway traffic (201)
13. where you try to accelerate to the speed of expressway traffic (201)
14. slowest legal speed allowed under ideal conditions (207)
15. speed used by most drivers (207)
16. lane used for slowing down after leaving expressway traffic (211)
17. ramp leading off the expressway (211)
18. used to warn others of a disabled vehicle (214)
19. condition of unconsciously driving too fast (216)
20. condition lulling a driver into drowsiness (216)

List B
a. acceleration lane
b. common speed
c. controlled-access highway
d. deceleration lane
e. emergency flares
f. exit ramp
g. highway hypnosis
h. merging area
i. minimum speed limit
j. rumble strips
k. velocitation

Chapter 12
Adverse Conditions

You're the Driver!

Snow, ice, heavy rain, and other adverse conditions can create visibility and traction problems for you. When you drive in adverse conditions, you will have to use special techniques to avoid conflicts.

Imagine that you are the driver in the situation pictured here. Should you use your low-beam or high-beam headlights?

Do you think the pedestrian is ready to move out of the way for traffic?

If the brown car ahead of you stops for the pedestrian, could you stop in time to avoid a collision?

How could you check traction?

If your car starts to skid, how could you correct that problem?

Using special techniques when driving in adverse conditions helps you prevent conflicts. These techniques are discussed in this chapter.

Objectives

12-1 Reduced Visibility

1. Explain how you can see ahead clearly when driving in adverse conditions. (222)
2. Summarize the techniques for safe night driving. (222)
3. List precautions to take to increase your visibility. (224)
4. Explain the importance of the IPDE process when visibility is reduced. (225)

12-2 Reduced Traction

5. Describe traction conditions during rain and snow. (226)
6. Explain how to check traction on icy roadways. (228)
7. Explain how to drive safely on other reduced traction roadway surfaces. (229)
8. Tell how to regain control of a car that is skidding. (230)
9. Tell how to use the controlled braking technique. (232)

12-3 Other Weather Conditions

10. Explain how to control a car in windy conditions. (234)
11. List precautions for driving during hot weather and cold weather. (235)
12. List suggestions for maintaining car control during winter driving. (236)

12–1 Reduced Visibility

To apply the IPDE process effectively, you must have a clear view ahead of and around your car. If darkness or poor weather restrict your view, your chances of having a collision increase.

Car Windows
Moisture can build up on the inside of your car's windows when it rains or when humidity levels are high. Windows start to steam up from the inside. Use your defroster or air conditioner or open the side windows to circulate fresh air.

Snow, ice, or frost can build up on your car windows. Clear your windows *before* driving. After your windows are clear, use your defroster to keep them clear.

Windows and headlights also get dirty more quickly in bad weather. Clean them often. Smoking and the vapors from plastic materials used in instrument panels, seat covers, and interior linings can cause a film to form on the inside of windows. Clean the inside of your windows regularly.

Sun Glare
Bright sunlight in the early morning or late afternoon can create glare problems as shown here. Wear sunglasses or use the sun visor to cut glare and eyestrain.

If the sun is behind you, be alert to the possibility that other drivers might not see you. Predict the problems sun glare can cause drivers approaching or following you. They could miss your turn signal or might not even notice you are there.

Dawn and Dusk
Sunlight levels are reduced just before the sun rises or after it sets. At these times, cars, motorcycles, and even trucks without headlights can be very hard to see. Protect yourself

by using your low-beam headlights, even though it might not seem dark enough to use lights. Do not drive using only parking lights. Other drivers could be confused as to whether or not you are moving. In some states, it is illegal to drive with only parking lights on.

Night
Night driving severely limits your ability to see. At night, you must work harder to use the IPDE process. Compare the two pictures on page 223 to see how much more is visible during daylight hours.

Headlights When driving at night with no other vehicles ahead of you, use high-beam headlights to see farther. Switch to low-beam headlights as soon as you see an oncoming vehicle's headlights or the taillights of a vehicle you are following. This precaution prevents temporarily blinding the other driver.

Use low-beam headlights at night during adverse weather. Using high-beam headlights in heavy rain, snow, or fog, causes more light to reflect back into your eyes, makes seeing more difficult, and limits your sight distance.

Meeting Cars Take these actions if an oncoming driver fails to use low-beam headlights after you switch to your low-beam headlights:

1. Make sure the car is far enough away so that the driver can react. Briefly flick on your high-beam headlights to remind the oncoming driver to use low-beam headlights.
2. If the oncoming driver still is using high-beam headlights, slow down and glance at the right edge of the roadway as a guide for your lane position.

3. Glance ahead frequently to check oncoming traffic. Do not look directly at the high-beam headlights.

Overdriving Headlights The term *overdriving headlights* means driving at a speed that makes your stopping distance longer than the distance lighted by your headlights. Avoid overdriving your headlights, especially when driving in fog, heavy rain, snow, or on a slick roadway.

Use the 4-second rule to see if you are driving within the range of your headlights. Follow these steps to make your check:

1. Choose a fixed point ahead of your car at the time the point appears within your lighted area.
2. Count off four seconds.
3. If you just reach the fixed checkpoint after four seconds, your speed is correct. Your stopping distance is within the range of your headlights.

Fog

The small particles of water in fog reflect light, causing visibility problems. Your ability to see is reduced. Always use low-beam headlights in fog, as this truck driver is doing. You will be better able to see ahead and to help others see you.

Fog can cut down on your ability to judge distance. Vehicles and other hazards might be closer than you think.

Maintain an added space cushion between yourself and possible hazards.

Slow down before you enter a patch of fog. Stay alert and be prepared to slow or pull off the roadway completely and stop, if necessary. If you pull off the roadway and park, use your emergency flashers to warn other drivers that you are not moving.

Rain

Heavy rain reduces your ability to see and be seen. Heavy rains blown by high winds can reduce visibility still more. Turn on your windshield wipers to clear windows, and defrosters to keep your windows from steaming up.

Turn on your low-beam headlights and reduce your speed in heavy rain to help others see you. Be alert for others who might not have turned on their headlights. Rain combined with darkness can make it very hard to see. Pull off the roadway completely if rain becomes so heavy that it is extremely difficult to see. Wait for the rain to stop. Remember to use your emergency flashers.

Rain also can create problems for cyclists and pedestrians. These roadway users might be anxious to reach their destinations. They might take chances they would not take normally. Stay alert, and be ready to avoid them.

Snow

The top picture on page 225 shows how wind-driven snow blocks vision and covers roadway markings. Heavy snow can pile up and block your rear window, reducing visibility. Slush or ice also can build up on your windshield wipers. If so, pull off the roadway and clean the wiper blades.

Use low-beam headlights when it snows, even in daytime. Reduce speed to maintain control and to give others time to respond. If snow covers the roadway, do not crowd the center. This action has the effect of narrowing the roadway and could lead to a head-on collision.

Applying the IPDE Process

When visibility is reduced, you need more time to respond to hazards and complete the IPDE process. Take these actions during adverse conditions, such as those shown in the bottom picture:

► Slow down.
► Scan and search the traffic scene carefully.
► Be ready to take actions to avoid a conflict.

Review It

1. How can you improve visibility during dawn and dusk?
2. During night driving, when should you switch from high-beam to low-beam headlights?
3. Which headlights should you use during poor weather?
4. What should you do when applying the IPDE process in bad weather?

Rain, snow, ice, or loose sand and gravel on a dry roadway can reduce traction. Poor visibility combined with poor traction can make driving conditions very dangerous.

Wet Roadways

Rain-slick roadways affect more drivers than any other reduced traction condition. The combination of low visibility and standing water can create a high-risk situation.

When Rain Starts As raindrops start to fall, they mix with dust and oil on the roadway to make a slippery surface. Traction is reduced greatly until this mixture is washed away. Even then, tires do not grip wet pavement as

well as they grip dry pavement. Reduce speed to maintain control.

When it rains, the roadway is drier where the car ahead of you has left tracks. Drive in those tracks for better traction and control.

Hydroplaning This driver runs the risk of losing car control. The tires are riding on the surface of the water, not the roadway. Steering and braking control could be lost. The car tends to travel in a straight line when the driver tries to turn.

This condition, *hydroplaning,* is caused by a combination of standing water, speed, and tire condition. If the tires are new and inflated properly, their deep treads will cut through water and grip the roadway. However, even with good tires, hydroplaning can start at about 50 mph. Worn, bald, underinflated tires can start to lose their grip on the roadway at 30 mph or less. Snow or slush in combination with standing water can increase your risk of hydroplaning.

Take these actions to avoid hydroplaning when you must drive through water:
► Reduce speed.
► Use properly inflated tires with good tread.

Deep Water Avoid driving through deep water whenever possible. If you cannot avoid deep water, take these steps to prevent stalling:

1. Check the water depth by watching other cars and looking at objects such as fire hydrants, fence posts, and parked cars. If the water is up to your bumper, *do not enter the water.* Turn around, and use another route even if you must drive several miles out of your way.

2. If the water is lower than your car's bumper, drive slowly so that the water building up in front of your car has time to part. (Downshift to a lower gear in a stickshift car.) Cars should proceed one at a time so that the higher center of the roadway can be used. Avoid low, soft roadway shoulders.

3. When driving through the water, use light pressure on your accelerator. At the same time, brake gently with your left foot to build friction on the brake pads to help dry them.

4. After leaving the water, tap your brake pedal lightly to check for wet brakes. If your car pulls to the side or does not slow, drive for a short distance, applying light pressure on your brake pedal. The friction from the brake pressure will generate heat to dry your brakes.

Snow

Changing temperatures and different snow textures can produce different levels of traction. When fresh snow falls at low temperatures, traction can be fairly good. When traffic packs the snow down in places such as intersections, traction is reduced. Packed snow is much like ice. Skids can occur easily.

Some of the worst traction conditions occur near freezing temperatures (32°F) when snow starts to turn to watery slush. The combination of snow and water can create very slippery surfaces.

Driving Techniques on Snow

Gentle actions are the key to maintaining car control when driving on snow. Gentle steering and light braking produce the best results. Put your car in motion gently to best use the limited amount of traction between your tires and the roadway. If your drive wheels start to slip, release your accelerator. Start again gently.

To improve traction on snow, use snow tires on the wheels that power your car. Many states also allow *tire chains*, as shown in the first picture. They are placed over the tire tread to increase traction on snow- or ice-covered roadways.

Rocking a Car You can loosen your car's wheels from snow by *rocking the car*. If your car is stuck in deep snow, you can usually rock it free.

Follow the steps below to rock a car. This technique also can be used in sand and mud.

1. Turn your front wheels straight ahead to reduce the resistance of the snow against your tires.
2. Apply gentle acceleration to move your car forward. *Do not spin your wheels*.
3. Let up on your accelerator the instant your car stops moving forward. Pause only long enough to let the engine slow. Shift to REVERSE, and move backward.
4. Continue this back-and-forth movement until your car has cleared tracks that are long enough to drive out of the deep snow. The driver in the second picture is about to move forward in tracks cleared by rocking.

Ice

If it is raining while temperatures are falling, ice can form on the roadway. Freezing can begin without any visible change on the roadway surface. When ice begins to form, expect roads to get icy quickly. Ice and sleet make driving extremely dangerous.

Temperature can change the amount of traction on ice. At very cold temperatures (near 0°F), traction is somewhat better than at warmer temperatures. When ice is at or near the freezing point (32°F), traction can be poor. If water forms on the ice, car control can be reduced greatly.

Pump your brakes lightly to check traction in icy areas. Perform this check only at low speeds, away from traffic. If you car starts to slide, slow down gradually.

Windows and wipers also can ice up. If you cannot keep your windows ice-free with wipers and defrosters, pull off the roadway and clear them manually. In such severe conditions, it might be best not to drive at all.

If you must drive, be alert for these three situations. Be prepared for:

► **Ice on Bridges** The roadway surface on this bridge has frozen first. Cold air circulates above and below the roadway on a bridge. Therefore, ice usually forms first on bridges and overpasses.

► **Ice in Shade** When driving on a sunlit roadway, be alert for ice on a shaded part of the roadway. Water from melting snow and ice can freeze in these shaded areas.

► **Ice in Tire Tracks** Snow can pack and then turn to ice in the normal tracks of travel within your lane. You might be able to avoid these slippery tracks by moving a little to the right in the unused portion of your lane. You might increase your traction by driving on loose snow, sand, or gravel on the edge of the roadway.

Gravel Roadways Loose gravel on some roadways, like the one in the top picture, can act like marbles under tires and cause skids. Well-packed wheel paths form on heavily traveled gravel roadways. Drive in these paths for better traction and control. When you must move out of the wheel paths to drive on loose gravel, slow and hold your steering wheel firmly.

Leaves During the fall, wet leaves on the roadway can reduce traction and affect stopping and steering control. When nearing wet leaves, as shown in the middle picture, slow down. Steer gently, and be prepared to brake.

Construction Areas In construction areas such as the one in the bottom picture, trucks and other equipment can leave mud, dirt, or sand on the roadway. Slow, steer gently, and obey workers' directions in these areas.

When following a truck that is carrying loose material, be alert for material falling from the truck onto the roadway. Prepare to slow, and steer around the material as needed.

Other Reduced Traction Surfaces

Any low-traction surface will increase your stopping distance. On a dry roadway, you can stop in a reasonable distance. However, when traction is reduced, your stopping distance increases.

229

Skidding

Your car can skid on snow, ice, or smooth, dry pavement. Differing levels of traction and speed can combine to produce a skid. Therefore, always be aware of available traction. Adjust speed *ahead* of time. Avoid hard and sudden steering, braking, and accelerating.

Skidding can be frightening. Many drivers who skid panic and freeze at the wheel. However, you can prevent worse trouble by quickly responding with the correct and precise actions the instant you sense a skid starting. In any skid, remember: *Do not give up.* Always try to drive out of a skid. Become familiar with the three types of skids discussed here.

Power Skid   If your tires start to spin when you accelerate, ease off your accelerator. Sometimes your tires can spin because of the fast-idle setting on the engine. If so, shift to NEUTRAL and tap the accelerator to reduce the engine's idle speed.

This is how a skid looks to a driver.

Braking Skid   Your car can skid if you lock your wheels by braking too hard. If so, release your brake a little to unlock your wheels and regain control. *Locked wheels provide no steering control.*

Sideways Skid   If the rear of your car skids to the right or left, take these actions quickly:

1. Ease off your accelerator or brake. You must keep your wheels rolling to maintain steering control.
2. Steer in the direction that the rear of your car is skidding. Steer just enough so that your car continues in a straight line. *Do not overcorrect for the skid by steering too much.*

3. Your car might continue to skid from side to side, or fishtail, after you have corrected for the first skid. If so, steer in the direction of the other skids as they occur until you have gained control. Execute steering actions in one smooth, continuous motion.

Imagine you are the driver in the situation shown here. In the left pictures on page 231, the rear of your car skids to the right; you steer right. In the center pictures you have a second skid to the left; you steer left. The right picture shows how you have corrected the skids.

This is how your car is skidding.

Corrected Sideways Skids

This is how you steer.

Skidding in a Curve

If you enter a curve too fast, your tires might not have enough traction to hold you in the curve. You might be able to drive through a curve at a modest speed on dry, smooth pavement. However, if the curve has ice and snow, as shown here, you might not be able to maintain control.

Take these steps if the rear of your car skids to the outside of the curve:

1. Ease off your accelerator or your brake. Keep your tires rolling to maintain steering control.
2. Steer in the direction the rear of your car is skidding.

3. Once you correct the skid, continue to reduce your speed. Center your car in your lane.

If you are correcting a skid in a curve and must leave your lane, keep on trying to regain control. You might have to slip off the edge of the roadway to bring your car under control. However, slipping off the roadway is better than losing control of your car.

To prevent skidding in a curve, you need only to reduce your speed *before* you enter a curve. Once in the curve, steer gently through it.

Controlled Braking

Even though you drive defensively, sometimes you might have to make a quick stop to avoid a conflict. A quick stop can lock your wheels, causing a skid and a loss of steering control.

Use *controlled braking* to make a quick, yet controlled, stop. Controlled braking is a technique of applying your brakes to slow or stop quickly without locking your wheels. Follow these steps to use controlled braking:

1. Step on your brakes hard enough to slow your car rapidly, but not hard enough to

lock your wheels. You must keep your wheels rolling to maintain steering control while slowing.

2. If your car starts to skid, ease up on your brakes until your wheels start rolling. Then step on your brakes again.

3. Repeat this "on-off-on" brake-pumping action until your car is stopped.

Applying the right amount of brake pressure is the difficult part of controlled braking. Braking too hard will cause you to skid. Braking too lightly will not stop you fast enough.

This chart shows braking distances at 20 mph. Notice how various surfaces and tires can make a difference in stopping distances.

Review It
1. What occurs when your car hydroplanes?
2. Where can you expect ice to form first on a roadway?
3. What should you do when driving on gravel roadways?
4. How can you prevent skidding in a curve?
5. Why must you keep your wheels rolling when braking to a stop?

Braking Distances at 20 mph

Surface	Tire/Condition	Distance
concrete	dry	20 feet
concrete	wet	26 feet
packed snow	reinforced chains	38 feet
packed snow	snow tires	52 feet
packed snow	conventional tires	60 feet
glare ice	reinforced chains	75 feet
glare ice	conventional tires	149 feet
glare ice	snow tires	151 feet

233

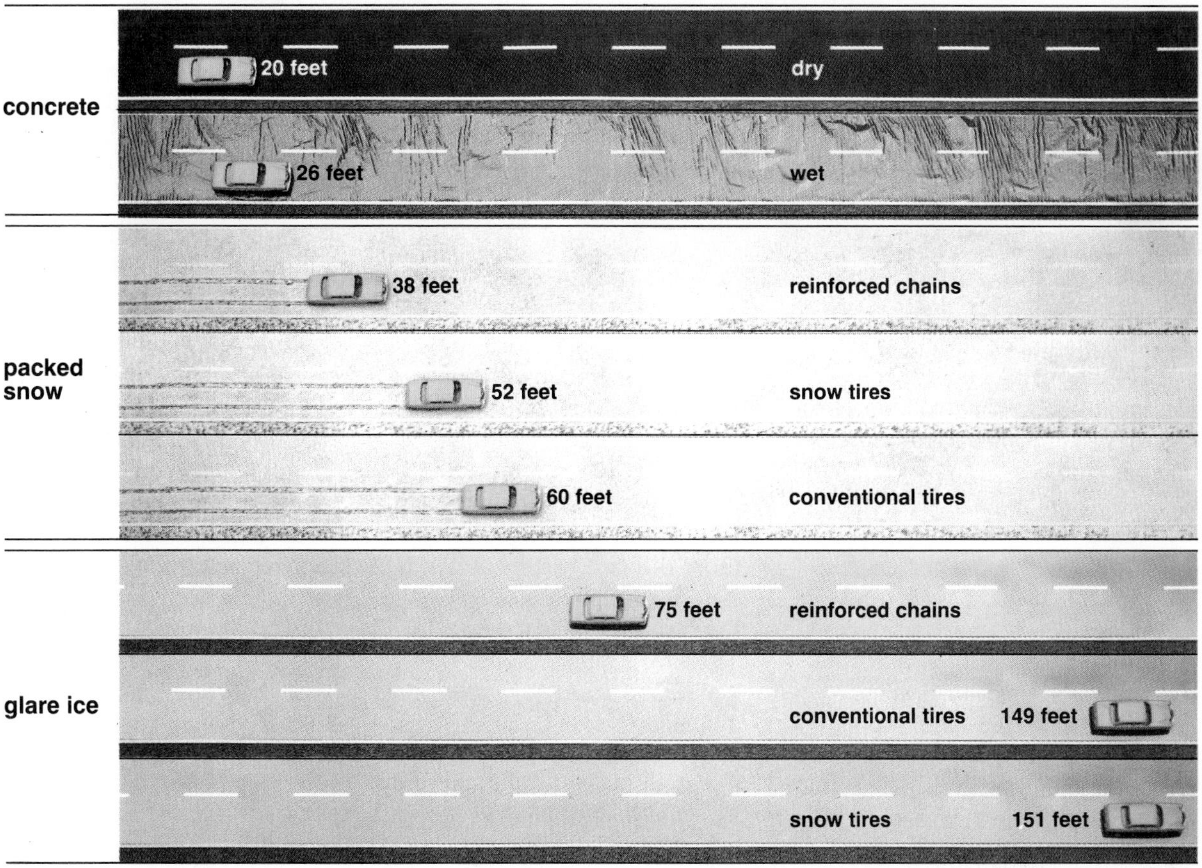

12-3 Other Weather Conditions

Driving under normal weather conditions can be difficult. You must use special techniques for driving during extreme weather conditions.

Wind

Strong winds can reduce car control. If you pass a truck, as the driver is doing in the first picture, a blast of wind could reduce your control. You could have the same problem when coming out from under a bridge, as shown in the second picture. Slow down, and keep a firm grip on your steering wheel to maintain control.

Head and tail winds can also cause problems. You might need to accelerate more than normal when driving into a head wind. Steering also is more difficult in a head wind. A tail wind pushes your car forward and builds speed. Therefore, brake earlier than usual, and allow yourself more distance to stop in a tail wind.

Different types of vehicles handle differently in high winds. Small, light cars and motorcycles might be difficult to steer and keep in the lane. Vans, campers, and cars pulling trailers also might have handling problems at highway speeds. Trailers can sway or weave in the wind. A car-top carrier makes any car harder to handle in high winds. In windy situations, give others room to maneuver safely. Predict that they might reduce speed to maintain control.

Hot Weather

Cars are designed to be driven in hot weather. Most cars' cooling systems use a radiator, water pump, and fan to cool the engine. However, in extreme conditions, your engine might develop problems.

Gasoline is a liquid when it is pumped into your engine. During very hot weather, the gasoline might boil and turn into vapor, causing a condition called vapor lock. Your engine cannot use vaporized gasoline. If your engine becomes vapor-locked, turn it off and let it cool. You should be able to restart it then.

Your temperature light warns that your engine is producing more heat than your cooling system can handle. Your temperature light might go on when you are:

► pulling a heavy load uphill.
► in stop-and-go traffic.
► using the air conditioner.

If your temperature light goes on, turn off your air conditioner if it is on and turn on your heater. The added heat will be uncomfortable, but this action helps cool your engine.

If your temperature light stays on, park your car and turn your engine off. Let your engine cool first, and then check for leaks in the cooling system. Do *not* open the radiator on a hot engine.

Cold Weather

Very cold weather also can create problems. During cold weather, be ready to take these precautions.

► **Keep Moving on Snow and Ice** In winter, you will meet other drivers whose vehicles have stalled or are otherwise disabled, as shown here. Try to avoid getting stuck behind them. Slow ahead of time to steer around a disabled vehicle, but keep moving.
► **Be Alert for Exhaust Leaks** During cold weather, you probably tend to keep your windows shut tightly. If there is a slight exhaust leak, carbon monoxide can build up inside your car. Open a window slightly to let in some fresh air and prevent carbon monoxide build-up. If you get stuck in snow, make sure the exhaust pipe is not blocked.
► **Do Not Race a Cold Engine** Racing a cold engine can increase engine wear. Do not run a cold engine at high speeds.
► **Do Not Set the Parking Brake** After driving through icy or slushy conditions, do not set the parking brake when you park your car. The parking brake could freeze. Use the PARK gear position with automatic transmission or REVERSE with manual transmission.

Suggestions for Winter Driving

Control of your car depends on the traction between your tires and the roadway. You need a larger space cushion on roadways covered by ice and snow. Follow these guidelines to keep your car under control during winter driving:

► **Keep Windows Clear** Remove snow or ice before driving. Be sure the windshield wipers and the defrosters work properly.

Be sure to clear snow off the roof, hood, and trunk, as this driver is doing, so it does not blow off and block your own or others' vision. Clear snow off of headlights and taillights so others can see these lights as clearly as possible.

► **Reduce Speed According to Conditions** Go as slow as necessary until you are sure you have control of your car and can stop when necessary.

► **Get the Feel of the Roadway** Test your brakes gently at low speeds to determine how much traction you have.

► **Keep a Safe Following Distance** Allow more room between yourself and the vehicle ahead.

► **Leave a Window Partly Open** This action helps keep your windows from fogging up. You also have a continuous supply of fresh air.

► **Watch for Danger Spots Ahead** Bridges and shaded areas might freeze first.

► **Use a Lower Gear Under Very Slippery Conditions** To maintain control, use a lower gear when slowing on an icy or a slippery roadway. Keep your tires rolling.

► **Avoid the Use of Cruise Control** Do not use cruise control on icy or slippery roadways. You could skid if you had to press your brake pedal to release cruise control.

Review It

1. Which actions should you take to maintain control in a strong cross wind?
2. What should you do to try to cool an overheated engine?
3. What should you do if you are unsure of how much traction there is on a slippery roadway?

Safe Driving Tips

► Clean windows for better vision in bad weather. Replace your windshield wiper blades when you notice they leave streaks on the windshield.

► Check the level of windshield washer fluid frequently in poor weather. Keep a spare container of windshield washer fluid in your trunk.

► Clean headlights, taillights, and front turn-signal lights often in bad weather. This action helps other drivers see you better.

► Take the tip when drivers approaching you in daylight have windshield wipers and headlights on. You probably will encounter rain in the next few miles.

► Slow down in a head wind to maintain control and save fuel.

Chapter Summary

1. Use the defroster or air conditioner, and open a side window to circulate air and clear steamed-up windows. Clear frost, sleet, and snow from all windows before driving. (12–1)

2. Use high-beam headlights at night when no other vehicles are ahead of you. Switch to low-beam headlights when meeting or following another vehicle. (12–1)

3. Use low-beam headlights when driving in fog, rain, or snow. (12–1)

4. Allow more time to apply the IPDE process when visibility is reduced. (12–1)

5. Rain and snow greatly reduce the amount of traction your car has on a roadway. (12–2)

6. Tap your brakes lightly to check traction on an icy roadway. If your car starts to skid, slow down. (12–2)

7. When driving on a gravel roadway, slow and hold your steering wheel firmly. When wet leaves, mud, or dirt cover the roadway, slow and prepare to brake and steer gently. (12–2)

8. Ease off your brake or accelerator, and steer in the direction the rear of your car is skidding to regain control in a skid. (12–2)

9. For controlled braking, brake hard enough to slow your car, but not so hard as to lock your wheels. If you skid, ease up on your brakes until your wheels start turning, and then brake again. (12–2)

10. Slow and grip your steering wheel firmly when driving in strong winds. (12–3)

11. Avoid overheating your engine during hot weather. During cold weather, be alert for exhaust leaks. Do not race a cold engine. (12–3)

12. Take these precautions during winter driving: keep windows clear; adjust speed to roadway conditions; keep a safe following distance; keep air moving inside your car; avoid using cruise control. (12–3)

Think About It

It is not uncommon to hear of a collision involving ten or more cars in foggy conditions. What can cause this type of collision?

Decision Making

1. What actions should the driver take in this skidding situation?

2. In this winter situation, what problem could the roadway on the bridge present? What precaution should the driver take when approaching this bridge?

3. What visibility and traction problems could the driver have in this situation?

4. What actions should you take to avoid being blinded by the headlights from the oncoming car?

Chapter 12 Test

Multiple Choice Copy the number of each sentence below on a sheet of paper. Choose the letter that best completes the statement.

1. To help others see you better during dawn and dusk, use your
   (a) high-beam headlights.   (b) brake lights.
   (c) low-beam headlights.   (d) emergency flashers.   (222)
2. You are overdriving your headlights when you
   (a) are using your high-beam headlights.
   (b) cannot see roadway signs.   (c) are driving at the speed limit.   (d) cannot stop within the distance lighted by your headlights.   (223)
3. When driving in fog, use your
   (a) high-beam headlights.   (b) low-beam headlights.   (c) emergency flashers.   (d) parking lights.   (224)
4. After driving through deep water, check your car's
   (a) acceleration.   (b) brakes.   (c) oil level.
   (d) lights.   (226)
5. Dry out wet brakes by
   (a) speeding up and letting them air dry.
   (b) parking and letting them dry.   (c) braking repeatedly, but gently, at low speeds.   (d) having a mechanic service them.   (226)
6. In cold weather, ice forms first on
   (a) hilltops.   (b) gravel roadways.   (c) bridges and overpasses.   (d) driveways.   (228)
7. Locked wheels cause a loss of
   (a) space cushion.   (b) gear-shift ability.
   (c) lights.   (d) steering control.   (230)
8. The best corrective action when skidding is to
   (a) steer in the direction the rear of your car is skidding.   (b) steer straight.   (c) steer in either direction.   (d) do not steer; let your car come out of the skid by itself.   (230)
9. A strong tail wind
   (a) requires more acceleration than normal.
   (b) makes stopping more difficult.   (c) decreases speed.   (d) increases fuel consumption.   (234)
10. Try to cool an overheated engine by
    (a) turning on your air conditioner.   (b) turning on your heater.   (c) opening your windows.
    (d) turning on your defroster.   (235)

Completion Copy the number of each sentence below. After each number, write the letter of the word or words that complete the sentence correctly.

11. When driving into the sun, ____ can be a problem.   (222)
12. Switch to ____ when meeting an oncoming vehicle at night.   (222)
13. Use the ____ to see if you are driving within the range of your headlights.   (223)
14. Drive in the tracks left by the vehicle ahead to get better ____ in rain.   (226)
15. Snow tires provide ____ traction for driving on snow or ice than regular tires.   (227)

   a. four-second rule
   b. glare
   c. less
   d. low-beam headlights
   e. more
   f. traction

Vocabulary Copy the number of each phrase below. Match the definition in List A with the term it defines in List B.

List A
16. stopping distance exceeds the area lit by headlights   (223)
17. tires riding up on the surface of standing water   (226)
18. devices to increase traction   (227)
19. maneuver to free your car from snow, mud, or sand   (227)
20. slowing or stopping quickly without locking your wheels   (232)

List B
a. controlled braking
b. hydroplaning
c. overdriving headlights
d. rocking the car
e. stopping time
f. tire chains

Chapter 13
Emergencies

You're the Driver!

Emergency situations develop suddenly. You might have only a fraction of a second to make the correct move. In these critical situations, you need special driving skills. Even under the best conditions, you must be alert to avoid being involved in a collision.

Imagine that you are driving the red car on the right. The white car pulls out in front of you.

What should you do?

Why should you not swerve to the left?

If you were driving the white car, what action would you take to help reduce the force of impact?

Vehicle malfunctions or driver errors can cause emergencies. In either case, you must be prepared to act quickly to avoid or minimize a collision.

This chapter discusses emergencies that are the result of vehicle malfunctions and driver errors. You can learn how to handle different kinds of emergency situations.

Objectives

13–1 Vehicle Malfunctions

1. List actions to take if a tire blows out. (242)
2. List the steps to follow if the brakes fail. (244)
3. Describe what to do if the accelerator sticks. (245)
4. Tell what to do if the engine fails or overheats. (246)
5. Describe what to do in case of steering failure. (247)
6. List actions to take if a raised hood blocks your forward vision. (247)
7. List the steps to take if the car catches fire. (248)
8. Describe what to do if your car stalls on railroad tracks. (249)

13–2 Driver Errors

9. Describe how to return to the roadway if your car runs off the roadway. (250)
10. Explain when to use an emergency swerve. (251)
11. Explain how to avoid or minimize head-on, side, and rear-end collisions. (252)
12. Tell how to escape a car that is sinking in water. (255)
13. Tell what to do if you enter a curve too fast. (255)

Good maintenance can prevent most vehicle malfunctions. A vehicle often gives warning signs before real trouble occurs. When you notice any warning signs, make the necessary repairs promptly. Refer to Chapter 17 to learn about car maintenance.

Vehicle equipment sometimes will malfunction with no warning. A sudden malfunction in a moving vehicle can create an emergency. You can handle an emergency more successfully if you know what to do. You also will reduce your risk of serious trouble in traffic.

Tire Failure

Tires wear, even under ideal driving conditions. All tires need to be replaced eventually. Many tire failures occur when the tires are well worn.

Tires wear more quickly under unfavorable driving and poor maintenance conditions. Long trips, high speeds, and hot roadway surfaces increase wear. Hard, abrupt braking and fast, sharp steering shorten tire life. Bumps, potholes, and poor roadway surfaces add to tire stress and can cause sudden damage to the tires. Unbalanced wheels and poor front-end alignment can cause tires to wear unevenly. Underinflation is also a major cause of tire wear.

Blowout A *blowout* occurs when a tire loses air pressure suddenly as you are driving. With tubeless tires, the sudden air loss often occurs around the rim of the tire. A blowout might occur if the tire hits a pothole or an object on the roadway. Older tires or badly worn tires also can blow out.

When a front tire blows out, the car pulls strongly in the direction of the deflated tire. Therefore, you must steer firmly against the pull of the car to keep the car on its intended path. A left-front blowout is especially dangerous. Note in the left-front blowout pictured here that the car pulls left toward the lane of oncoming traffic.

When a rear tire blows out, the back of the car can fishtail. When fishtailing occurs, the rear of the car swerves first in one direction, and then in the other, until steering is controlled. The fishtail movements are often irregular and abrupt. Handle a rear blowout like a skid. Steer in the direction that the rear of the car is skidding.

Take these actions when a tire blows out:
1. Grip the steering wheel firmly.
2. Ease up on the accelerator to slow the car. *Do not brake.* Braking can cause the car to swerve. Let the car slow gradually.
3. Check the traffic situation as you gain control of the car.
4. Drive off the roadway slowly, braking gently.
5. Turn on emergency flashers. Drive on the flat tire until you find a safe and suitable place to stop. You might ruin the tire, but stopping suddenly in traffic could cause a collision.

Changing a Tire Even though you might be an auto club member, you should know how to change a tire. Tire-changing instructions often are included in the owner's manual. These instructions also might be found in the spare-tire compartment or inside the trunk lid.

You need a jack in order to change a tire. A *jack* is a hand-operated device to lift and hold one corner or side of the car. Never put yourself in a position where the car could fall on you when it is elevated on the jack. A car is heavy and could slip off the jack.

Follow these steps to change a tire:

1. Park on a level spot away from traffic. Turn on the emergency flashers. Set the selector lever in PARK; use REVERSE in a stickshift car.

2. Set the parking brake.
3. Block the wheel that is diagonally opposite the flat tire. Carry two blocks of wood or two bricks in your car for this purpose. Otherwise use rocks or whatever else is available. Place one block firmly in front of the wheel and another block firmly behind the wheel. This precaution keeps the car from rolling when it is raised on the jack.
4. Ask your passengers to get out of the car and move to a safe place away from the roadway. They should not block other drivers' views of the emergency flashers.
5. Take out the spare tire and jack.
6. Assemble the jack. Position it according to the instructions.

7. Jack up the car partway. The flat tire should still touch the ground firmly enough so that the wheel cannot turn.
8. Remove the wheel cover. Loosen the *lug nuts,* the devices that hold the wheel to the car.
9. Jack up the car until the tire completely clears the ground.
10. Remove the lug nuts. Place them in the wheel cover or other safe place.
11. Remove the wheel with the flat tire. Place the wheel to the side.
12. Mount the wheel with the spare tire, as this person is doing. Rock the wheel gently into position.
13. Replace and tighten the lug nuts by hand.
14. Lower the car and remove the jack.
15. Use the lug wrench to tighten all the nuts again. Replace the wheel cover.
16. Put the flat tire and tire-changing equipment into the trunk. Remove the blocks.

Replace or repair the flat tire as soon as possible. If your spare tire is a lightweight or limited-mileage tire, drive on it only as necessary until you repair or replace the regular tire.

Brake Failure

Most cars have a two-part braking system. Each part controls two wheels. If one part fails, the other part still brakes two wheels. The brake warning light comes on to signal the partial failure. If both parts fail at the same time, your foot brake will have no braking power at all.

Total Brake Failure   Total brake failure rarely happens. When total brake failure does occur, the driver is usually braking hard for a stop. If brake failure occurs, follow these steps immediately:

1. Pump the brake pedal fast and hard. Pumping might temporarily restore enough brake-fluid pressure to slow or stop your car. You will know after three or four pumps if your brakes are going to hold.
2. At the same time, apply the parking brake hard. While applying the parking brake, pull and hold the parking-brake release lever out or hold the button at "off," as in the picture. By doing this, you can quickly release the parking brake for a moment if the car begins to skid. The parking brake, a separate braking system, brakes only two wheels. Generally, the parking brake controls the two rear wheels.

3. Downshift to the lowest gear. Downshifting uses the braking power of the engine to help slow your car.
4. Scan for a safe place to slow down. You can still steer and swerve the car. If necessary, rub the wheels against the nearest curb to reduce the speed of the car. You also might steer into something soft, such as bushes, to reduce speed. If a collision is unavoidable, steer for a sideswipe rather than colliding head-on into something solid.

Power Brake Failure   Brake "failure" with power brakes is usually the loss of the power that helps you brake. The power stops if the engine stops running. However, the brakes

have not failed. You simply must push the brake pedal harder than when the engine is running.

Other Brake Failures   When brakes overheat, they can lose some of their effectiveness. This condition, called *brake fade,* occurs after long, continuous, hard braking. To regain full braking ability, stop and let the brakes cool.

Driving through water also can cause temporary brake failure. See Chapter 12 for how to dry wet brakes.

Accelerator Stuck

The accelerator is stuck if the engine does not return to idling speed when you release the accelerator. A wadded floor mat pushed under the accelerator can cause the pedal to stick.

A more serious cause is a broken accelerator spring. If this spring breaks, the accelerator opens completely and stays open. The accelerator pedal might be flat on the floor.

A stuck accelerator is a critical emergency. While driving at a steady speed, you have no warning that the accelerator is stuck. You discover that there is a problem when you need to turn or stop. You must quickly bring your car under control.

Take these actions should the accelerator stick:

1. Apply the brakes, as shown here. This step is the normal action that you are already prepared to take for a stop or turn.
2. Choose an escape path that leads to a safe place off the roadway. Continue braking to control the car.
3. Shift to NEUTRAL. Depress the clutch with a manual transmission. The engine will race faster, but power is removed from the wheels. With an automatic transmission, the engine and transmission can be damaged, but a collision might be avoided.
4. Follow your escape path to your chosen place safely off the roadway.

5. Turn off the ignition when you are off the roadway and no longer need to change directions.
6. Stop the car and secure it.

Freeing the Accelerator   If you are in a low-traffic area, you might try to free the accelerator while driving. Put your toe under the accelerator pedal and lift. A passenger might also try to help you. Do not tap the accelerator while driving. It might stick farther down and cause the car to go even faster. Never reach down with your hand to lift the pedal while driving. You cannot drive safely from this position.

From a stopped position, take these actions:

► Remove any obstructions, such as a wadded floor mat, that are under the pedal.
► Tap the accelerator repeatedly to clear it.
► Put your toe or hand under the accelerator and lift.

After freeing the accelerator, test it with the engine running and the car parked before you drive again. If a broken spring is the problem, do not drive until it is repaired. You cannot fix a broken spring by lifting the accelerator pedal.

Engine Failure

Usually you have little warning that your engine is going to sputter or stop due to ignition or fuel-system failure. When engine failure occurs, move out of traffic to a safe place.

Follow these steps if your engine stops suddenly:

1. Shift to NEUTRAL to keep moving when the engine first sputters or stops.
2. Begin moving out of traffic toward the right shoulder. Turn on the emergency flashers. Do not brake. Use hand signals for slowing and changing lanes.
3. Try to restart the engine while you are moving. If the engine starts, shift into a forward gear and proceed. If it does not start, move safely onto the shoulder or to the curb before stopping, if possible. Try again to start the engine.

   If you cannot move onto the shoulder or to the curb, stop on the roadway. Use your emergency flashers while trying to start the engine.
4. If the engine still fails to start, raise the hood and leave emergency flashers on to signal a breakdown. You and your passengers should get out of the car. Stand safely off the roadway to wait for help, as pictured here.

If you become disabled in such risky locations as over the crest of a hill or on a curve, put out flares or other warning devices to alert other roadway users.

You can move some stalled stickshift cars a short distance. Turn the ignition switch to the "start" position with the clutch pedal out and the transmission in FIRST gear.

Engine failure also affects the performance of power steering and power brakes. You need more effort to steer and brake when the engine is not running.

Flooded Engine   An engine floods when too much fuel and not enough air reach the engine. A flooded engine often results if you pump the accelerator repeatedly when trying to start the car. You might smell fuel when the engine is flooded.

Follow these steps to start a flooded engine:

1. Hold the accelerator pedal to the floor to let air in and to clear excess fuel from engine.
2. While holding the accelerator down, turn the ignition switch on steadily for 5 to 10 seconds. If the engine does not start within that time, wait several minutes, and try again.
3. When the engine starts, release the accelerator gradually to help clear excess fuel from the engine.

Engine Overheats   A number of factors can cause an engine to overheat. Sometimes even a well-maintained engine overheats in hot weather or in stop-and-go traffic.

Take these steps if your engine overheats:

1. Turn off the air conditioner if it is on. This action helps lighten the load on the engine.

2. Turn on the heater to draw off heat from the engine. You might be uncomfortable, but often this one action will lower engine temperature.

3. During stops, shift to NEUTRAL. Press the accelerator gently to speed up the engine slightly, but do not race the engine.

Shifting to NEUTRAL lightens the load on the engine. Accelerating increases fan and water pump speeds for cooling the radiator. This acceleration also increases coolant flow through the heater.

4. If the temperature light stays on, move to a safe place. Stop, turn off the engine, and let the engine cool. Do not attempt to add water to the radiator until the engine has cooled.

Steering Failure

Complete failure of the steering system seldom occurs. However, complete steering failure is extremely serious when it happens.

Total Steering Failure Take these actions if your steering fails completely:

1. Use your horn and emergency flashers to communicate your emergency to other drivers.

2. Stop as quickly and safely as possible. Lift your foot from the accelerator. Do not brake. Braking could cause the front wheels to turn sharply. Instead, use the parking brake. To avoid a skid, hold the parking brake release "off" to allow a quick on-off action with the parking brake.

3. Shift to a lower gear.

Power-Steering Failure A failure in the power-steering system is the most common type of steering "failure." Power-steering failure occurs when the engine dies, when the power-steering fluid in the system is low, or when a drive belt breaks. The steering mechanism still works, but you must exert much more effort to steer.

Loss of Forward Vision

If you have lost forward vision, you must act promptly to regain visibility. Do not swerve. Continue to drive in the path you remember.

The Hood Flies Up This emergency usually occurs because the hood is not securely latched. Stop the car in a safe place if the hood is down but vibrating, or if it is not level with the top of the fenders. Release the hood and close it again. Be sure that the hood is latched securely.

Take these actions if the hood flies up while you are driving:

1. Look through the crack below the open hood, as seen here.

2. If you cannot see under the hood, quickly roll down the window. Look in the direction that you are driving.

3. Continue to drive. Turn on the emergency flashers. Pump the brakes gently to warn other drivers of your emergency.

4. Slow down, and drive off the roadway at a safe location.

Headlights Fail   If you are driving at night and your headlights start to flicker, move quickly and carefully off the roadway to a safe place. Follow these steps if your headlights fail entirely:

1. Slow down, and then continue to drive in the path you remember.
2. Try the dimmer switch, interior light, parking lights, emergency flashers, and the turn signals. Try turning the headlights from low to high. Some circuits might still work. If so, use whatever lights are available to help you drive off the roadway to a safe location.

3. Use the light from street lights, lighted signs, buildings, or other vehicles to help you see. Move off the roadway to a safe place when the car has slowed down.

Windshield Is Splashed   Your windshield might be splashed with slush or mud from other vehicles. Snow from a snow blower could also cover your windshield.

Immediately turn on your windshield wipers to clear your windshield. Slow down at once, and try to remember your path until you regain visibility. Use your windshield washers as needed.

Car on Fire
A car fire can be dangerous and hard to extinguish. The fire can involve fuel, oil, grease, ordinary combustibles, electrical equipment, or a combination of causes. Carry an A-B-C type fire extinguisher that is designed to control such fires. Notify the local fire department of any vehicle fires.

Engine Compartment Fire
Many vehicle fires start in the engine compartment. Take these actions in case of fire:

1. Quickly steer the car out of traffic and off the roadway to a safe, open area. Stay away from buildings and service stations. Turn off the ignition to cut off the engine's electrical supply.
2. Have passengers get out of the car immediately and move at least 100 feet away from the car.
3. Estimate how serious the fire is. You might see flames and smoke around the hood, as pictured here. The hood might be hot to the touch. In both situations, do not try to put out the fire. Leave the hood closed. Move away from the car while waiting for the fire department. The fuel tank could explode.

If you estimate that the fire is small enough to control and you have an A-B-C type fire extinguisher, take these steps:

1. Use a rag to protect your hands. Lean away from the car. Turn your face away to protect yourself from the heat and flames. Carefully open the hood. Once the hood is up, the fire will burn freely as it gets more air.
2. Direct the fire extinguisher on the area of the fire. Water is not effective in putting out oil and fuel fires.
3. Never try to disconnect the battery or work with your hands under the hood while it is still hot.

Fire is possible in any collision where the engine compartment is smashed. As precautions, turn off the ignition, and get passengers out and away from the car. Loose electrical wires, leaking fuel and oil, and a hot engine combine to create a potential fire situation.

Passenger Compartment Fire
A passenger-compartment fire usually is caused by a carelessly handled match, lighter, or burning tobacco product. Such fires smoulder, but rarely flame up. Pull safely off the roadway. Use water or a fire

extinguisher to put out the fire. Make sure that the fire is completely out. Upholstery fires often restart.

Car Stalls on Railroad Tracks
An anxious driver might slow down too much while crossing railroad tracks and stall the engine. Take these actions if your car stalls on the tracks:

1. If no train is coming, try to restart the car. It will probably start. If you hurry too much, you might flood the engine. If the engine floods, hold the accelerator to the floor as you restart the engine. Keep looking for trains.
2. If you cannot restart the engine, have passengers leave the car immediately. They should walk a safe distance away from the tracks and the crossing. Tell passengers to watch for trains.
3. Shift to NEUTRAL and push the car off the tracks.

4. With some stickshift cars, you can move the car a short distance. Shift to FIRST or RE-VERSE, let the clutch out, and turn the ignition to "start."
5. If a train is coming, abandon your car. Quickly move away from the tracks in the direction from which the train is approaching. This precaution helps you avoid injury from flying fragments.

Review It
1. What actions should you take if a tire blows out?
2. What should you do if the brakes fail?
3. What actions should you take if the accelerator sticks?
4. What should you do if the engine fails or overheats?
5. What actions should you take if the steering fails?
6. What should you do if a raised hood blocks your vision?
7. What actions should you take if the car catches on fire?
8. What should you do if your car stalls on railroad tracks?

13–2 Driver Errors

Driver errors cause many more emergencies than vehicle malfunctions. Errors from inexperience, lack of attention, or poor decisions often create driving emergencies. Any driver can be put in an emergency situation by the unpredictable act of another driver.

Identifying an emergency, making correct decisions, and maneuvering skillfully will help you avoid a collision. Developing automatic responses to emergencies is part of the total driving task.

Off-Road Recovery

When a front wheel drops off the roadway, your first reaction might be to steer back sharply to the roadway. This action could be dangerous. The shoulder could be lower than the roadway or the shoulder could be rough or soft. The wheels that are still on the roadway have much better traction than the wheels that are on the shoulder. The car will tend to pull to the shoulder of the roadway.

Avoid quick steering to get back on the roadway. This action can cause a car to swerve across the roadway into a lane of traffic.

Take these actions for an off-road recovery:

1. Hold the steering wheel firmly. The greater the drop-off between roadway and shoulder, the greater amount of steering control you need. Keep your car heading straight.
2. Let up on the accelerator and brake gently. Slow to 5 or 10 mph.
3. Position your car so it straddles the roadway edge, as in the top picture.
4. Select a place to return to the roadway where the roadway and shoulder are nearly level.
5. Check for traffic. Signal and return to the roadway when no oncoming traffic is near.
6. Steer sharply toward the roadway to start your recovery. The middle picture shows you must make a sharp turn to return to the roadway.
7. Countersteer sharply the instant the front tire comes back on the roadway, as in the bottom picture. You *countersteer* when you steer in the opposite direction.
8. Center your car in the lane. Cancel your signal. Adjust speed to traffic flow. If traffic is heavy when you go off the roadway, drive entirely off the roadway. Stop and wait for an opening in the traffic flow.

Sometimes an obstruction, such as a bridge or pole, might be on the shoulder ahead. In

this case, act quickly to make a recovery. You have neither time nor space to slow down properly or to look for a level spot. Grip the steering wheel firmly. Countersteer *immediately* when the front wheel touches the roadway.

Emergency Swerving

Swerving is a last-second emergency means of avoiding a collision. Swerve only when you judge that braking hard will not prevent a collision. At speeds over 30 mph, you can sometimes swerve to a new path in less distance than the distance you need to stop.

The Stop-Swerve Decision

This picture shows a dangerous situation. The driver of the yellow car might hit the brakes to stop. In some situations, this action will be the only choice. However, the driver might hit the brakes and slide into an object. When moving at 30 mph or above, the traction created by the car's tires can move the car sideways faster than braking traction can stop it. Make this check when deciding to swerve around an object: Be sure that no other vehicle is in the lane that you will enter.

The stop-swerve decision is not an easy one to make. Swerve only as a last resort. If a pedestrian steps in front of you at the last second, you might be forced to make a stop-swerve decision.

Use the IPDE process to protect yourself and possibly

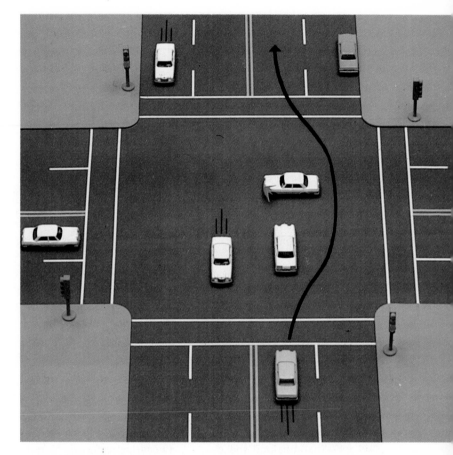

reduce the number of stop-swerve situations you encounter. In addition, allow an adequate space between yourself and the vehicle ahead.

Executing an Emergency Swerve
Follow these steps if you decide to swerve:

1. Identify possible escape paths. Choose the best escape path.
2. Grip the steering wheel firmly.
3. Turn the steering wheel sharply in the direction of the swerve.
4. In the same rhythmic motion, countersteer to stabilize your car. Straighten the wheel, and continue to steer in your path.

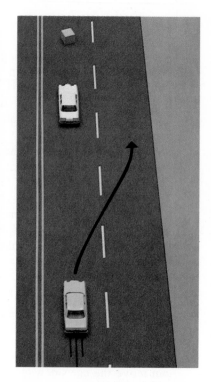

How Sharply to Swerve? The amount of time available to swerve determines how sharply you must swerve. Two factors—distance and speed—determine how much time you have to swerve.

Distance to the object is the first factor that determines how sharply to swerve. These pictures show how sharply you must swerve when the stopped car is close. When the stopped car is farther away, the swerve will be less severe and easier to execute.

Speed is the second factor that determines how sharply to swerve. As speed increases, the amount of time in which to swerve is reduced. You must swerve more sharply to get around a stopped vehicle at 40 mph than at 20 mph.

Minimizing Effects of a Collision

Whenever a collision is about to occur, you should:
► Above all, not give up. Keep control of your car. Any change of speed or direction that lessens the impact also lessens the damage.

► Steer for something "soft" if you leave the roadway. Look for bushes, a snowbank, or an open field.
► Steer for a sideswipe collision rather than a head-on collision. In a sideswipe collision, only the sides of the cars touch. If possible, sideswipe a car going in your direction rather than an oncoming car.
► Avoid objects, such as trees and parked vehicles, that will stop your car suddenly.
► Act quickly after a collision. Get passengers out and away from your car in case a fire starts.

Threat of a Head-On Collision

A head-on collision produces the highest force of impact of any collision. Try to avoid a head-on collision at all costs. Take these steps when you are threatened with a head-on collision:

1. Keep driving. Slow down as much as possible, but do not lock the wheels when braking. Slowing down lessens the force of impact and also gives the other driver space and time to recover control.
2. Blow the horn and flash the headlights. These actions might alert an inattentive or sleepy driver who is driving toward you in your lane. Begin to brake and move to the right if the driver does not heed your warning.
3. Steer right toward the shoulder. Do not steer left. The other driver likely will try to steer back into the proper lane, as in the top picture. Prepare to drive entirely off the roadway to the right, if necessary. Look for a soft impact spot, such as a bush, if you do not have a clear escape path.
4. If you cannot avoid the collision, try to sideswipe rather than collide head on. Chances of surviving a sideswipe collision are far better than in a head-on collision.

Threat of a Side-Impact Collision

The driver of the red car in the bottom picture might find it difficult to avoid being hit from the side. However, by accelerating, the driver might avoid the passenger compartment being crushed.

Take these steps to avoid or lessen the effect of a side-impact collision:

1. Brake or accelerate quickly. Do whichever seems more likely to prevent or lessen the collision. Try to avoid a collision directly into the passenger compartment.
2. Blow the horn to alert the other driver.
3. Change lanes or swerve away from the impact. Be aware of the traffic situation around you. Your swerve should not cause a more severe collision.

Threat of a Rear-End Collision
You are quite defenseless while your car is standing still. The driver in this picture realizes that the car approaching from the rear is coming too fast. The car might not be able to stop in time. Take these actions if you are threatened with a rear-end collision:

1. Flash your brake lights early to alert the driver approaching from behind.

2. As the car nears, release your brakes and move a few feet forward. This precaution gives the driver approaching from behind more stopping distance.

3. If the intersection is clear, accelerate across the intersection. Again, you give the driver approaching from behind more space to stop. If your lane is not clear, turn right promptly, if possible.

4. If a collision is unavoidable, release your brakes just before the collision occurs. This step helps soften the impact. Brake immediately after the collision to avoid sliding into another traffic lane or into another car.

Roadway Emergencies

Unusual and unexpected roadway emergencies, such as this large pothole, can cause you to lose control of your car. Objects on the roadway, sharp curves, and driving into deep water can cause emergencies.

Potholes in the Roadway

Freezing and thawing of water in roadway cracks breaks up the roadway, creating potholes. Vehicles driving over these water-filled cracks speed up the development of potholes. Potholes often have sharp edges that can severely damage tires. You can lose control of your car when you hit a pothole at a high speed.

Watch for potholes and avoid them whenever possible. Drive carefully around a pothole, not over it. Stay in your own lane as you avoid potholes in the roadway.

If you must drive through a pothole, drive slowly to prevent tire damage. By driving slowly, you can better keep control of your car.

Car in Deep Water   Act quickly if you drive or plunge into deep water. A car often will float for a few minutes. The engine end of your car is heavy and might sink first. Take these actions if your car goes into deep water:

1. Unfasten your safety belt. Check your passengers.
2. Open the window that is farthest out of the water. Power windows might short circuit in the water so open these windows immediately.
3. Exit promptly through the open window.

If the windows will not open, exit through a door. Do not panic when the door is slow to open. Pressure will equalize as water from outside the door enters your car. You then can open the door.

If your car is underwater, some air will be trapped toward the highest side of your car. Try to get a full breath or two of air while locating a window or door that is facing up. Open the window or door and leave your car.

If trapped in your car underwater, turn on your headlights. This step can help rescuers find your car more quickly.

Sharp Curve   You might unintentionally go into a curve too fast on a strange roadway, especially at night. The standard warning sign does not indicate how sharp the curve is. Also, the warning sign might not give you a suggested safe speed.

Take these actions if you enter a curve too fast:

1. Brake as soon as you realize your problem. If you are not yet in the curve, brake firmly. If you are in the curve, brake gently, but do not lock the wheels.
2. About halfway through the curve, accelerate gently to help stabilize your car.

Manuevering a curve at a high speed is dangerous. A bad spot in the roadway or driving in the wrong lane might lead to a collision.

Object on the Roadway An object on the roadway creates a hazard, whether it is a box, leaves, or an animal darting onto the roadway. A cardboard packing box in the street might not appear to be dangerous. Neither does this pile of leaves that were raked from a yard. However, avoid these and other objects on the roadway. You might not be able to identify the contents of the box. You cannot see a rake or other object in the leaf pile. In addition, both empty boxes and leaf piles attract children as places to play.

First check traffic, and then decide whether to pass, brake, straddle, swerve, or drive over the object. Choose to straddle the object only if your car can clear it. Avoid swerving left across the center line because you could encounter oncoming traffic. Drive over an object only as a last resort.

Review It
1. How should you safely return to the roadway if your car runs off the roadway?
2. Under what conditions should you make an emergency swerve?
3. What should you do to minimize the impact of a head-on collision? side-impact collision? rear-end collision?
4. How should you escape a car that is sinking in deep water?
5. What actions should you take if you enter a curve too fast?

Advancements in Traffic Safety

Anti-lock brake systems help minimize many reactions to vehicle malfunctions and driver errors. This computer-assisted system helps you maintain control of your car in an emergency.

Anti-lock brake systems sense when each wheel's brakes lock up. The sensors electronically release and reapply the brake until you release the foot brake. Brake lockup is prevented.

Any combined braking and steering reponse to a vehicle malfunction or driver error is safer with anti-lock brakes. The wheels continue to roll as the non-lock brakes slow the car. You can steer even while braking hard and still keep control of your car without skidding.

Chapter Summary

1. Maintain vehicle control when a tire blows out. Grip the steering wheel firmly and decelerate as you safely leave the traffic flow. (13–1)
2. Total brake failure rarely occurs. If it does occur, pump the brakes, apply the parking brake, and shift to a lower gear. Watch for a safe place in which to slow down. (13–1)
3. Try releasing a stuck accelerator pedal by placing your foot under it and lifting. If you cannot lift the pedal or are in a high-traffic area, brake and shift to NEUTRAL. Drive to a safe place off the roadway. Stop and secure the car. (13–1)
4. Shift to NEUTRAL if your engine stops. Move to the shoulder of the roadway as quickly and as safely as possible. If your engine overheats, turn off the air conditioner and turn on the heater. Shift to NEUTRAL and move to the shoulder of the roadway. (13–1)
5. If steering fails completely, shift to a lower gear. Use an "on-off" technique with the parking brake to slow your car as quickly as possible. (13–1)
6. If forward vision is blocked by a raised hood, look through the space below the open hood or out the side window. Reduce speed and move off the roadway to a safe location. (13–1)
7. In case of a car fire, get everyone out of and away from the car. Call the fire department, if possible. A small fire sometimes can be put out with a fire extinguisher carried in the car for this purpose. (13–1)
8. If your car stalls on railroad tracks, try to restart it only when no train is in sight. If possible, push the car off the tracks. Abandon your car immediately if a train is coming. (13–1)
9. If your car has run off the roadway, grip the steering wheel firmly. Let up on the accelerator and brake gently. Turn sharply back onto the roadway and then countersteer. (13–2)
10. Swerve only in a last-second effort to avoid a collision or if braking might cause you to skid. Be sure the areas around you are clear before you swerve. (13–2)
11. Avoid or minimize a collision by maintaining car control, changing speed or direction, and following a selected route. (13–2)
12. Escape a car that is sinking in deep water by opening a window or door, and exiting. (13–2)
13. Brake as soon as you realize that you have entered a curve too fast. Use a gentle action to reduce speed and keep steering control. Accelerate gradually after regaining control. (13–2)

Think About It

You are going 45 mph on a four-lane divided highway. The driver behind you passes you on the left. The driver then cuts in front of you and brakes hard. You brake hard, but skid to the left. How can you recover from this emergency?

Decision Making

1. The white car has just had a left front tire blow out. What steps should the driver take to handle this emergency situation?

2. You are traveling 30 mph. You brake for the stop ahead, but then realize that your brakes do not work. What should you do to stop the car?

3. The driver cannot possibly stop in time to avoid hitting the bicyclist. What should the driver do?

4. You are driving the white car. Both you and the driver in the gray car are traveling 30 mph. The other driver is not aware of your car. What can you do to prevent a collision or keep the collision from being too serious?

Chapter 13 Test

Multiple Choice   Copy the number of each sentence below on a sheet of paper. Choose the letter that best completes each statement or answers each question.

1. If a rear tire blows out, the car can
   (a) stop.   (b) fishtail.   (c) pull to the left.
   (d) pull to the right.   (242)
2. What type of location do you need to safely change a tire?
   (a) level   (b) wet   (c) busy   (d) uphill   (243)
3. If the accelerator sticks while driving, do not
   (a) lift the pedal with your toe.   (b) apply the brakes.   (c) lift the pedal with your hand.
   (d) shift to NEUTRAL.   (245)
4. Which gear position should you use to keep the car moving when the engine suddenly stops?
   (a) PARK   (b) DRIVE   (c) NEUTRAL   (d) LOW (246)
5. To start a flooded engine, you should
   (a) pump the accelerator pedal.   (b) turn the ignition switch without pushing the accelerator pedal   (c) open the hood so more air can reach the engine.   (d) push the accelerator pedal to the floor and turn the ignition switch.   (246)
6. The *first* thing you should do in case of an engine compartment fire is
   (a) get all passengers out of the car.   (b) steer the car off the roadway to a safe, open area.
   (c) call the fire department.   (d) estimate how serious the fire is.   (248)
7. Which type of collision is the most damaging?
   (a) side-impact   (b) head-on   (c) sideswipe
   (d) rear-end   (253)
8. If you cannot avoid being struck by another car from behind, you should
   (a) brake hard.   (b) fasten your safety belt.
   (c) blow the horn.   (d) release the brakes.   (254)
9. If your car is sinking in water, you should
   (a) escape through a window or door.   (b) break the windshield.   (c) get down on the floor.
   (d) yell for help.   (255)
10. When you realize you have entered a curve too fast, you should
    (a) steer toward the shoulder.   (b) countersteer.
    (c) brake gently.   (d) brake firmly.   (255)

Completion   Copy the number of each sentence below. After each number, write the letter of the word or words that complete the sentence correctly.

11. When total brake failure occurs, use the ____ to help slow down the car.   (244)
12. If your car stalls on railroad tracks, try to ____ it if no train is coming.   (249)
13. When a ____ drops off the roadway onto the shoulder, keep the car going straight.   (250)
14. You should ____ only when you determine that braking hard will not prevent a collision.   (251)
15. When faced with an oncoming vehicle in your lane, steer to the ____.   (253)
    a. front wheel
    b. left
    c. parking brake
    d. restart
    e. right
    f. swerve

Vocabulary   Copy the number of each phrase below. Match the definition in List A with the term it defines in List B.

List A
16. occurs when a tire on a moving vehicle loses air pressure suddenly   (242)
17. device that lifts a corner or side of the car for changing a tire   (243)
18. small pieces of hardware that hold the wheel onto the car   (243)
19. condition that occurs from long, continuous, hard braking   (244)
20. to turn the steering wheel in the opposite direction   (250)

List B
a. blowout
b. brake fade
c. countersteer
d. jack
e. lug nuts
f. wheel cover

Unit 4
Your Responsibilities as a Driver

Your responsibilities as a driver in the highway transportation system directly affect you and other roadway users. This picture shows one such responsibility. Keeping tires inflated to their recommended pressure helps increase tire lifespan, but also helps you maintain control of your car.

This unit discusses how physical and emotional conditions can affect a driver's ability. You will learn how alcohol and other drugs can seriously affect a driver's ability. Finally, this unit discusses your responsibilities as a car owner, and how to make owning a car as economical and enjoyable as possible.

Chapter 14
Driver Condition and Risk

You're the Driver!

Imagine that you have just completed an afternoon of bicycle riding as these people have done. You feel physically healthy and mentally alert. This sense of well-being is as important to your driving as it is to your other daily activities.

If you were going to drive this car, on which physical sense would you most depend?

How could you protect yourself from the effects of carbon monoxide while driving?

If you were in a traffic jam, what techniques could you use to control your emotions?

What could you do to control a high-risk driving situation?

This chapter discusses your physical and emotional abilities as they relate to driving. You can learn how to lower the risks associated with driving. Apply the skills discussed in this chapter to improve the way you manage and control driving situations.

Objectives

Your senses are important when using the IPDE process. You use your ability to see, hear, smell, and feel to know what is occurring around your car.

Seeing

Most of your driving information is perceived through your eyes. You must be able to see clearly and quickly to be a safe, responsible driver. Your brain directs your eyes to focus on objects in and around your path of travel. Information is sent to your brain and is combined with stored information. As a result, you can identify hazards, predict conflicts, decide how to adjust your speed and position, and execute your decisions.

Visual Acuity You must be able to read gauges on your instrument panel, and in the next instant identify oncoming traffic. This ability to see things clearly near and far away is called *visual acuity*.

A person with normal visual acuity is said to have 20/20 vision. A person with 20/20 vision can read 3/8 inch letters on an eye chart from 20 feet away. Estimate your visual acuity by placing this page 20 feet away. You should be able to read the term IPDE in the block above.

IPDE

You must pass a visual acuity test in order to obtain a driver's license. Most states require a minimum visual acuity of 20/40 to drive. A person with 20/40 vision must be twice as close to an object to see it as clearly as a person with 20/20 vision must be to the object. If you must wear glasses or contact lenses to pass the vision test, then you must wear them whenever you drive.

Color Vision Color vision gives you the ability to tell one color from another. Not being able to distinguish colors is *color-blindness*. Being able to see the colors red, green, and yellow is important since these colors give the messages stop, go, and slow or caution.

Men inherit color-blindness more often than women. The most common type of color-blindness is the difficulty distinguishing red from green. While the picture below is not an actual color-blindness test, it shows what part of a test for color-blindness might look like.

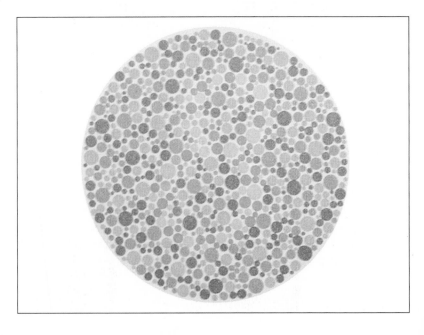

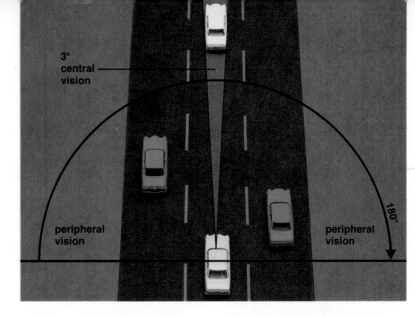

A color-blind driver can compensate by:

► remembering the order of the lights in a traffic signal. If the lights are vertical, the red light is at the top. If the lights are horizontal, the red light is on the left.
► knowing what traffic signs mean by their shapes.
► reading all signs that appear with traffic signals.
► checking all traffic, especially cross-traffic, before proceeding at traffic signals.

Field of Vision Your *field of vision* is all the area that you can see around you while looking straight ahead. From a stopped position, most people can see about 90 degrees to each side. This width is a half circle, or 180 degrees, as shown above.

However, you can only see clearly in your area of *central vision*. This straight-ahead part of your field of vision is a small, 3-degree, cone-shaped area. As you learn to drive, your brain begins to direct your central vision toward events that pertain to your driving task.

The vision area left and right of central vision is called side vision or *peripheral vision*. Good peripheral vision attracts

your attention to possible hazards, which your central vision then identifies as you look at the hazard. A narrow field of peripheral vision (140 degrees or less) is called *tunnel vision*. A driver with tunnel vision must compensate with more frequent head and eye movements. The picture below shows how objects to the side might look at expressway speeds to a driver with tunnel vision.

Objects recognizable but blurred.

Area of central vision, objects in sharp focus.

Objects recognizable but blurred.

Depth Perception The ability to judge the distance between yourself and other objects is *depth perception*. Distance judgments in driving involve your moving car and other vehicles and objects. When you are in a moving car as shown to the right, you have more difficulty judging the distance of another moving object.

A driver can compensate for poor depth perception by:
► using a following distance greater than 2 seconds.
► allowing for additional clear distance ahead before passing.
► using known distances, such as city blocks or the space between utility poles, to judge distances.
► allowing greater distances at night than in daytime. Darkness hides many guides you would use in daytime.

Night Vision The ability to see at night varies from person to person. Some people who see clearly in the daytime have poor night vision. Not being able to see well at night is *night blindness*.

All people see less at night than in daylight. Your eyes have a different system for seeing at night. Colors are harder to identify. Details of objects do not appear as sharp as in daytime.

Your vision at night is limited to the area lit by headlights and streetlights. In rural areas, you might be in total darkness except for the area that is lighted by your headlights. You might not be able to see anything to the sides, and might be less able to read signs and roadway markings.

Compare the pictures below. Both pictures show the same situation. The only difference is that one picture was taken at night and the other was taken during the day. Notice that you cannot see as much at night. Your ability to judge distances accurately also decreases.

Use these guides to improve your ability to see at night:

► Travel at slower speeds, beginning at sunset.
► Use a following distance greater than 2 seconds.
► Glance to the shoulder of the roadway to avoid looking directly at bright lights.
► Drive at night only if your eyes are rested.
► Keep the windshield and the headlights clean.
► Keep the interior car lights turned off.
► Do not wear sunglasses at night.

Glare   Glare occurs in the daytime when you look at shiny surfaces that reflect bright sunlight. At night, glare occurs when you look directly at bright lights or shiny surfaces that reflect bright lights. The term *glare resistance* describes the ability to continue seeing when looking at bright lights. Glare resistance varies from person to person.

Sudden glare can temporarily blind a person, especially at night. Headlights turn toward you at intersections. Bright lights appear from over hills and around curves. The pupils of your eyes open wide at night to let in light. When your eyes are suddenly exposed to bright lights, as in the picture below, the pupils become smaller. You might be temporarily blinded before your pupils become larger again after the bright lights pass.

The term *glare recovery time* describes the time your eyes need to regain clear vision after being affected by glare. Often your pupils take five to ten seconds to open fully. At 40 mph, your car will travel almost 300 feet in 5 seconds.

Take these precautions to avoid or recover from glare:

► Avoid looking directly at bright lights. Use the right edge of the roadway as a guide.
► Use side vision rather than central vision to check your position and the location of oncoming cars.
► Anticipate glare situations and glance away.
► If you are impaired by glare, slow until your vision clears.
► Wear sunglasses, and use your car's visor in bright sunlight.

Car Design and Vision Roof supports and your rearview mirror can block part of your vision. Develop the habit of looking around these blocked areas as you drive. Do not hang objects from the rearview mirror or place objects either on the instrument panel or on the rear window ledge where they could block your view. In a collision, these objects could hit the car's occupants.

Other Senses and Driving
Sometimes you will have to depend on senses other than vision to avoid trouble. In complex driving situations, you might have to use more than one sense at a time.

Hearing Your sense of hearing can alert you to the sounds of honking horns, train whistles, emergency-vehicle sirens, and the engines and brakes of trucks and buses. You can also get an early warning of mechanical problems with your car by listening for unusual noises.

Drivers who have sounds blocked from them can be dangerous to themselves and to others. Driving with closed car windows and with the radio, air conditioner, or heater on might make a driver unaware of critical traffic sounds.

Car Speed and Vision As car speed increases, the need for accurate vision also increases. Yet, at higher speeds, you have less time to see clearly. Your field of vision is also narrowed. When you drive at 55 mph, your clear side-vision area is less than half as wide as when you drive at 20 mph.

Objects on the sides become blurred and distorted as your speed increases. This blur, or *speed smear*, as shown here, has an effect much like tunnel vision. Your eyes tend to focus far ahead where the roadway appears to come to a point. You see less and less of what is happening on the sides. At higher speeds, increase the number of times you glance to the sides.

Deaf drivers know that they must see what they cannot hear. They compensate by using their eyes more than drivers who are not deaf. In general, the driving records of deaf drivers are among the best.

Smelling Your sense of smell can identify an overheated engine or something burning in the car. Pure carbon monoxide has no smell. However, you can get an early warning of this deadly gas if you smell exhaust fumes inside your car.

Feeling Certain sensations can give you clues to the movement of your car. You can sense whether you are veering right or left or changing speed. Your sense of balance reminds you that you are going around a curve as shown in the picture. A sudden vibration of the car or jerk of the steering wheel might warn you of a mechanical problem or a change in roadway surface.

Review It

1. What is your field of vision? What part of your field of vision provides you with your clearest vision?
2. What can you do to compensate for poor depth perception?
3. How do your senses of seeing, hearing, smelling, and feeling help you drive?

Experienced drivers learn how to respond to temporary and permanent disabilities. Many times driving is possible with a moderate to severe disability.

Temporary Disabilities

Sometimes you must drive even though you are not at your physical best. You can compensate for some temporary disabilities. With other disabilities, you should not drive.

Fatigue   Fatigue lessens your fitness to drive. Mental or physical work, emotional stress, or loss of sleep can cause fatigue.

Fatigue dulls your senses and slows both mental and physical processes. If you are fatigued, you will need more time to identify hazards. You might delay and make inaccurate predictions. Your actions are often abrupt and uncoordinated when you are tired. You might even drive faster or slower than normal.

Fatigue can also cause drowsiness, as shown here. Drivers who fall asleep at the wheel cause many collisions.

Rest is the only safe remedy for fatigue. However, people often need to drive when they are tired. If you are tired after work or school, take a break for a few minutes before you drive. Choose a quiet, less congested route home.

Take these actions to compensate for fatigue on long drives:

► Rest before you start.
► Change drivers often.
► Stop regularly for light refreshments. Walk or jog.
► Open a window for fresh air.
► Wear sunglasses in bright sunlight and for snow glare.
► Use your orderly visual search pattern to keep your eyes moving.
► Listen to the radio, sing, or talk with your passengers.
► Stop in a safe place if you feel drowsy. Lock the car and take a nap.

Temporary Illness or Injury

Any illness, even a cold, can impair driving to some extent. A temporary physical injury, such as a broken bone or a sprained ankle, can also impair your driving. These temporary conditions can cause discomfort and pain, limit physical movement, lessen endurance and strength, dull your senses, or a combination of these disabilities.

Take these actions if you must drive when you have an illness or injury:

► Choose a quiet route.
► Use reduced speeds.
► Drive within your abilities.

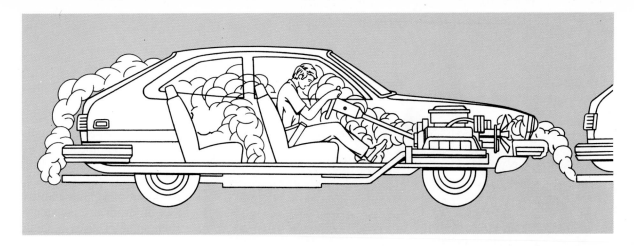

Effects of Medicines Many medicines have side effects that can interfere with your driving ability. A medicine to reduce headache pain or relieve hay fever, for example, might also cause drowsiness, dizziness, or reduced alertness.

If you take medicine, consider these points before you drive:
► Read the label. Learn the possible side effects. Ask your pharmacist or physician about side effects.
► A medicine can affect you differently at different times.
► If possible, drive home before taking the medicine.
► If you must drive after taking medicine, choose a quiet route.
► Compensate for any side effects. Do not drive if your driving ability is seriously affected.

Carbon Monoxide Part of the exhaust fumes from your car is *carbon monoxide,* a colorless, odorless, and tasteless gas. Carbon monoxide is present in all exhaust gases from gasoline engines.

You can sometimes detect carbon monoxide in a car because it is mixed with other exhaust fumes that have an odor. However, you cannot tell how concentrated carbon monoxide is by the odor of the exhaust fumes.

Small amounts of carbon monoxide can cause drowsiness, headaches, muscular weakness, mental dullness, and nausea. Too much carbon monoxide can cause death.

Be alert for the danger of carbon monoxide in heavy traffic and in such enclosed areas as tunnels and underground parking facilities. Your car's heater or air conditioner vents might draw in exhaust fumes from the car ahead, as shown here. The open rear window of a station wagon might create a slight vacuum that pulls in exhaust fumes.

Take these actions to prevent carbon monoxide exposure and combat its effects:
► Avoid running the engine inside a garage. Move your car outside after starting the engine.

► Keep your car well ventilated.
► In stop-and-go traffic, keep a half-car length or more between yourself and the vehicle ahead of you.
► In traffic jams, especially in enclosed areas, turn off the engine when possible.
► Check your exhaust system regularly.
► Move a person who is overcome by carbon monoxide into fresh air. Get medical help.

Smoking Be aware that smoking while driving is dangerous. Besides distracting the attention of the driver from the driving task, smoking also raises the carbon monoxide level in a driver's blood.

Discourage your passengers from smoking. Carbon monoxide from tobacco smoke can affect even nonsmokers in an enclosed area such as a car. If someone does smoke in your car, open a window to provide fresh air.

Permanent Disabilities

Many people have permanent disabilities. Special car equipment and controls can help many of these people compensate for their disabilities. Still others are able to drive because they can control their disabilities with medication. Certain impairments make it impossible for some disabled people to drive.

Older Drivers As a nation, we are healthier and living longer. More and more older drivers will use our roadways in the future. Some older drivers might have physical limitations. However, they can more than compensate for these limitations by adjusting their driving based on prior experience.

Physical Disabilities State agencies license drivers with many types of physical disabilities. Each case is considered on an individual basis.

Special equipment can allow a disabled person to operate all car controls, as this driver is preparing to do. Some adapted controls are quite simple while others are options already available on a car. For example, a person who does not have the use of his or her left leg can drive an automatic-transmission car equipped with a hand-operated dimmer switch.

Chronic Illnesses A *chronic illness* is an ailment that lasts over a period of years. Some chronic illnesses, such as high blood pressure, have little effect on driving. Other illnesses, such as heart disease, could seriously impair a person's ability to drive.

Certain chronic illnesses require regular medication that also can have side effects that interfere with driving. Some people are subject to sudden loss of consciousness or muscular control. Before these individuals receive a driver's license, they must provide medical proof that their chronic illness is under control.

Stress worsens some chronic illnesses. Persons with these illnesses should not drive in heavy traffic or in other stressful driving situations. Whatever the illness or disability, everyone who can perform the driving task safely and successfully has the privilege of being licensed to drive.

Review It

1. How can you compensate for the effects of fatigue?
2. How can you avoid and combat exposure to carbon monoxide?
3. How can a chronic illness affect your driving?

14–3 Emotions and Driving

The word *emotion* is used to name a strong feeling. Anger, fear, and joy are examples of emotions. Emotions can and do add a special quality to life.

How Emotions Affect Driving
Emotions influence the way you think and act. When emotions affect your thoughts and actions, they can change the way you normally drive.

Mental Effects of Emotions
Strong emotions can interfere with your ability to think and reason. When strong emotions affect you, your ability to make decisions is reduced. Your chances of making a mistake increase. The effect that an emotion has on your ability to drive depends upon the strength of the emotion and the effort you make to resist the effects of the emotion.

In some situations, a strong emotion can cause you to fix your attention on one event. You might miss other important events in the driving scene. In other situations, you might experience several strong emotions in a short period of time. One emotion can lead to another. In the left picture, the driver in the front has just cut over to the right lane and started to slow. This action could startle following drivers. During this difficult driving situation, strong emotional feeling could turn to anger. The following drivers must control their emotions. They should increase the space between themselves and the car ahead.

Physical Effects of Emotions
Strong emotions also can cause changes in your bodily functions. Under emotional stress, your heartbeat increases, your breathing quickens, your digestion slows, and your palms sweat. Your body prepares itself for the stressful event.

You can expect some emotional stress in your everyday life. However, continued emotional stress can exhaust you. Imagine you are driving in the situation shown in the right picture. You should be on the alert for the way rush-hour traffic can cause stress and fatigue in you and other drivers.

Anger While Driving When you drive, you usually rely upon a set of assumptions or expectations. You assume that others will drive and act in a safe, responsible manner. When you must change your expectations, you might be tempted to react angrily.

In normal driving, other drivers will interfere with your planned speed or path of travel. They will slow in front of you or change lanes improperly. Sometimes you might think that everyone is trying to irritate you. As a result of these and other unplanned actions, you might become angry. Anger occurs more often to more drivers than any other emotion. Anger can range from mild irritation to furious rage.

In this picture, the driver is angry at the people who are talking and blocking his way. The driver is angry because he might be late for an appointment. If the driver is not able to maintain emotional control, he might remain angry long after the people have cleared the street.

Anger can impair your ability to brake, steer, and accelerate smoothly. If you are angry, you might not see everything you should see. You might force other drivers to stop or swerve abruptly. These last-second actions can cause conflicts and added stress not only for you, but for other drivers.

Other Emotions and Driving
Sorrow, depression, and anxiety are other emotions that can adversely affect driving. These emotions slow body processes and reduce mental alertness.

Anxiety differs from anger. You might be anxious if you are driving in an unfamiliar, difficult situation. You might

have trouble identifying hazards when you are confused. Sometimes, you might feel panic-stricken. As a responsible driver, you can work to recognize anxiety and try to avoid it. You can realize that you are in a difficult situation, and try your best to cope.

Excitement and happiness are emotions that also can prevent you from fully concentrating on your driving task. A happy, excited driver can be just as impaired as an angry driver. After an intense event, such as a football game, be sure that strong emotions do not impair your driving ability.

Emotions and the IPDE Process
The successful use of the IPDE process requires total concentration on the driving task. Your emotional condition can drastically affect your driving ability. The event triggering the emotion might not be related to your driving. Emotions such as apathy or sorrow, or depression tend to lessen your mental alertness and distract you from driving well. Since emotions can cause you to focus your concentration on a single event, you might be unable to concentrate fully on the driving task.

Look at the picture, and think how emotions could affect your driving if you were beside the truck. The car ahead has been slowing and forcing you to slow. The truck has just decided to pass the car. You are not sure what the driver ahead is going to do. Another truck is behind the truck that is passing. The driver ahead and the truck drivers could cause you to make these mistakes when using the IPDE process:

▶ **Identify** If the emotional stress is strong enough, your attention could be focused on the trucks. You might not identify a sudden change in speed by the car ahead.

▶ **Predict** If you are unsure of the drivers around you, you will not be able to make accurate predictions.

▶ **Decide** Under such emotional stress, you probably have not been able to think of your decision options. In this tight situation, your best option might be to move toward the shoulder to the right.

▶ **Execute** When emotional stress reduces your ability to identify, predict, and decide, you might have a hard time executing the right decisions. You need time to use the IPDE process. In a tight, high-stress situation, you need even more time to use the IPDE process effectively.

Passengers and Emotions   Peer or group pressure, a very strong force, can be good or bad, depending upon the situation. In a baseball game, team spirit can help win the game. In school, pride can help students achieve. In a car, your friends can strongly influence the way you feel, think, and drive.

In most group situations, one or more people need to assume responsibility and lead the group. When you are driving, you must be the leader and take control. You are the one responsible for protecting your passengers.

In this picture, the championship game has just ended. Everyone is going to a celebration party. The driver in this situation will be under special pressures. Emotions will be running high. It might be hard for the driver to concentrate on the driving task. Friends might encourage the driver to hurry. To make sure that nothing goes wrong, the driver must be the leader. The driver must maintain control over the situation.

Passengers can help the driver maintain control while driving. Listed here are actions you can take to assist a driver:

► Avoid saying or doing anything that might upset the driver.

► Discourage the driver from taking reckless actions. Do your best to prevent others from encouraging dangerous driving behavior.

► Be prepared to intervene if the driver is endangering others by reckless driving. Encourage the driver to let someone else drive, or refuse to ride in the same car. Do what you must do to protect yourself and others.

► Do not hesitate to thank a driver for doing a good job of driving in a difficult situation. Next time, you might need the same support.

How to Control Emotions

During a long, exciting match point in a tennis game, spectators discipline themselves to keep from applauding until the point is finished. In driving, you must develop this same type of emotional discipline. You must not let emotions lessen your driving ability.

Techniques for Coping with Emotions High-stress driving situations can cause emotions to surface. The techniques below can help you to control your emotions while driving in a variety of situations:

► Drive in an organized manner. Learn and use correct driving procedures until they become habits. You then will be more likely to execute the right action, even under emotional stress.
► Anticipate emotion-producing situations, and adjust your expectations. Say to yourself, "I know there will be delays during rush hour, so I will adjust the amount of time that it will take me to get home. I will not let the actions of others bother me."
► Make a self-check. If you are emotionally upset before you enter your car, tell yourself, "I am angry, but I will not drive angrily."

► Do not drive when you are not in control.
► Adjust your route or time of travel to avoid irritating traffic situations.
► If you are tired, make a special effort to control your emotions. A tired person can become upset easily.
► Analyze your mistakes. Decide whether or not emotions might have interfered. Plan ahead so that the same mistakes will not be a problem in the future.

Goal of Emotional Control

Emotions are complicated and powerful forces. Learning about emotions and how to control them is something most individuals work at all their lives. Maintaining an attitude of "I will always work to control my emotions" is a big step toward actually mastering your emotions. If you can control your emotions and maintain your driving ability, you will earn the respect of others as shown here.

Review It

1. How can anger affect your ability to drive?
2. How can you help a driver when you are a passenger?
3. What can you do to control your emotions while driving?

14-4 Driving Ability and Managing Risk

Look out for the hurried driver who passes a left-turner and risks causing a collision.

All activities involve some risk. Activities such as participating in a sport, mowing the lawn, and driving a car all expose you to some risk.

Risk

The probability of being involved in a collision determines the amount of risk in driving. You increase or decrease your risk by changing the level of control you have over your car. Likewise, other roadway users can increase or decrease your chance of having a collision.

Risk and Driving If a person has not learned to adjust to high-risk situations, that person might decide to take unnecessary chances. People who take unnecessary chances in high-risk situations demonstrate *risk-taking behavior.*

Taking a chance in a situation where a mistake will not hurt you is usually safe. But, taking a chance in such a situation as driving a car can be deadly. Before driving, you must be mature enough to adjust your behavior so that you do not drive into or create high-risk situations.

High-Risk Situations In the top picture on this page, the driver of the yellow car has created a high-risk situation. In the bottom picture, the driver of the car has increased the risk at this intersection. In both situations, the drivers could have lowered the risk by adjusting their driving.

Sometimes it seems that a route you travel day after day holds no risk.

When it seems quiet ahead . . .

. . . beware of potential risk.

Some drivers are willing to take chances on different days on the same roadway. For example, if you were driving an injured friend to the hospital, you might drive in a hurry. An hour later, you probably would not drive home in the same manner. You would drive more cautiously.

Driving the same way over and over again on the same roadway is a trap that an experienced driver can fall into. Look at the top picture on this page and imagine that you are driving toward the yellow car. If you drive on this one-way street day after day, you might think that the yellow car could not turn toward you. If you assume that the yellow car will not turn, you could create a high-risk trap.

Whether you take a chance intentionally or not, the result is the same. Your chance of having a collision increases.

How to Control Risk

You must try to control and reduce your risk in any driving situation. To do so, you must measure your risk, and then act to reduce it.

Assessing Risk   In any driving situation, you should always be able to measure some risk. By using the IPDE process, you can determine how risky a situation might be. When making this assessment, you need to consider:

► the condition of your car.
► your driving ability.
► how others might react.

As you drive, your ability to use the IPDE process will increase over the years. Mature, responsible drivers have learned through experience how to drive responsibly. As you drive, you must be alert in all situations. Even a routine, low-risk situation, like the one shown in the middle and bottom pictures, can turn into a high-risk situation. The hedge is blocking the view of the driver to the right. If you had not assessed this situation as a possible high-risk situation, a conflict might have occurred.

mile. You can protect yourself by putting a little more distance between yourself and that driver.

Imagine that you are the driver moving away from the STOP sign in the picture. In this situation, each of the drivers could increase the risk. When you drive into a similar situation, tell yourself, "I will not let them take control of this situation." By slowing and using distance as your defense, you can lower your risk in this situation.

Review It

1. When might a high-risk driving situation occur?
2. What can you do to lower the risk in a driving situation?

Reducing Risk   As is true with any well-developed, high-level skill, safe driving starts with a solid plan. To lower your driving-related risk, you need to think about your driving. You need to tell yourself, "I will always work to maintain control of my car."

Use these techniques to maintain control of your car and lower your driving risk:

▶ Use your safety belt.
▶ Check that you are fit to drive. Be sure that you are not too tired to drive and that your emotions are under control.

▶ Be sure that your car is in good condition. If your car has a problem, it can be harder for you to get out of a high-risk driving situation.
▶ Always check the roadway and traffic ahead. Learn to adjust to bad weather and darkness.

By using the IPDE process continually, you can lower your risk of driving situations before you enter them. Imagine that you see a driver cut off another driver. You can assume that the driver who cut in too closely will make another mistake within the next

Safe Driving Tips

► *Avoid nervous pumping of the accelerator while waiting at a traffic light. This action can increase engine wear and wastes fuel.*
► *When fatigued or under severe emotional stress, you need more time to think and act. To gain more time while driving, slow down and increase your space cushion.*
► *To avoid conflicts, do not make emotional, last-second decisions when driving in heavy traffic.*

► *Always use your safety belt, no matter what your physical or emotional condition. Strongly encourage your passengers to also use their safety belts.*
► *If you become fatigued while driving, stop and rest. Do not rely on chemical stimulants to keep you alert.*

Chapter Summary

1. Your field of vision is all the area you can see around you when looking straight ahead. Central vision is the small area straight ahead of you in which your vision is clear. (14–1)
2. Compensate for poor depth perception by increasing your following distance and by allowing extra clearance before passing. Use known distances to judge distance, and allow greater distances at night. (14–1)
3. Your eyes gather most driving-related information, but your other senses also gather driving-related information. (14–1)
4. Fatigue dulls your senses and slows mental and physical responses. Rest often, avoid driving for long periods, and keep eyes moving to fight fatigue. (14–2)
5. Avoid carbon-monoxide exposure by not running the engine in a garage and by keeping your car well-ventilated. Increase your distance between cars in heavy traffic, and check the exhaust system regularly. (14–2)
6. Such chronic illnesses as heart disease can impair driving ability. Such illnesses as high blood pressure have little effect on driving. (14–2)

7. Anger reduces your ability to steer, brake, and accelerate smoothly. All emotions can interfere with the driving task. (14–3)
8. Aid a driver by limiting distractions and discouraging reckless behavior. Offer to drive if the driver is impaired. (14–3)
9. Control your emotions by driving in an organized manner, anticipating emotion-producing situations, and adjusting your expectations. Do not drive if you are emotionally upset. (14–3)
10. You create a high-risk driving situation each time you take a chance. (14--4)
11. Lower your risk in a driving situation by being fit to drive, and being sure your car is in good shape. Always check the roadway and adjust by increasing your distance between yourself and others. (14–4)

Think About It
It is not uncommon to find a driver with several traffic violations over a short period of time. Why do you think this happens?

Decision Making

1. Where should you be directing your clear central vision in the next few seconds of driving?

2. What factor ahead could cause you to be impaired for a few seconds? What could you do to avoid being impaired?

3. These people are having an argument. How could the argument affect the driver's ability to drive?

4. How are these passengers affecting the driver? What should they be doing to help?

Chapter 14 Test

Multiple Choice   Copy the number of each sentence below on a sheet of paper. Choose the letter that best completes each statement or answers each question.

1. The sense that drivers use most is
   (a) hearing.   (b) seeing.   (c) smelling
   (d) feeling.   (264)
2. Most drivers can see to each side approximately
   (a) 180 degrees.   (b) 90 degrees.
   (c) 360 degrees.   (d) 45 degrees.   (265)
3. What temporary disability dulls your senses and lowers your ability to drive?
   (a) a minor cut   (b) fatigue   (c) a sprained ankle   (d) a rash   (270)
4. Under sudden, strong emotions, your body
   (a) prepares for a stressful event.   (b) cools down.   (c) is tired.   (d) does not change.   (273)
5. When using the IPDE process in a high-stress situation, you need
   (a) less time.   (b) more time.   (c) no additional time.   (d) half the time.   (275)

Completion   Copy the number of each sentence below. After each number, write the letter of the word or words that complete the sentence correctly.

6. A person with ____ cannot see well to the sides.   (265)
7. The side-vision area to the left and right of your central vision is your ____.   (265)
8. The ability to continue seeing when looking at bright lights is ____.   (267)
9. The blur and distortion of objects on the sides as speed increases is called ____.   (268)
10. The ____ of medicine might decrease your driving ability.   (271)
11. Your blood's carbon monoxide level can increase due to ____.   (271)
12. A strong ____ can reduce a driver's thinking ability.   (273)
13. The emotion that occurs more often to more drivers than any other emotion is ____.   (274)

14. A driving situation's ____ can be measured by the probability of a collision.   (278)
15. In high-risk situations, drivers might take ____ that they would not normally take.   (278)

a. anger
b. chances
c. emotion
d. glare resistance
e. happiness
f. peripheral vision
g. risk
h. side effects
i. smoking
j. speed smear
k. tunnel vision

Vocabulary   Copy the number of each phrase below. Match the definition in List A with the term it defines in List B.

List A
16. ability to see clearly   (264)
17. inability to tell colors apart   (264)
18. all the area you can see around you as you look straight ahead   (265)
19. area you see clearly straight ahead   (265)
20. ability to judge distances   (266)
21. inability to see well at night   (266)
22. time needed to regain clear vision after being blinded by glare   (267)
23. deadly, colorless, and odorless gas   (271)
24. an ailment that lasts for years   (272)
25. taking chances   (278)

List B
a. carbon monoxide
b. central vision
c. chronic illness
d. color-blindness
e. depth perception
f. field of vision
g. glare recovery time
h. night blindness
i. risk-taking behavior
j. tunnel vision
k. visual acuity

Chapter 15
Alcohol, Other Drugs, and Driving

You're the Driver!

As you drive by the people pictured here, you realize they are celebrating a special occasion. Some people serve alcoholic beverages as well as other beverages on these occasions.

When a party is over, most guests will drive away in their cars as these people plan to do. The effects of alcohol or other drugs on drivers who used them might prevent some of them from driving safely.

What factors might help determine whether a person uses alcoholic beverages at such a celebration?

What mental and physical driving abilities are impaired when a person uses alcohol?

What can drinkers and non-drinkers do to reduce or avoid the risk of alcohol-impaired driving?

How might the implied-consent law affect drivers who are arrested for driving while intoxicated?

This chapter discusses the effects of alcohol and other drugs. Read this chapter to gain knowledge that can help you decide about drinking and driving.

Objectives

15-1 Alcohol Affects Driver Performance

1. Explain how alcohol affects mental and physical abilities needed for driving. (286)
2. Describe factors that determine the effects of alcohol. (289)
3. Define blood-alcohol concentration. (290)
4. Explain five myths about the use of alcohol. (292)

15-2 Laws Governing Alcohol Use

5. Explain the levels of intoxication and how these levels can be measured. (293)
6. Explain what is meant by implied-consent laws. (294)

15-3 Other Drugs and Driving

7. Explain how depressant, stimulant, and hallucinogen drugs can affect a driver. (296)

8. Describe the effects of combining alcohol with other drugs. (296)

15-4 Alcohol, Other Drugs, and Peer Pressures

9. Tell how peer pressure might affect one's decision about drinking and driving. (297)
10. Tell why everyone should share the responsibility of preventing friends from driving after drinking. (299)

15–1 Alcohol Affects Driver Performance

A major problem that society faces today results from the use of alcohol and other drugs. The problem of drinking and driving becomes a greater concern for society each year.

Alcohol Facts
Alcohol is one of the most commonly used drugs in our society, although not everyone realizes it is a drug. The word "alcohol" is the commonly used term for the chemical substance ethanol, grain alcohol, or ethyl alcohol.

The effects of alcohol vary from person to person. Some people who drink might do so without harmful effects. For others, drinking might lead to serious problems. One of the most serious problems is that of the drinking driver. The demands of the driving task are so great that each driver needs to be in the best condition possible. Although there is always some risk in driving, a person whose driving skills are reduced by alcohol often does not even realize what the risks are. That driver is a hazard to him- or herself and other roadway users.

Consider these facts about alcohol and driving:
► Alcohol is a major factor in nearly 50 percent of all traffic deaths.

► Nearly half of those killed in alcohol-related collisions had not been drinking.
► This chart shows that approximately 60 percent of alcohol-related deaths involve young people 16 to 20 years old.
► Teenage and adult drinking patterns differ in one very serious aspect: Much teenage drinking is done in cars, while much adult drinking is done in the home or at social occasions.
► Between 10:00 P.M. and 3:00 A.M. on Friday and Saturday nights, at least one of every ten drivers is drunk. In fatal collisions involving only one vehicle, two-thirds of the drivers are legally drunk.
► Driving and riding with other young drivers is the greatest hazard that young people must survive to reach adulthood.

Everyone needs to know how alcohol affects the mental and physical abilities needed for safe driving. Nondrinkers will be interacting with intoxicated drivers on the roadways. People who drink need to know the importance of not drinking before driving.

Alcohol Affects Mental Abilities
Alcohol begins to affect a person's abilities almost the moment it enters the body. Alcohol is not digested. It is

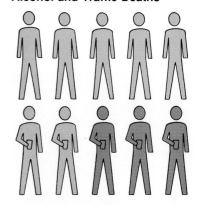

Alcohol and Traffic Deaths

■ Traffic deaths not related to alcohol

■ Alcohol-related traffic deaths

■ Alcohol-related traffic deaths involving youth

Nearly fifty percent of traffic deaths are alcohol related.

Nearly sixty percent of alcohol-related traffic deaths involve 16 to 20 year olds.

absorbed directly and quickly into the bloodstream through the walls and lining of the stomach and small intestine. Some alcohol is even absorbed through the tongue and surrounding tissues when it enters the mouth.

Once alcohol reaches the bloodstream, it quickly reaches the brain because of the large blood supply to the brain. Alcohol has its greatest effect on the brain. Mental abilities are affected first; then physical abilities become impaired.

The area of the brain first affected controls judgement and reason. Inhibitions are reduced. Physical abilities are affected next. The third area impaired controls seeing abilities and speech. When the entire brain is affected, the person might become unconscious.

Alcohol Affects Physical Abilities

As more alcohol enters the bloodstream, the area of the brain that controls muscular movements and body control begins to slow down. Even after the driver recognizes danger, the brain takes longer than normal to process the information and react to the danger. Brain messages to different parts of the body might even be confused.

Reaction Time and Coordination The muscular reactions of a driver who has been drinking can become slow and clumsy. Steering and braking movements can become uncoordinated. The driver might oversteer, brake late, or not brake at all. These actions cause drinking drivers to be involved in many serious collisions.

Alcohol is more likely to affect the actions of a beginning driver than the actions of a more experienced driver. A beginning driver lacks experience, and his or her skills are less automatic. A beginning driver is more likely to be seriously affected by alcohol.

Judgment and Reason This picture shows how alcohol first affects the part of the brain that controls judgment and reasoning, the part needed most for safe driving. As a result, the driver has a decreased ability to reason clearly and make sound judgments. However, the driver actually feels as though thinking and judging abilities are sharper and quicker than usual. This error in self-judging adds even greater risk to the driving task. After only one drink, such as one beer or one glass of wine, a person's driving ability can be diminished. As the amount of alcohol in a person's body increases, that person's driving ability decreases.

The IPDE process is affected when judgment and reasoning abilities are reduced. An alcohol-impaired driver is less able to interpret correctly what he or she sees. This driver is likely to make errors in judging distance, speed, space and shape, and is more likely to make poor decisions.

Alcohol also weakens a driver's *inhibitions,* inner forces of personality that hold back or restrain one's impulsive behavior. As alcohol content in the body increases, a driver's inhibitions weaken. The person might drive too fast, take needless risks, and even drive into emergency situations without knowing or caring.

Seeing Abilities   Just as alcohol impairs a driver's judgment, reasoning, reaction time, and coordination, so does alcohol affect a driver's ability to see clearly. Night vision, peripheral vision, color vision, and depth perception all are impaired.

Pedestrian as seen by a driver at night.

Pedestrian as seen by a drunk driver at night.

Because alcohol distorts vision, it reduces the effective use of an orderly visual search pattern. A drinking driver's eyes are more likely to fixate in a stare, thus reducing the scanning and searching process. At the same time, both visual acuity and peripheral vision are reduced.

After one or two drinks, a person's eyes need more light to see dimly lit objects. At night, a driver who has not been drinking can see the pedestrian pictured here. The second picture shows how the pedestrian might appear to a drinking driver at night. The drinking driver might not see the pedestrian at all.

Alcohol also affects the reflex action of the eyes. At night, this impairment can be critical. As headlights of oncoming vehicles come closer, the pupils of the eyes normally become smaller to shut out the excess light. As the headlights pass, the pupils enlarge again to let in all available light. After a few drinks, this reflex action is impaired. The pupils do not become small in time as the bright lights approach and are slow to open after the bright lights pass. As a result, the driver can be temporarily blinded.

Seeing blurred or multiple images occurs after heavy drinking. The eyes normally pick up two separate images of an object. The brain quickly coordinates these images so that the person sees only one image. After several drinks, however, coordination of the images becomes impaired. The person might see several images such as two center lines on the roadway. An oncoming car might even appear to be on both sides of the roadway at the same time.

Alcohol also impairs depth perception. A drinking driver might perceive something as far away when it is actually very close. Accurate depth perception is needed to judge:
► distance and speed of oncoming vehicles.
► space from vehicles ahead.
► distance from signs and signals.

As a person continues to drink, the center of the brain might become impaired. This center, called the medulla, controls breathing and heartbeat. Death can occur if large amounts of alcohol, consumed in a very short time period, reach the medulla. Usually, a person becomes unconscious and stops drinking before this point.

Amount of Alcohol in Standard Drinks

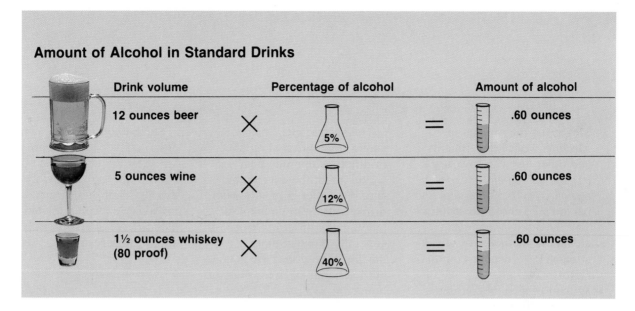

	Drink volume		Percentage of alcohol		Amount of alcohol
	12 ounces beer	×	5%	=	.60 ounces
	5 ounces wine	×	12%	=	.60 ounces
	1½ ounces whiskey (80 proof)	×	40%	=	.60 ounces

Managing the Effects of Alcohol

The same amount of alcohol does not affect all people the same way. Alcohol does not even affect one person the same way in every situation. Alcohol might affect a person more at one particular time than at other times. However, the effects of alcohol in any person begin with the first drink.

These factors determine the degree of impairment caused by alcohol:
► number of drinks a person consumes
► amount of alcohol in each drink
► amount of time over which a given amount was consumed
► amount and type of food in the stomach at the time of drinking
► person's weight
► person's physical and emotional condition
► person's age and drinking experience.

Controlling intake can reduce the effects of alcohol. This action is the first step toward controlling impairment and reducing the driving risk.

Amount of Alcohol in a Drink
People who drink and then drive can be a hazard not only to themselves but to other roadway users. Even a small amount of alcohol can increase the driving risk. Some people who are not familiar with alcohol research might doubt these statements. However, both experiments and experience have proven them true.

This chart shows standard serving sizes of three different drinks: a mug of beer, a glass of wine, and 1-1/2 ounces of liquor in a cocktail. Each amount is considered "one drink." Each drink contains approximately the same amount of alcohol.

The term "proof" describes the strength of liquor. Divide a liquor's proof number by two to determine the liquor's approximate percentage of alcohol. The chart shows that 80-proof whiskey is about 40 percent alcohol. A 100-proof liquor is about 50 percent alcohol.

The 12 ounces of beer and the 5 ounces of wine contain about the same amount of alcohol as the 1-1/2 ounces of liquor. Drinking 12 ounces of beer can impair a person's abilities as much as 5 ounces of wine or 1-1/2 ounces of liquor in a cocktail.

Some lower-calorie, "light" beers have a lower alcohol content than some regular beers. Some cocktails have a higher alcohol content than 1-1/2 ounces of liquor. This higher or lower alcohol content is due to other alcoholic and non-alcoholic beverages being combined with the basic liquor in mixed drinks.

Measuring the Amount of Alcohol Police departments and other agencies measure a person's *blood-alcohol concentration* (BAC) to determine the person's level of intoxication. The BAC tells the percent of alcohol in the person's bloodstream. BAC depends on three factors:
► amount of alcohol consumed
► period of time during which the alcohol was consumed
► the person's body weight.

The first chart below shows BAC standards. Each drink adds approximately .02 to .03 percent to the person's BAC. The average person needs only to consume about two drinks in an hour to reach .05 percent and become an unsafe driver. However, to base drinking and driving decisions *only* on a BAC chart is dangerously misleading.

The second chart below shows how different numbers of drinks within one hour would affect the average person. A smaller person, a new drinker, or a physically ill or emotionally upset individual is generally affected more quickly. The drinks are standard servings of beer, wine, or liquor.

Since only one drink can begin to affect the IPDE process, a responsible driver can choose not to drink before driving. Half of all teenagers involved in alcohol-related collisions have a BAC of only about .02 percent.

BAC Standards
(percent alcohol in bloodstream)

BAC	Condition
.01-.04%	Affected
.05-.09%	Impaired
.10%	Intoxicated

Effects of Alcohol on Behavior

This chart shows how different numbers of drinks in *one* hour's time would affect the average person. The drinks are standard servings of beer, wine, or liquor.

Number of drinks in one hour	BAC	Effects
1 serving 	.02 -.03%	Inhibitions are lessened. Judgment and reasoning begin to be affected.
3 servings 	.05 -.09%	Unable to think clearly. Judgment and reasoning are not reliable. Muscular coordination is impaired.
4 servings 	.10 -.12%	After four drinks, hearing, speech, vision, and balance are affected.
5 servings 	.13 -.15%	Most behaviors are affected. Body parts seem to "not work together." Walking without stumbling is difficult. Unmistakable intoxication.

Controlling Intake A person can avoid alcoholic beverages at a social gathering by choosing to drink soft drinks or other beverages rather than alcohol-based drinks. A person can also set down an unwanted drink and walk away from it.

For people who do decide to drink, responsible friends can take these actions to help them to control alcohol intake:
► Get them involved in activities other than drinking.
► Encourage them to decide on a limit of drinks in advance and stick to it.
► Ask them to avoid drinks with a high concentration of alcohol.
► Suggest that they leave part of a drink in the glass. An empty glass invites a refill.
► Encourage them to sip a drink very slowly.
► Suggest that they not drink more than one alcoholic beverage in an hour.
► Make them aware of their physical and emotional conditions.

Controlling Impairment
Alcohol is absorbed into the body very quickly, but it is very slow to leave. Alcohol continues to circulate throughout the body until it is oxidized and removed by the liver. A very small amount of alcohol is also removed by the kidneys, breath, and sweat glands.

How much time is needed after drinking to be fit to drive again? A person's system oxidizes, or burns, alcohol at the rate of approximately three-fourths of a standard drink in one hour. A person who has one drink needs about one hour and fifteen minutes to rid the body of the alcohol in that drink. After consuming three drinks in an hour, a person needs over four hours for the body to oxidize and eliminate most of the alcohol. A person should not drive during those time periods. *Only time can reduce the body's BAC and that person's degree of impairment.*

A person's BAC increases when intake and absorption rate of alcohol is greater than the body's ability to oxidize and eliminate the alcohol. This chart shows that BAC continued to increase even after the person stopped drinking. Note too, that alcohol remained in the body for about ten hours after the person stopped drinking. The person's BAC had reached .15 percent.

People who make the decision to drink can use this information to help to control alcohol impairment:
► Food eaten before and while drinking slows the body's alcohol absorption.
► Drinks should be spaced at least one hour apart.
► Loud talk or unsteady coordination are signs of alcohol impairment.

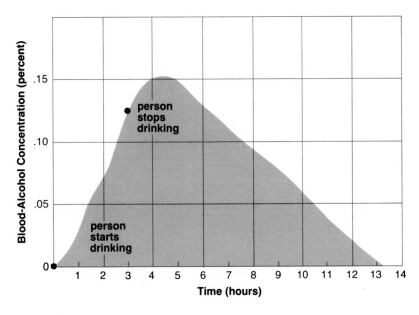

291

Myths About Alcohol

Many people do not realize that these ideas about alcohol are not true:

► **I can burn off alcohol by strenuous activity.** Only time can reduce the effects of alcohol. Even very strenuous activity is ineffective in reducing BAC because the sweat glands release only a small amount of alcohol.

► **I can sober up by drinking black coffee and taking a cold shower.** Even the stimulation of black coffee and a cold shower cannot reduce BAC. The person might seem more alert after coffee or a shower, but BAC is not reduced.

► **I will not be affected because I am only drinking beer.** A 12-ounce bottle or can of beer contains as much alcohol as an average cocktail.

► **Alcohol will not affect me because I have built up a tolerance to it.** By the time a person's BAC level reaches .10 percent, that person is intoxicated and cannot expect to be able to drive safely.

► **I can drive better after a few drinks.** This mistaken reasoning might occur after a person has been drinking, and judgment and reasoning are already affected.

Reducing Driving Risk The surest way to eliminate the risk of driving under the influence of alcohol is to not drink and drive. Some people think they can be responsible drinkers and still drive safely. However, they cannot be sure that their judgment and responses are totally unimpaired.

FRIENDS DON'T LET FRIENDS DRIVE DRUNK

Most people realize that driving after drinking is not a responsible act. However, some drivers take a calculated risk and drive after drinking. As a responsible driver, here are some ways you can help reduce the risk of drinking and driving:

► Refuse to ride with drivers who might be impaired.

► As this sign says, be a friend. Do not let your friends drive drunk.

► Support strong enforcement of DUI and DWI traffic laws.

Review It

1. Which abilities are first affected by alcohol?
2. What factors determine the degree of impairment caused by alcohol?
3. What is meant by blood-alcohol concentration?
4. What are five myths regarding alcohol?

15-2 Laws Governing Alcohol Use

Many states have raised their legal drinking ages to 21 in an effort to reduce alcohol-related fatalities. A major problem still exists when states border a state that has an under-21 drinking law. Young people who live near the border of the state with the lower drinking-age law might drive to that state and buy alcoholic beverages. These people then drive back to their home state, often very late at night, under the influence of alcohol. This practice of under-age drinking has greatly increased the injury and fatality rate of alcohol-related collisions.

Levels of Intoxication

Most states have set the level of intoxication at a BAC of .10 percent. A driver with this

BAC could be charged with *driving while intoxicated* (DWI). A DWI charge can be made, and the driver convicted, on the basis of BAC evidence.

In some states, a lesser charge, *driving under the influence* (DUI), can be made if the driver's BAC is between .05 and .09 percent. However, this charge cannot be made without other supporting evidence of reduced driving ability.

Tests for Intoxication

Law enforcement agencies place a high priority on enforcing DUI and DWI laws. They also place an increased emphasis on training officers to recognize impaired drivers. Several tests can be used to evaluate a person suspected of

DUI or DWI. Tests can be given in the police station, or on the roadside where the suspected offender has been stopped.

Chemical Testing Chemical analysis of blood, urine, or breath can accurately determine BAC. The breath test is a widely used and simple analysis. One type of breath test uses a machine called a breathalyzer. The person blows through a tube into the breathalyzer. The machine performs a chemical analysis of the breath to determine the person's BAC.

The *intoxilyzer* is a machine similar to the breathalyzer. First, the person breathes into the intoxilyzer's tube as instructed by the machine, as this person is doing. Then the intoxilyzer determines BAC by the amount of infrared light absorbed by the breath. Finally, the person's BAC is indicated on both the intoxilyzer's screen and on a paper printout.

Field Sobriety Testing Law-enforcement officers in many states can give a *field sobriety test* when they suspect a driver of DUI or DWI. A field sobriety test is a series of on-the-spot, roadside tests which helps an officer detect driver impairment.

The tests might include a variety of procedures. Some states might include only one or two tests, while other states include several tests. A variety of coordination tests and eye checks might be included in such a field sobriety test. In many states DWI convictions can be based on field sobriety test results.

One such test is the horizontal-gaze nystagmus test. The term *nystagmus* refers to the involuntary jerking of the eyes as the person gazes to the side. Most people show some nystagmus as their eyes track from straight ahead to the side. The horizontal-gaze nystagmus test determines the point where the jerking begins. As a person's BAC increases, the jerking begins at an earlier point. Trained officers measure where nystagmus begins.

Implied-Consent Law

All states have an *implied-consent law*. This law states that when a person receives a driver's license, he or she automatically gives consent to be tested for BAC if arrested on suspicion of DUI or DWI. Implied-consent laws help authorities control problems related to alcohol and driving. However, each driver's cooperation is also important.

If a driver is stopped, and then refuses to be tested for BAC, that driver's license can be suspended. The license can be suspended even if the driver is not convicted of DUI or DWI. When the driver agrees to be tested for BAC, test results are used to determine intoxication.

Penalties for Conviction
Penalties for DUI and DWI convictions vary from state to state. The most common penalty is suspension of the person's driver's license for a specified period of time. Other legal penalties include fines, imprisonment, or both. In many cases, fines are more severe if the person was driving while intoxicated, and then was involved in a collision. If a fatality resulted from a collision, the driver could be found guilty of manslaughter. A driver who has been convicted of DUI or DWI also pays a much higher premium for automobile insurance for many years after getting his or her license back.

Review It

1. What percent BAC is the level of intoxication in most states?
2. What is an implied-consent law?

15–3   Other Drugs and Driving

Different drugs affect people in a variety of ways. Two factors that determine the effect of a drug are the kind of drug and amount of the drug used. Regardless of the type of drug used, nearly all drugs affect a person's driving ability. Drug use can so affect a person's IPDE process that the person loses all ability to identify and predict clearly, and to decide and execute correctly.

Types of Drugs

Most drugs are classified according to the effect they have on the central nervous system and bodily functions. Some drugs depress or slow down the central nervous system; others stimulate or speed it up. Other drugs can alter a person's thinking process and personality.

When buying any medicine, check the labels for warnings of what effects the drug might have on driving performance, as these labels show. The labels of most medicines list their possible side effects. When a label says, "Might cause drowsiness or dizziness," do not use the drug before driving. Some labels might even say, "Do not drive after using." As a responsible driver, do not ignore such cautions.

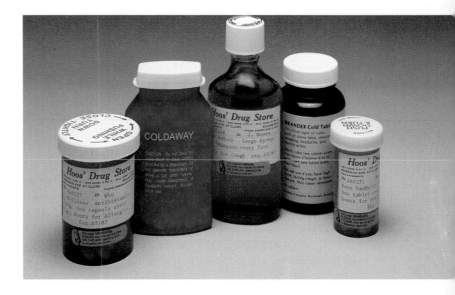

Over-the-Counter Drugs

Drugs that can be legally obtained without a doctor's prescription can affect a person's driving abilities. Such a drug, called an *over-the-counter drug* (OTC drug), is widely advertised and displayed.

Many OTC depressant drugs provide relief from colds, hay fever, allergies, and headaches. Side effects from OTC drops, sprays, syrups, and pills can include drowsiness, dizziness, slowed reaction time, and poor judgment. OTC drugs can increase driving risks and reduce a person's ability to drive safely. These drugs are all the more harmful because their effects on driving are often unexpected.

Prescription Drugs

A drug that can be purchased legally only when ordered by a doctor is a *prescription drug*. Most prescription drugs are stronger than OTC drugs. Many prescription drugs have very strong effects on the way a person feels and acts. Whenever you must take a prescription drug, ask your doctor how that medicine might affect your driving ability.

Depressants	Stimulants	Hallucinogens
alcohol barbiturates codeine heroin methadone morphine sleeping pills tranquilizers	amphetamines cocaine	marijuana LSD PCP

Depressants A *depressant* is a drug that can slow down or depress the central nervous system. Some people use depressants to relieve tension, reduce anxiety, treat high blood pressure, and calm nerves. This chart lists several examples of depressants.

A depressant slows down both mental and physical processes. A depressant's effect is similar to the effect of alcohol, also a depressant. Reflex actions are slowed and coordination becomes clumsy. A driver can become very relaxed, lose inhibitions, and have difficulty identifying, predicting, and deciding accurately.

Stimulants A *stimulant* is a drug that can speed up a person's central nervous system. The chart lists two examples of stimulants.

At first, a stimulant can give a feeling of energy and alertness and can even prevent sleep. However, this effect does not last long, and the person can become nervous and irritable. A driver using a stimulant can develop a false sense of alertness and self-confidence, thus increasing driving-related risks.

Hallucinogens A *hallucinogen* is a drug that alters a person's thinking, distorts vision, perception, and other senses. The chart lists three examples of hallucinogens.

Marijuana enters the bloodstream quickly and affects the brain and central nervous system. A marijuana user might become easily distracted. Abilities to judge distance, time, and space are reduced; coordination is impaired. How long the impairment from marijuana lasts is a critical issue. Unlike alcohol, which the body can eliminate over a period of hours, the chemicals in marijuana can remain in the body for several weeks. A marijuana user might feel that the effects have worn off and safe driving is possible after a few hours. In reality, driving abilities remain impaired for some time.

LSD and PCP are strong hallucinogens. They cause a user to be confused and unable to concentrate or think clearly. Use of any type of hallucinogen drug can distort a person's sense of direction, distance, and time.

Combining Alcohol with Other Drugs

Using alcohol and other drugs at the same time can be especially dangerous. When some drugs are combined with alcohol, the effects of both drugs are multiplied, rather than just added together. The effect is as if one plus one equals three or more, instead of just two. Alcohol usually makes the effect of the other drug even more powerful.

Consider a driver who is taking aspirin or an antihistamine for a cold. If that driver also uses alcohol, the combined effects on that driver's IPDE process and total driving ability usually are greater than the separate effects of the individual drugs.

While many alcohol-drug combinations increase driving risk, some combinations can be fatal. For example, drinking alcohol while under the effects of tranquilizers or barbiturates severely depresses the central nervous system and can lead to death.

Review It
1. What three different ways can a drug affect a person?
2. What happens when alcohol is combined with other drugs?

15-4 Alcohol, Other Drugs, and Peer Pressure

While many people choose not to drink, they must deal with the fact that our society is a drinking society. Availability and pressures regarding the use of alcohol and other drugs are probably greater than ever before, especially for young people. Influences and pressures directed at young people are often very difficult to cope with or resist.

Peer Pressure and Drinking

The influence of others of a similar age on a person is called *peer pressure*. These feelings and pressures can be very forceful influences on a person's actions.

In most cases, peer pressure is a positive influence on young people as they begin to make critical decisions about their lives. Peer pressure produces positive results when students are encouraged to join such school activities as sports, theater, academic clubs, or service groups.

Needing to belong is a natural feeling for most people. However, some people worry a great deal about what others think of them. This excessive need to belong can result in a person doing things against his or her beliefs just to be accepted by the group. This behavior is a negative result of peer pressure.

Wanting to identify with or belong to a group is not wrong. It is more mature and important, however, to be guided by your own beliefs and values than to give them up for group approval. This is especially true about giving in to peer pressure to use alcohol or other drugs when one will be driving.

Peer-Group Counseling Many schools have organized student programs for *peer-group counseling*. This type of counseling uses peer leadership to help others make decisions and determine goals. These high-school students are involved in peer-group counseling. Students are trained as peer-group leaders. They learn specific skills for helping others deal effectively with problems or concerns. Counseling sessions are usually informal discussions or "rap sessions."

Even with help from others, some people still have trouble following their own beliefs about drinking and driving when pressured by friends. A person might face peer pressure to be "one of the group" and drink before driving. A person needs strength of character and a strong image of self-worth to withstand pressures from friends and others.

Other Influences   Teenagers today probably face greater pressures involving the use of alcohol and other drugs than ever before. However, family viewpoints and religious beliefs continue to be strong influences when young people are confronted with pressures and decisions regarding alcohol and other drugs. Organizations that fight the problem of alcohol and driving include Mothers Against Drunk Drivers (MADD), Alliance Against Intoxicated Motorists (AAIM), and Students Against Driving Drunk (SADD).

Deciding About Drinking

Almost every person is in a situation at some time where alcohol is available. Each person must make his or her own decision whether or not to drink. The best decision a person can make is not to drink, especially if the person will drive later.

Individuals who decide not to drink alcoholic beverages never need to worry about alcohol impairing their driving performance. However, nondrinkers must share general concern about those people who do drink and then drive.

Consider that:
► An average of one of every fifty drivers on the roadway is DUI or DWI. During weekend nights, the average climbs even higher, to about one in ten.
► The number of DUI and DWI drivers on roadways in some communities goes even higher during pre-dawn hours, to about one in four.
► After midnight, over 90 percent of all one-car collisions involve a drinking driver.

Responsibility to Others When people find themselves in situations where alcoholic drinks are served, their first responsibility is for their own actions. However, a person's responsibility increases when the situation involves drinking and driving.

The host of any party has the responsibility of providing a variety of food, soft drinks, and activities, as seen on page 298. If anyone at the party is drinking, the host must remember that alcohol first affects judgment and reasoning abilities. People who are drinking might not have the ability to judge the effects the alcohol is having on themselves. Most people who have had too much to drink do not recognize it, and rarely admit it.

To what extent should a person take responsibility for the actions of others? Some people feel that doing so is interfering in other people's lives. However, most people wisely realize that they are being caring friends when they prevent friends from driving after drinking. All drivers must understand what a hazard a drinking driver can be to other roadway users.

Everyone should accept the responsibility of trying to keep a drinker from driving. The drinker has the prime responsibility of not driving after drinking. Anyone who serves alcoholic beverages carries the next greater responsibility. Concern must be not only for the drinking driver, but also for others who might be injured or killed as a result of the actions of the drinking driver.

You must be able to recognize signs of too much drinking in order to share the responsibility for friends who drink. Since alcohol affects different people in different ways, no set pattern can determine a

person's impairment. Look for these signs of impairment:
► walking unsteadily or stumbling
► slurred unclear speech
► talking louder than usual
► inability to gain eye contact with others
► losing track of time or day of week
► any behavior that is the opposite of normal behavior for that person.

Remember that only one drink can cause a person's BAC to reach .03 percent. Driving abilities can be impaired even at that BAC. Collision risk increases greatly as drinking increases. By the time BAC reaches .06 percent, just over the level for impaired driving, the chances of a collision have doubled. At .10 percent BAC, the level of intoxication in most states, collision risk has increased six times.

A responsible person does not let friends drive drunk, as this sign indicates. Keeping a drinking person from driving is the responsibility of everyone.

What You and Others Can Do

A nondrinker has decisions to make about keeping drinking friends from driving. Sometimes the best action is to call a taxi to take a friend home, as these people have done.

A nondrinker might also have to decide whether or not to ride with a drinking driver. Try to persuade the drinker to let you drive. If you cannot prevent a drinker from driving, refuse to ride with him or her. Try to find other transportation to get home safely. Stay where you are if necessary.

The effects of alcohol are harmful, if not deadly, especially when operating a motor vehicle. Heavy drinkers are the major cause of alcohol-related collisions that result in death or injury. However, social drinkers share the responsibility for alcohol-related collisions. Responsible drivers should decide not to become a part of the drinking-driving problem, but contribute to its solution. The drinking driver is 6 to 25 times more likely to be involved in a collision than a non-drinker.

Review It

1. How might peer pressure affect a young person's decision about drinking?
2. What decision might a nondrinker need to make about a friend who has been drinking?

Safe Driving Tips

Be alert for intoxicated drivers, and increase your space cushion as needed. Intoxicated drivers often exhibit these characteristics of poor driving ability:

▶ *Drivers might travel too fast or too slow. They might have difficulty maintaining a steady speed. They might make quick or abrupt starts and stops.*
▶ *Drivers might have difficulty making turns. They might run over a curb or turn into the wrong lane.*
▶ *Drivers might have trouble steering. They might weave from side to side, straddle lane lines, or cross the center line.*
▶ *Drivers might not obey traffic signs and signals. They might overshoot or run STOP signs.*
▶ *Drivers might not signal, or give the wrong signal.*

Chapter Summary

1. Alcohol affects judgment and reasoning first. Inhibitions weaken and muscular reaction slows. Coordination becomes clumsy, and seeing abilities are impaired. (15–1)
2. The effects of alcohol are influenced by intake, amount of alcohol in one drink, amount of food in the stomach, amount of time drinking, body weight, and physical condition. (15–1)
3. Blood-alcohol concentration (BAC) is the percent of alcohol in a person's bloodstream. (15–1)
4. Myths about alcohol use include: strenuous activity burns alcohol, black coffee and a cold shower sober a person, a person cannot get drunk on beer, a drinker can build up tolerance, and drinking helps a person drive better. (15–1)
5. The level for DWI is .10 percent BAC in most states. Authorities use chemical testing and field-sobriety testing to measure BAC. (15–2)
6. Implied-consent laws mean that when a person gets a license, he or she automatically agrees to be tested for BAC if arrested on suspicion of DUI or DWI. (15–2)
7. Depressants slow down mental and physical processes. Stimulants cause drivers to develop a false sense of alertness and confidence and to increase risk-taking. Hallucinogens distort vision and perception and reduce abilities to judge distance, time, and space. (15–3)
8. Combining alcohol with other drugs multiplies the effects of both, rather than just combining the effects of each. (15–3)
9. Peer pressure might affect decisions about drinking and driving because of the need to belong to a group. (15–4)
10. Everyone should share the responsibility of preventing friends from driving after drinking because an alcohol-affected driver is a hazard to every roadway user. (15–4)

Think About It
Explain the meaning of this statement: "The depressive action of alcohol is progressive."

Decision Making

1. Several passengers are trying to prevent a friend from driving after drinking. If the friend does insist upon driving, what choices do the passengers have to protect their own safety?

2. This driver has been stopped by the police for suspicion of driving while intoxicated. What types of tests might the officer request the driver to take? What can these tests detect and measure?

3. These two people have just left a party where each drank several cans of beer. The driver plans to pass the car ahead. What effects might the beer have on the driver's ability to pass safely?

4. The person above has just received a driver's license for the first time. What has this new driver automatically consented to do by receiving this license?

Chapter 15 Test

Multiple Choice Copy the number of each sentence below on a sheet of paper. Choose the letter that best completes each statement or answers each question.

1. Forces that restrain inpulsive behavior are
   (a) psychological impairment.   (b) inhibitions.
   (c) reflexes.   (d) visual acuity.   (287)
2. The amount of alcohol in 12 ounces of beer compared to 1-1/2 ounces of liquor is
   (a) about the same.   (b) much less.   (c) much more.   (d) somewhat more.   (289)
3. How long does the human body take to rid itself of the alcohol in one drink?
   (a) about 24 hours   (b) about 1 hour and 15 minutes   (c) 3 hours   (d) 45 minutes   (291)
4. Which drug can you purchase legally without a prescription?
   (a) over-the-counter drug (OTC drug)
   (b) morphine   (c) LSD   (d) PCP   (295)
5. What drug can be legally obtained only with a doctor's prescription?
   (a) aspirin   (b) antihistamine   (c) cough syrup
   (d) prescription drug   (295)

Completion Copy the number of each sentence below. After each number write the letter of the word or words that complete the sentence correctly.

6. The area of the brain first affected by alcohol is the area that controls ____.   (287)
7. The percent of alcohol in a person's bloodstream is that person's ____.   (290)
8. The level for intoxication in most states is ____.   (293)
9. With supporting evidence, a driver in some states can be convicted of ____ with a BAC of .05 percent.   (293)
10. The term ____ refers to the involuntary jerking of the eyes.   (294)

    a. blood-alcohol concentration (BAC)
    b. driving under the influence (DUI)
    c. judgment and reason
    d. nystagmus
    e. .10 percent
    f. .15 percent

Vocabulary Copy the number of each phrase below. Match the definition in List A with the term it defines in List B.

List A

11. percent of alcohol in the bloodstream   (290)
12. in most states, driving with a BAC of .10 percent or higher   (293)
13. computerized machine that analyzes and determines BAC in breath   (293)
14. permission to be tested for BAC if arrested for suspicion of DUI   (294)
15. roadside tests given by police officers to detect driver impairment   (294)
16. drug that slows down the central nervous system   (296)
17. drug that speeds up the central nervous system   (296)
18. drug that distorts visual perception and other senses   (296)
19. influence of friends or social group to do things only for the sake of group acceptance   (297)
20. peer leadership to help others make decisions and determine goals   (297)

List B

    a. blood-alcohol concentration (BAC)
    b. depressant
    c. driving while intoxicated (DWI)
    d. field sobriety test
    e. hallucinogen
    f. implied-consent law
    g. intoxilyzer
    h. peer-group counseling
    i. peer pressure
    j. soft drink
    k. stimulant

Chapter 16
Buying and Insuring a Car

You're the Driver!

Many young people dream of having a car of their own. With so many types of cars available, as seen here, how can you choose one to meet your needs? Should you buy a car with an automatic or a manual transmission?

How will you pay for a car?

How much will it cost to own and maintain a car for a year?

From whom should you buy a car?

How can you get accurate information about which cars deliver the best mileage in both city and highway driving?

What is a fair price to pay for a car?

What amount of insurance coverage is necessary, and how much will it cost?

This chapter discusses questions that can help you determine whether you can afford to own a car. The chapter also discusses another important aspect of car ownership—your responsibilities if you are involved in a collision.

Objectives

16–1 Buying a Car

1. Describe the responsibilities of owning a car. (306)
2. List the costs of owning and driving a car. (306)
3. Explain how to choose a used car. (308)
4. Describe the steps to take when buying a used car. (309)

16–2 Insuring a Car

5. Explain how car insurance works. (312)
6. Explain what is covered by each type of insurance: liability, collision, comprehensive, medical, uninsured motorist, towing, and no-fault. (312)
7. List factors that affect the cost of car insurance. (312)

16–3 If You Have a Collision

8. List the immediate steps to take if you are involved in a collision. (315)
9. List follow-up steps to take after a collision. (316)

16-1 Buying a Car

Owning a car offers you freedom to come and go on your own. Owning a car also means responsibility for the car's purchase, maintenance, insurance, and fuel expenses.

Do You Need a Car?

Are your present needs for transportation great enough that you should own a car now? Are there alternatives to buying a car? Answers to these questions can help you decide if your reasons for buying a car justify the expenses of owning a car.

If you are a student, you might have to work many hours to earn the money for a car. Working reduces the time available for study, sports, and social activities. A student who works to support a car often earns lower grades. Therefore, you might decide not to buy a car at this time.

Cost of Owning a Car

The actual total cost of owning and driving a car might be more than you expect. Even when careful records are kept, the total annual cost might be hard to identify. Some of the major expenses include:

▶ **Purchase Price** The price of a car is the amount of money the owner wants for the car. Read newspaper ads to see what different types of cars can cost.

▶ **Depreciation** No matter how much or how little you use a car, its value drops steadily. This decrease in value is called *depreciation*. In most cases, the newer the car, the more it depreciates.

▶ **Other Costs** Operating costs include fuel, oil, tune ups, battery, tires, and repairs. Parking and toll fees add to the cost of owning a car. Finally, the cost of insurance, license and registration fees, and interest on your car loan must be considered. However, saving to buy a car eliminates the cost of interest on a car loan.

Many of these expenses increase annually. Yearly cost depends on how many miles you drive, where you drive, and your fuel-mileage rate. It could cost you $2,500 to $3,000 to drive a $2,000 used car 10,000 miles annually. These

costs are estimates; your annual cost could be lower or higher.

What Kind of Car to Buy

If you decide you need and can afford a car, what kind should you buy? Think about your answers to these questions when deciding what kind of car to buy:

► What will the car be used for?
► Is the car intended for just one or two passengers and some packages, towing a trailer, or for additional purposes?
► How many miles will you drive each year?
► Will the car be used for long trips or mainly for short trips?

Car Size The size of the car, such as these four cars, is an important factor in your decision to buy a car. Consider these factors:

► A smaller car often gets better mileage than a larger car. However, most smaller cars offer less protection in a collision than larger cars.
► A smaller car might not ride as comfortably as a larger car.
► A larger car can carry more passengers and packages than a smaller car.

Engine Size and Type A small engine in a compact car is usually economical. However, if you choose air conditioning, power brakes, and power

steering, the small engine might not be the best choice. A larger engine uses more fuel than a small engine.

A diesel engine delivers higher fuel mileage than a gasoline engine. However, the initial cost of a diesel engine is more than a gasoline engine. The resale value of a car with a diesel engine is often lower than that of a car with a gasoline engine.

Transmission An automatic transmission is nearly as fuel efficient as a manual transmission. However, the cost of repairing an automatic transmission might be higher.

Cars that Save Fuel Many smaller cars are called "economy" cars and can be more fuel efficient. One car might deliver 20 miles per gallon (mpg); another lighter-weight car might give as much as 45 mpg. If you drove 10,000 miles in a year, the first car would consume 500 gallons of fuel, while the other car would burn 222 gallons of fuel. At $1.00 to $1.50 per gallon, the car that used the extra 278 gallons of fuel would cost $278 to $417 more to drive per year.

MONTHLY PAYMENT (3 years)				
Amount Borrowed	Interest Rate Charged			
	10%	12%	14%	16%
$2000	$64.54	$66.47	$68.40	$70.32
$3000	$96.80	$99.64	$102.50	$105.47
$4000	$129.07	$132.86	$136.71	$140.63

Amount Borrowed	Total Amount Paid (loan amount plus interest on loan)			
$2000	$2323.44	$2392.92	$2462.40	$2531.52
$3000	$3484.80	$3587.04	$3690.00	$3796.92
$4000	$4646.52	$4782.96	$4921.56	$5062.68

Buying a Used Car

If a new car costs too much, you might consider buying a used car. Used cars are available from private owners and car dealers.

Buying from a private owner can cost less. You can talk to the owner and try to learn about the history of the car. A private owner seldom will repair the car or provide a *warranty*. A warranty is a written guarantee that the seller will repair the car for a stated period of time. A private sale is final in nearly all cases.

Used-car dealers usually have a variety of cars available. However, many used-car dealers do not have repair facilities. They might not provide a full warranty.

New-car dealers usually have the best selection of good used cars from those traded in for new cars. The new-car dealer's price might be somewhat higher than other sources, but a warranty is usually included.

In most states, a car dealer must post a warranty statement in the window of each car. The warranty must specify what parts are guaranteed and for how long the parts are guaranteed.

How Much Should You Pay?

The *blue book* lists the average price paid to dealers for various used cars. The price actually paid depends on the condition of the car. A dealer might charge more than the blue-book price if a car is in excellent condition, less for one that is in poor condition or has high mileage.

Additional Car Expenses Car ownership involves unexpected expenses. Regardless of the initial cost of a used car, be prepared to set aside at least $400 for repairs during the first year of ownership. Remember to budget the costs of insurance, licensing, and interest on the loan if you borrow the money to buy a car. Note in this chart that interest on a loan can significantly increase the cost of buying a car.

Choosing a Used Car

Selecting a used car takes time. When you find a car you like, check further to see if it is in good condition as these people are doing. Do not buy on impulse or be pressured into buying a car.

A car's outward appearance can differ from its operating condition. Be suspicious of a late-model car that is priced very low. The car might have been in a major collision. It might have been a police car or a taxi, with high mileage and hard use. Turning back a car's odometer is illegal, but it might still occur. If possible, try to talk with the previous owner to verify the odometer reading and condition of the car. Some states require car dealers to provide a mileage disclosure statement, certifying that the car's odometer reading is accurate.

Make these checks when considering a used car:

Outside and Inside Checks

► The doors should not sag. All doors should open and close from inside and outside. Locks should operate on all doors.
► Paint color should be uniform on all parts of the car.
► There should be little or no rust around fenders, under chrome trim, or around the headlights.

► The car should not lean to one side.
► A spare tire and a working jack should be in the trunk. Check for rear-end collision damage in the trunk.
► Open the hood. Check for collision damage on the inner fenders and frame.
► Check for oil spots under the car, and leaks from the engine or transmission.
► The front seat should feel firm when you sit on it. Worn upholstery might indicate high mileage or hard use.
► Check all pedals. Very worn, or very new pedals might indicate high mileage.
► Turn the steering wheel. With unassisted steering there should not be more than 2 inches of "play," steering wheel movement that does not move the front wheels. With power steering, there should be no play when the engine is running.
► Check that accessories work. Accessories include heater and defroster, lights, windshield wipers and washers, radio, and turn signals. If power seats, cruise control, power windows, or air conditioning are included, check that they work.
► Firmly press the brake pedal. There should be no loss of firmness as you continue to press the pedal.

Checks Under the Hood

► Check the radiator and fan for signs of collision damage. Check for leaks around hoses and the radiator.
► Check condition of fan belts as seen in this picture.
► Remove radiator cap. The radiator should be filled with coolant. There should be no oil on the bottom of the radiator cap.
► The battery and its cables should be free of corrosion. Battery should have no cracks.

► Start the engine. Listen for any unusual noises. Check for water and oil leaks while the engine is running.

Test Drive the Car   If the owner refuses to let you test drive the car or demands a deposit, forget the deal. Look for another car.

Make these checks during your test drive:
► Turn on the ignition switch. Check to see that all warning lights and signals work.

► Start the engine. It should start easily each time you turn the key. Warning lights should go out in a few seconds.
► Drive at low speed and test the brakes several times. The car should stop smoothly and straight.
► Turn some corners. The car should steer easily without play in the steering wheel.
► Accelerate moderately. The car should accelerate smoothly and without hesitation from 0 to 40 mph.
► Test the brakes at various speeds. Brakes should not pull to one side or grab in a stop-and-go fashion.
► Drive at 25 mph on a rough roadway. The car should not rattle or feel very unstable.
► Note any indications of low oil pressure, overheating, or other warnings from lights or gauges.

Check by Mechanic   If the car passes your tests, have a mechanic of your choice make a final check. A car clinic will check the car thoroughly for a moderate fee.

Repairs to Consider When Buying a Used Car

You will need to fix defects if the seller will not repair the car. Consider these costs as you determine the actual purchase price:

Least Expensive Repairs

► Air filter is dirty.
► Battery cables are corroded; low battery-fluid level.
► Body has chipped paint and small rust spots.
► Fan belts are frayed or worn.
► Hoses are cracked or soft.
► Oil and oil filter are dirty.
► Thermostat is faulty.
► Transmission fluid is low.
► Windshield wiper blades are hard or worn.

Moderately Expensive Repairs

► Acceleration is uneven; car hesitates.
► Automatic transmission fluid is dark-colored or smells burnt.
► Car body is damaged.
► Car leans to one side due to broken spring.
► Doors, hood, or trunk do not open and close smoothly.
► Engine starts hard or idles roughly.
► Shock absorbers need replacing.

► Brakes or wheel bearings need repair or replacement.
► Hood, trunk, or doors do not fit properly.
► Ignition wires need replacing.
► Jack and spare tire missing.
► Paint is faded or worn through; large rust spots.
► Radiator is clogged, needs cleaning, or replacement. Radiator leaks.
► Tires need replacing.
► Upholstery needs cleaning or repair.
► Windows are broken or do not operate smoothly.

Too Expensive to Consider Buying

► Transmission does not shift smoothly; jerking motion when shifting.
► Automatic transmission slips when accelerating.
► Brakes grab or pull to one side.
► Clutch slips or chatters.
► Engine smokes when accelerating or braking.
► Frame needs repair.
► Gears make noise when accelerating, slowing, or turning.
► Heater or air conditioner does not operate properly.
► Large oil leaks.
► Radiator contains oily water.
► Seats sag.

Before You Close the Deal

Pay for the car in full (cash deal), if possible. If you must borrow money, carefully shop for a car loan. Talk to various *lending agencies,* such as banks, credit unions, and savings and loan associations. If you are buying a car from a dealer, the dealer might offer a loan. However, the interest rate might be higher than at a lending agency. Bargain for a lower purchase price if the dealer finances the loan.

Never close the deal if something needs repair, unless you get a written agreement that the repair will be done. Have the repair work written into the sales contract.

Review It

1. What are some responsibilities of car ownership for a student?
2. What major expenses must you consider if you buy a car?
3. What should you consider when deciding the kind of car to buy?
4. What steps should you take when buying a used car?

The largest expense in owning a car can be paying for damages due to a collision. Each state has a *financial responsibility law*. This law requires you to prove that you can pay for damages you cause that result in death, injury, or property damage. In some states, you can prove your ability to pay for damages by depositing cash or posting a bond.

Most individuals choose to protect themselves by purchasing insurance. Some states have mandatory insurance laws that require every licensed driver to be insured. These states do not allow drivers to post a bond or deposit cash.

What Is Car Insurance?

You buy insurance by paying a *premium*, a specified amount, to an insurance company. A *policy* is an agreement or contract between you (the policyholder) and your insurance company. Some typical policies are shown here. If you are involved in a collision, you pay a *deductible*, a set amount of damage costs as stated in your policy. Your insurance company agrees to pay (up to specified limits) the balance of the costs of injuries to persons and damage to property.

Kinds of Coverage

The most important type of coverage is *liability insurance*. One type of liability insurance, bodily-injury coverage, protects the driver at fault against claims providing for another person's health. A second type of liability insurance, property-damage coverage, protects the driver at fault against claims for replacing a person's property. The chart shows other types of insurance which protect you and your passengers from other expenses.

No-Fault Insurance

A claim can take years to settle when blame for a collision must be determined. In some states, insurance companies have *no-fault insurance*, a type of insurance that does not raise the question of fault. No-fault insurance eliminates much of the need for legal suits. Minor claims can be settled more easily under no-fault insurance.

In most cases, the insurance company of the driver at fault in a collision pays for injuries and property damage to others. Under no-fault insurance, the insurance company provides its policyholder medical coverage (up to specified limits), regardless of who is at fault.

Establishing Insurance Rates

Premium rates are determined by the amount paid out in claims. Each state regulates rates to assure fair costs for insurance coverage.

How Rates Are Determined

The premium you pay for insurance coverage depends on such factors as:

▶ **Collision and Violation Record** A driver with recent convictions for moving violations tends to have more collisions.

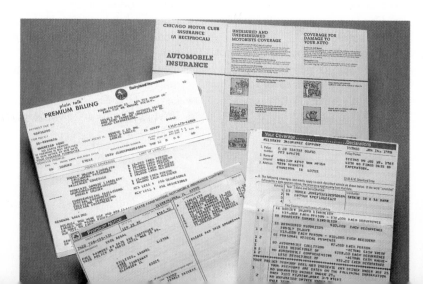

Car Insurance

Kind of Insurance	Coverage	Claim Includes	Minimum Amount	Notes
Bodily-injury liability	Pays claim against owner if someone is killed or injured and owner is at fault.	Hospital and doctor bills Legal fees Court costs Loss of wages	States normally specify minimum: $10,000-$15,000 for one person; $20,000-$30,000 for several persons.	Required in many states. Needed by all car owners. Minimum coverage required is generally too low.
Property-damage liability	Pays claim against owner if property of others is damaged and owner is at fault.	Other car and possessions in car. Damage to house, telephone pole, and traffic light.	States normally specify minimum: $5,000-$10,000.	Required in many states. Needed by all car owners.
Uninsured-motorist*	Pays for injuries to you and your passengers in case of hit-and-run collision or uninsured motorist.	Hospital and doctor bills Legal fees Court costs Loss of wages (Does *not* cover property damage.)	Usually same as bodily-injury liability.	Required in many states. Needed by all car owners.
Collision (usually requires comprehensive coverage along with collision.)	Pays cost of repairing or replacing owner's car when owner is at fault or when owner cannot collect from person at fault.	Repair or replacement of any car driven by owner or with owner's permission.	Insures for depreciated value of car. Owner decides on $100 to $500 deductible to reduce cost of premium.	Important for new or expensive car. Drop after 7-10 years of ownership or when value of car no longer justifies cost of coverage.
Comprehensive	Pays cost of repairing or replacing owner's car.	Fire Earthquake Theft Storm Flood Riots Wind Vandalism	Insures for depreciated value of car, usually with $100 to $500 deductible to reduce cost of premium.	Important for new or expensive car. Drop after 7 to 10 years of ownership.
Medical-payments	Pays medical costs for you and your passengers injured in any collision, regardless of fault.	Pays all immediate medical costs (generally in addition to other medical insurance).	Insures for $500 to $5,000 per person.	This insurance does not require a legal process to determine fault, while bodily-injury coverage usually does.
Towing	Pays cost of towing or minor repair to disabled car.	Dead battery Out of gas Flat tire Accident (regardless of cause or fault).	Usually pays amount validated by towing company.	Good to have. Not needed if owner belongs to automobile club with towing service.

*Note that uninsured-motorist insurance covers collision-related injuries *only*, not property damage. Some states now allow insurance companies to offer uninsured-motorist property damage insurance.

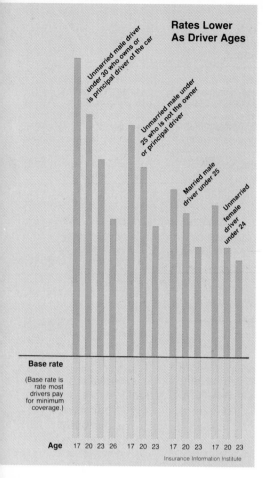

Rates Lower As Driver Ages

Unmarried male driver under 30 who owns or is principal driver of the car

Unmarried male under 25 who is not the owner or principal driver

Married male driver under 25

Unmarried female driver under 24

Base rate

(Base rate is rate most drivers pay for minimum coverage.)

Age   17 20 23 26   17 20 23   17 20 23   17 20 23

Insurance Information Institute

► **Age of Principal Driver** The principal driver is the person who drives the car the most. A principal driver under the age of 25 pays higher premiums.

Insurance records show that young drivers have more collisions, in proportion to their numbers, than older drivers. Drivers age 16 to 24 represent about 22 percent of all licensed drivers. However, these same drivers are involved in 36 percent of all injury-causing and fatal collisions. For the number of miles driven, young drivers have nearly twice as many fatal collisions as drivers over

25. Since young drivers average only half as many annual miles as older drivers, the actual collision rate for all types of collisions for young drivers is four times greater.

► **Miles Driven** The greater the mileage, the more the car is exposed to the possibility of a collision.

► **Sex of Driver** This chart shows that young male drivers pay higher premiums because they drive more, have more collisions, and their collisions tend to be more severe than collisions involving older drivers.

► **Marital Status** A driver who is married tends to have fewer collisions than an unmarried driver.

► **Where the Driver Lives** Premiums are generally higher in cities than in rural areas.

► **Type of Car** Premiums on expensive cars are higher because repair costs are higher.

► **Driver's Claim Record** Higher and more frequent claims, especially for collision and comprehensive coverage, result in higher premiums.

Reduced Premiums for Special Groups Some insurance companies reduce premiums for a driver who:

► has had no claims or moving violations for three years.

► has more than one car insured by the same company.

► has successfully completed a driver-education course.

► is a student and maintains a "B" grade average.

Assigned-Risk Insurance
An insurance company might cancel the policy of a driver who has a serious collision or several traffic violations. Revocation or suspension of the driver's license can also result in policy cancellation.

A driver whose insurance has been canceled might not be able to obtain coverage at standard rates from another company. A high-risk driver might have to obtain *assigned-risk insurance*. This type of insurance provides minimum bodily-injury and property-damage liability coverage to a high-risk driver for a higher premium. After a specified number of years of collision- and violation-free driving, the driver can apply for standard insurance coverage at regular rates.

Review It
1. What is the purpose of car insurance?
2. What are the different types of car insurance?
3. What factors determine car insurance premiums?

16-3 If You Have a Collision

You might never be in a collision such as the one pictured here. However, you must be prepared to follow certain procedures should you collide with another vehicle, a pedestrian, or someone else's property.

Your First Steps

Each state has specific procedures that you must follow immediately when involved in a collision. All states require you to:

1. **Stop Immediately** If you are in a collision, you must stop immediately. Failure to stop is a serious offense. If possible, move your car to the side of the roadway, out of traffic. Never leave your car where it can block traffic unless your car is so damaged it cannot be moved under its own power. If you damage a parked vehicle even slightly, try to find the owner. If you cannot, write your name, address, and phone number on a note to the driver. Leave the note under a windshield wiper or attach it to the car so the driver will see it. Notify police even if the damage is slight.
2. **Aid the Injured** Send for paramedics if anyone is seriously injured. *Do not move an injured person unless there is danger of fire or another collision.*

Administer basic first aid for injuries such as severe bleeding, shock, and stoppage of breathing *if you have completed a certified first-aid course.* Use a first-aid kit or manual if one is available.

3. **Prevent Further Damage** Turn off the ignitions of the damaged vehicles to reduce the risk of fire. Warn oncoming traffic with flares or reflectors placed at least 100 feet ahead of and behind the collision site (500 feet away in high-speed traffic). If you do not have such devices, ask someone to stand at the side of the roadway and wave a flashlight or light-colored cloth to warn other drivers.

4. **Send for Police** You must call the police if anyone is injured or killed. Some states require you to call the police for any collision, regardless of injuries.
5. **Exchange Information** Get the following information from others involved in the collision: names, addresses, driver's license numbers, license plate numbers, and insurance company names and addresses.

Note the names and addresses of passengers, of the positions in which they were sitting, and of the extent of their injuries. Getting this information, and giving information about you and your passengers, is your responsibility.

Additional Steps

Take these additional steps following a collision:

▶ **Record Witnesses' Names and Addresses** Note the names and address of any witnesses to the collision. Make a sketch of the collision scene. Record such important facts as time, date, location, weather, and driving conditions as these drivers are doing. Note the name of the hospital where injured persons were taken. Note the name and badge number of the police officer at the collision scene.

▶ **Give Police the Facts** Give the police honest and accurate facts. Do not argue with the other driver or the police over who was to blame. Stay at the scene until all information has been noted. Take your car to a garage for repairs. Keep all towing and repair bills for future reference.

▶ **See a Doctor** Have a doctor examine you if you were shaken up or injured, even if you do not notice any special ill effects of the collision. An injury that appears minor can develop serious complications.

▶ **File Necessary Reports** Each state requires drivers involved in a collision to file a written report if someone was killed or injured, or if the property damage exceeds a set amount. Some states require a report to be filed within 24 hours of the collision; other states allow more time. The report usually is sent to the state's department of motor vehicles or licensing.

In addition, you must show proof of financial responsibility through current insurance coverage or a bond. Finally, notify your insurance agent promptly. Failure to notify your insurance company within the time specified in your policy can invalidate your claim.

Review It

1. What steps should you take immediately if you are involved in a collision?
2. What additional steps should you take following a collision?

Be a Fuel Saver

► Keep your car free of unneeded packages, books, and debris. Added together, these items can weigh as much as a passenger. Any additional weight reduces fuel economy.
► Government mpg figures are estimates of the fuel economy you can expect from a car. Your actual fuel economy depends on how you drive, the number of miles you drive, speed traveled, and the condition of the engine and other equipment.
► New tires make the steering feel better. When you replace worn tires, consider those types which give increased fuel economy.

► Use the phone instead of going in your car to talk to someone, to shop, or to pick up a small item. Use mail or a delivery service. Make efficient use of resources, including your time.
► Use other means of transportation such as public transportation, bicycling, and car pooling, instead of driving. Each alternative often costs less and uses less fuel than driving a car.

Chapter Summary

1. A student usually must work to pay for a car and its upkeep. The student's grades and social activities are often affected. (16–1)
2. The cost of owning a car includes purchase price, depreciation, fuel, repairs, license and registration fees, and insurance. (16–1)
3. If you cannot afford a new car, consider buying a used car. Buying from a private owner can cost less than buying from a car dealer. However, a private owner will seldom warranty a car. (16–1)
4. Take these steps when buying a used car: make outside and inside checks, check under the hood, test drive the car, have a mechanic check it, budget for repairs, arrange financing. (16–1)
5. Insurance is an agreement between a car owner and an insurance company to protect the owner from financial loss if a collision occurs. The policy states the conditions and limits of what the company will pay. (16–2)

6. Liability insurance covers injury or property damage to others. Uninsured-motorist and medical payments cover injury to the policyholder and his or her passengers. Collision, comprehensive, and towing cover repairs to the car. No-fault insurance covers injury to policyholders, their passengers, and their cars, regardless of fault. (16–2)
7. These factors affect the cost of insurance: age, marital status, sex of driver, car equipment and engine size, cost of car, miles driven, where owner lives, collision and violation record of driver, principal driver, and claims against company. (16–2)
8. Take these actions immediately after a collision: stop, aid the injured, prevent further damage to the cars, call the police, and exchange information. (16–3)
9. Take these actions following a collision: record information about witnesses and the collision, give accurate facts to the police, see a doctor if you were injured in any way, file necessary reports. (16–3)

Think About It
How can you prepare yourself to buy a car and reduce the chance of making a poor decision?

Decision Making

1. You are a high-school student working part-time to save for college. What are the arguments for and against buying a car?

2. Newspaper ads display the same year used-car model at similar prices from a private owner, a used-car dealer, and a new-car dealer. How would you decide which of the three cars to buy?

3. You were just involved in a collision. No one was injured. What procedures should you follow?

4. You find your car was vandalized. What kind of insurance will cover this damage?

Chapter 16 Test

Multiple Choice   Copy the number of each sentence below on a sheet of paper. Choose the letter that best completes each statement or answers each question.

1. The decrease in a car's value is its
   (a) premium.   (b) mpg.   (c) depreciation.
   (d) cancellation.   (306)
2. The least expensive repair you might have to make on a used car is to replace
   (a) a dirty air filter.   (b) shock absorbers.
   (c) a leaky radiator.   (d) tires.   (311)
3. Which insurance provides medical coverage for its policyholders, regardless of blame?
   (a) assigned-risk   (b) comprehensive
   (c) liability   (d) no-fault   (312)
4. Insurance sold to a driver whose license has been revoked or suspended is
   (a) liability insurance.   (b) assigned-risk insurance.   (c) no-fault insurance.
   (d) comprehensive insurance.   (314)
5. What should your first step be if you are involved in a collision?
   (a) Stop immediately.   (b) File report.
   (c) Exchange information.   (d) Aid injured.   (315)

Completion   Copy the number of each sentence below. After each number, write the letter of the word or words that complete the sentence correctly.

6. Turning back a car's odometer is ____.   (309)
7. The written agreement that describes the car you will buy is the ____.   (311)
8. Only ____ covers replacement of a stolen car.   (313)
9. Younger drivers usually pay ____ than older drivers.   (314)
10. Your premiums might ____ if you have a serious collision or traffic violation.   (314)

a. assigned-risk insurance
b. comprehensive insurance
c. higher premiums
d. illegal
e. increase
f. sales contract

Vocabulary   Copy the number of each phrase below. Match the definition in List A with the term it defines in List B.

List A

11. lists average prices of various used cars   (308)
12. guarantee for a limited time   (308)
13. banks, savings and loan association, credit unions, and finance companies   (311)
14. law requiring proof that the owner can pay for damages if involved in a collision   (312)
15. pays for claims for damage to other persons and property   (312)
16. pays medical expenses regardless of fault   (312)
17. written agreement which contracts for insurance coverage   (312)
18. price you pay for insurance coverage   (312)
19. amount the policyholder pays for damages   (312)
20. minimum-coverage plan for high-risk driver   (314)

List B

a. assigned-risk insurance
b. blue book
c. deductible
d. financial responsibility law
e. lending agencies
f. liability insurance
g. no-fault insurance
h. policy
i. premium
j. uninsured motorist
k. warranty

Chapter 17
Owning and Maintaining a Car

You're the Driver!

A car is a complex piece of machinery with many parts and systems. Each system is important to the car's safe and efficient operation. Like any other machine, your car can break down. Mechanical repairs can be expensive, and can cause you some inconvenience.

Preventive maintenance helps you avoid breakdowns. You can perform some preventive maintenance when you buy fuel. In this picture, one person is checking the oil level while the other person is filling the fuel tank.

If you were one of these people, would you know how to check the oil? battery and cables? coolant level? tire pressure?

How do you operate the service-station fuel pump to fill the tank?

You can make such checks at fuel stops, but you might not be able to perform major service or repairs. This chapter discusses how to respond to various warnings and how to plan repairs or adjustments.

Objectives

17–1 *Owner Maintenance*

1. Describe the warning signs for repair, replacement, or adjustment to keep these systems running:
   - ► power train   (322)
   - ► ignition and electrical   (323)
   - ► lubrication   (325)
   - ► steering and suspension   (325)
   - ► cooling   (326)
   - ► fuel and exhaust   (327)
   - ► brake   (328)

2. Tell how to start a car that has a dead battery.   (324)
3. Describe three types of tires and list guidelines for replacing tires.   (329)

17–2 *Preventive Maintenance*

4. Define preventive maintenance.   (331)
5. List preventive maintenance checks to make before and after starting the engine, while driving, when stopping for fuel, and when having the car serviced.   (331)

6. Tell how to find a qualified mechanic.   (333)

17–3 *Improvements for Saving Fuel*

7. Tell how car design can improve fuel economy.   (335)
8. Explain how to calculate miles per gallon of fuel consumption.   (336)

17–1 Owner Maintenance

Learning about the care your car requires can help to give you confidence to handle problems as they occur. Day-to-day servicing helps ensure that you will have few, if any, serious problems.

Engine and Power Train

The engine burns fuel to provide the power that moves the car. The power train transmits the power to the car's wheels.

How It Works   A spark produced by a *spark plug* ignites the air-fuel mixture in each combustion chamber or cylinder of the internal-combustion engine. The resulting explosion forces the piston down the cylinder. The crankshaft changes the up-and-down motion of each piston into rotary motion which turns the car's drive wheels. Some cars are rear-wheel drive while others are front-wheel drive, as shown to the right.

The major parts of the power train are the clutch (in a stickshift car), transmission, drive shaft, differential, and drive axle. The *transmission* has gears which enable the engine to deliver power to the drive wheels. Lower gears let the engine turn faster; higher gears let the engine turn more slowly.

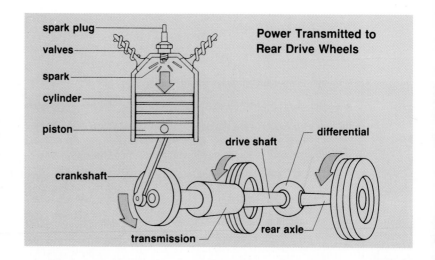

Power Transmitted to Rear Drive Wheels

spark plug, valves, spark, cylinder, piston, crankshaft, transmission, drive shaft, differential, rear axle

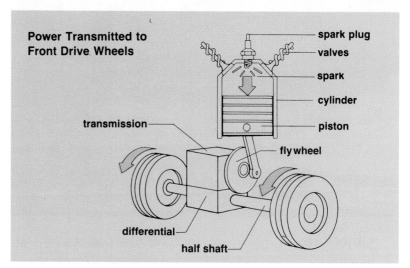

Power Transmitted to Front Drive Wheels

transmission, spark plug, valves, spark, cylinder, piston, flywheel, differential, half shaft

In a stickshift car, you shift gears by first pressing down the clutch pedal. The clutch disconnects the engine from the transmission so you can select another gear. In an automatic-transmission car, you select the gear, but shifting is done without a manual clutch.

The *drive shaft* is a long metal rod in rear-wheel-drive cars. The drive shaft carries power from the transmission to the *differential* in the rear of the car. The differential has gears which allow one rear wheel to turn faster than another when turning a corner.

In front-wheel-drive cars, the power is carried to the front wheels by two half shafts. The differential is located between the two half shafts.

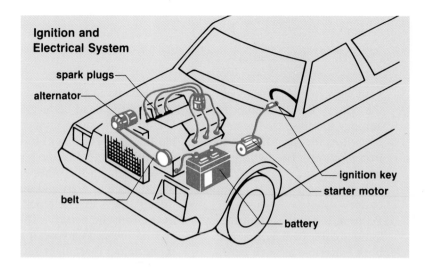

Ignition and Electrical System

- spark plugs
- alternator
- belt
- ignition key
- starter motor
- battery

Keeping It Running Drive at a moderate speed until the engine warms up. This action allows all engine parts to receive proper lubrication.

Help keep the engine operating properly by having a *tune up* performed once a year. The tune up should include cleaning or replacing of spark plugs and checking the emission controls, fuel filter, and air filter.

Check the automatic transmission fluid level at least once a month. While the warm engine is running, use the automatic-transmission dipstick to check the fluid level. The warning signs of low fluid level include jerky shifting or a pause before the car starts to move.

Ignition and Electrical System

The ignition system sets off combustion in the engine's cylinders. The electrical system is involved in the ignition process and also runs the lights and accessories.

How It Works Turning the ignition key sends an electric current from the battery to the electric starter motor that turns the engine. Once the engine is running, the *alternator* generates electric current. This picture shows that a belt drives the alternator. The electric current is delivered to each spark plug at the proper time to ignite the air-fuel mixture in each cylinder.

Keeping It Running Make sure the battery is kept in good condition. The car's starter, lights, and other equipment depend on the electrical power stored in the battery. Keep the battery terminals free of corrosion. Make sure battery cable connections are tight.

Some batteries are sealed and do not need the water level checked. Other batteries have vent caps and need to be checked regularly. If the battery's water level is low, remove the caps carefully and fill as needed.

A battery generates hydrogen, a very explosive gas. Never expose a battery to an open flame or electrical spark. Never let battery fluid (a strong acid) touch your skin or eyes. Severe injury can result. Wear eye protection and gloves when working with or around a battery.

If the alternator warning light stays on while you are driving, the alternator is not generating electricity. The problem might be a broken or loose belt, or a defective alternator. Have repairs made promptly.

Cold weather makes starting the engine more difficult because the battery has less power when it is cold. Keep the battery charged to avoid battery failure. If the starter does not turn the engine over quickly, have your mechanic charge or replace the battery. By doing so, you can avoid having the battery fail when you are not near a service station. Park in a garage, if possible, during cold weather to keep the car warmer and easier to start.

Lights Headlights, tailights, and turn-signal lights sometimes burn out. Check them by watching their reflection on a wall or garage door. Keep headlights aligned properly. If the headlight beams are aimed too high, they could temporarily blind an oncoming driver. Headlight beams aimed too low can reduce your sight distance at night or during low-visibility conditions.

Starting a Car That Has a Dead Battery If you turn the ignition key while in PARK or NEUTRAL and the starter makes no sound, the problem is usually a dead battery. In most cases, you can start your car by using jumper cables connected to a charged battery of the same voltage. Before attempting to jump the battery, open any vent caps to make sure that the battery fluid is neither frozen nor too low. *Do not attempt to start a car that has a frozen battery. The battery might explode.*

Follow these steps to jump a battery safely:

1. Position the cars so that the jumper cables easily reach both batteries, as seen here. Do not let the cars touch.
2. Turn off each car's engine and all accessories. Place each in PARK or NEUTRAL gear. Set each car's parking brake.
3. If either battery has vent caps, remove them to release accumulated hydrogen. Lay a heavy cloth over the vents in case the battery explodes and sprays acid.
4. Clamp the positive jumper cable (marked + or red) to the positive terminal of the good battery. Clamp the other end of the cable to the positive terminal of the dead battery.
5. Clamp the negative jumper cable (marked - or black) to the negative terminal of the good battery. Clamp the other end of the cable to a ground on the "dead" car's engine block, away from the battery. This ground prevents a sparking at the terminal that might set off an explosion. Keep the jumper cables away from engine parts that will move such as the fan and belts.
6. Start the car that has the good battery first. Then start the car that has the dead battery.
7. When the car with the dead battery has started, remove the cables in the reverse order that they were connected.
8. Replace the vent caps, if necessary. Throw away the cloth since it might have acid on it.

Car with dead battery   Car with good battery

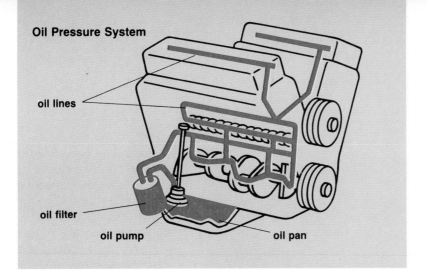

Oil Pressure System

oil lines

oil filter

oil pump   oil pan

Lubrication System

Lubrication is the use of grease and oil to reduce friction on a car's moving parts. Lubrication prevents damage from heat and helps keep the parts operating efficiently.

How It Works When the surfaces of two moving parts rub against each other, they create friction and heat. If engine friction is not reduced, the engine will burn itself out. Oil helps the engine operate efficiently by reducing friction, carrying away engine heat, and keeping engine parts clean. Grease is used to lubricate other parts of the car, such as the axles and the steering system.

Notice above that the *oil pump* forces the oil in the oil pan (located at the bottom of the engine) through the oil filter. The oil then flows through the oil lines to the engine's moving parts.

Keeping It Running Your car needs an oil change after being driven a certain number of

miles or after the length of time stated in your owner's manual. The used oil is drained and replaced with clean oil. The oil filter also is usually replaced. If you drive mostly on short, local trips, or on dirt roadways, you might need to change the oil and filter more often than recommended.

Cold weather makes oil thicker. Thick oil does not flow well. Therefore, your car will not start as easily as in warmer weather. Use a multiweight or synthetic oil all year to lessen engine problems.

If the oil pressure warning light or gauge indicates low oil pressure while you are driving, pull over to the side of the roadway, stop, and turn off the engine. *Do not drive your car.* Have the low oil pressure problem corrected before driving your car again. Insufficient oil pressure will quickly and seriously damage the engine.

Your car must be lubricated periodically. Check your owner's manual for a schedule of lubrication needs.

Steering and Suspension Systems

The steering system is vital to safe car control. The suspension system contributes to car control, steering, and riding comfort.

How They Work The steering system includes the steering wheel and steering column. The steering column carries the force used to turn the steering wheel to the front wheels.

The *springs* in the suspension system support the car to allow gentle up-and-down motion. Each *shock absorber* controls hard bouncing and helps keep the tire on the roadway.

Keeping Them Running Some steering problems can develop gradually and might not be recognized. Have any steering problem repaired immediately. Have a mechanic check the steering system if any of these problems occur:

► You feel "play" or excess movement in the steering (any "play" at all while the engine is running, for power steering; more than 2 inches of "play" for standard steering).
► Steering is difficult with properly inflated tires.
► You feel a "shimmy" or wobbling, or your car pulls to one side under normal conditions.

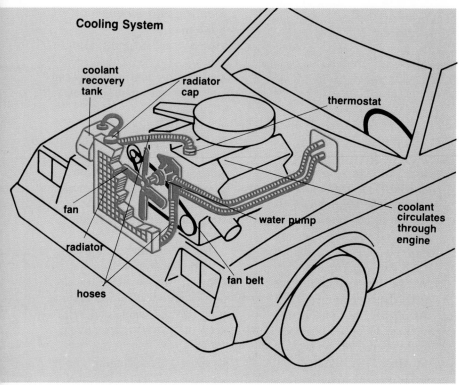

Cooling System

coolant recovery tank

radiator cap

thermostat

fan

water pump

coolant circulates through engine

radiator

fan belt

hoses

Cooling System

Although oil in the lubrication system removes some engine heat, additional cooling is needed. The cooling system provides that additional cooling ability.

How It Works The cooling system, as shown above, includes a fan, fan belt, radiator, water pump, coolant recovery tank, thermostat, heater, and hoses that connect the radiator to the engine. The *radiator* holds and cools the coolant, a mixture of antifreeze and water. The water pump draws coolant from the bottom of the radiator and forces it throughout the engine. The fan draws air through the radiator, helping cool the coolant in the radiator.

When the system's temperature is below the best operating level, the *thermostat* shuts off the flow of coolant. When the system's temperature rises to the correct operating temperature, the thermostat opens and coolant flows to cool the engine.

Keeping It Running Check your radiator's coolant level at least once each month. Check the coolant in the recovery tank before starting the engine, while the engine is cold.

Engine overheating can be caused by:
low coolant level
► loose or broken fan belt, or defective fan or water pump
► blocked radiator air flow
► frozen coolant in the system
► faulty thermostat.

If the temperature gauge or warning light indicates overheating, it might be necessary to add coolant. *Caution: Never remove the cap from a hot radiator.* Hot fluid and steam can spurt out and burn you. Pour the coolant in slowly while the cooled engine is running.

Colder weather and hotter weather require that the cooling system work at its best. Engine damage can occur if the coolant freezes in cold weather or boils over in hot weather. Have the cooling system, belts, and hoses checked regularly. The radiator should be cleaned and filled with the recommended amount of coolant to withstand both winter and summer temperatures.

Fuel and Exhaust Systems

The fuel system consists of a fuel tank, fuel line, fuel pump, air cleaner, fuel filter, and carburetor or fuel-injection system. These components are shown in the top picture. The exhaust system, shown in the bottom picture, includes the exhaust pipe, catalytic converter, muffler, and tail pipe.

How They Work The fuel pump draws fuel from the fuel tank through the fuel line. Fuel is then pumped through the fuel filter to the *carburetor* or *fuel-injection system*. Air is drawn through the air filter and mixed with the fuel to become a fine mist for combustion in each cylinder of an internal-combustion engine.

Exhaust gases leave the exhaust system through the tail-pipe at the back of the car. The muffler reduces noise from combustion explosions in the cylinders. The catalytic converter reduces pollution from the car's exhaust.

Keeping Them Running The carburetor might need cleaning and adjustment periodically to remain efficient. A fuel-injection system needs little

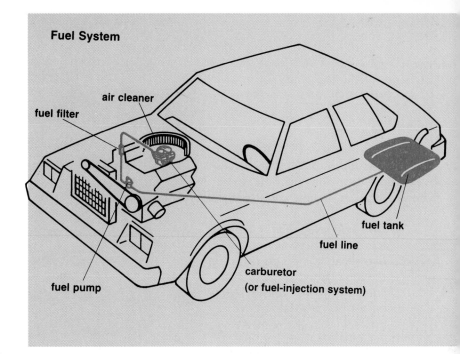

Fuel System

air cleaner

fuel filter

fuel tank

fuel line

carburetor
(or fuel-injection system)

fuel pump

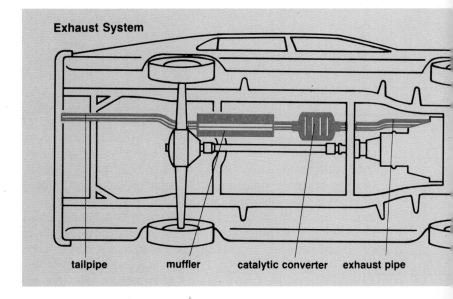

Exhaust System

tailpipe   muffler   catalytic converter   exhaust pipe

adjustment. A tune up usually includes a check of the air and fuel filters. Replace these filters according to the schedule in your owner's manual.

The exhaust system needs replacement when a part rusts out or is damaged. Ignoring a defect in the exhaust system creates noise and increases the risk of carbon monoxide poisoning of the car's occupants.

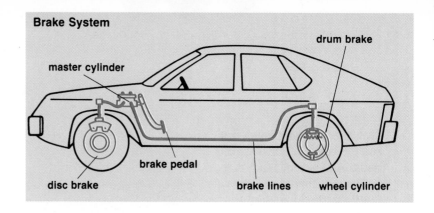

Brake System

Brake System

Good brakes are a vital safety component in any motor vehicle. How long the brakes last depends on how you use them.

How It Works The brake system's *master cylinder* contains two separate systems shown in the top picture. Each system controls two wheels. Pressure on the brake pedal forces brake fluid from the master cylinder through the brake lines to each wheel's cylinder. Each wheel's cylinder creates friction through brake shoes or brake pads to stop the wheel.

Many cars have a *disc brake* on each front wheel, and a *drum brake* on each rear wheel, as shown in the bottom pictures. On a disc brake, fluid pressure squeezes the pads against the turning disc. A drum brake works as fluid pressure squeezes the brake shoes against the inside of the brake drum. Friction between the system's parts slows and stops the wheels.

If a leak develops in the brake system, fluid will not reach one pair of wheels and the brake-warning light will appear. The dual master cylinder assures that the other two wheels will get fluid, and the brakes on those wheels will still work. However, stopping the car will take longer.

Drum Brake

Brake shoes are forced against hollow cylinder drum inside a wheel to stop the car.

The parking brake is a separate system. A steel cable usually connects the parking brake lever to the brakes on the rear wheels. The parking brake should be able to hold the car on a hill.

Keeping It Running Both disc brakes and drum brakes are self-adjusting. If the brake pedal goes too far toward the floor when you press the pedal hard, back up, stop, and move forward several times. Repeat this sequence several times. Apply the brakes firmly each time. If this procedure does not adjust the brakes, have the brake system inspected promptly.

Disc Brake

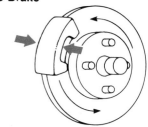

Pads press against sides of rotating disc inside a wheel to stop the car.

Keep the brake fluid in the master cylinder at the proper level. Watch for these warning signs of brake trouble:

► brake-warning light appears
► low brake pedal (less than 2 inches from the floor for power brakes; less than 3 inches for standard brakes when pressed firmly)
► "spongy" feel in brake pedal
► pulling to left or right when stopping when brakes are dry
► grabbing or sudden braking action
► squealing or chattering noises in the brakes
► need to pump brakes or push brake pedal harder to stop the car.

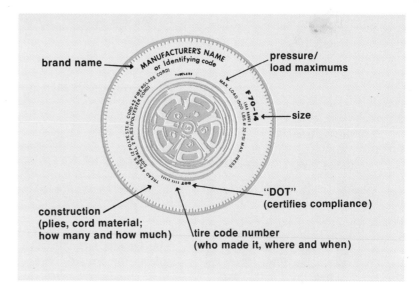

brand name → MANUFACTURER'S NAME or Identifying code

pressure/ load maximums

size

"DOT" (certifies compliance)

tire code number (who made it, where and when)

construction (plies, cord material; how many and how much)

Tires

A tire is made of rubber reinforced with layers of cord material under the tread. Each layer, called a ply, strengthens the tire and gives it shape.

Tire Construction

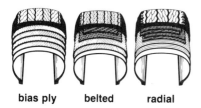

bias ply   belted   radial

A conventional bias-ply tire has no belt. All radial tires have belts, which improve mileage.

Types of Tires   A *bias-ply tire* has cord layers that crisscross at an angle. Bias-ply tires offer less tread mileage and are best suited to lower-mileage driving in local areas. A *belted tire* has special cord layers added to the bias-ply tire for improved strength and mileage.

A *radial tire* has plies, that run straight across the tire, and strengthening belts of steel or other material that circle the tire. Radial tires give improved tread mileage, traction, and fuel economy as compared to other tires. Note the construction of each tire type shown above.

Information about the tire's construction, size, and carrying capacity is clearly marked on the sidewall of the tire, as shown above. Note in the picture below how a paper label on the tread of a new tire shows additional information.

Replacement tires should be the same size and construction as the original equipment. Never use radial tires with any other type of tire on the same car. Radial tires do not react the same way as bias-ply tires.

Inflation and Tread   Maintain recommended air pressure in all tires. The air pressure marked on the tire sidewall will yield maximum fuel and tire mileage. Too little air in even one tire can make the car difficult to control. Low inflation causes tires to wear quickly and can cause tire failure.

A puncture or faulty valve stem can cause a slow leak and deflate a tire, causing your car to act as if it has a blowout. Change the tire and have the leak repaired.

Keep a good tire gauge in your car and use it regularly. Periodically check tire pressure when the tires are cool. Air pressure in a tire rises in warmer weather and falls in cooler weather. Air pressure increases when the car is driven, even for a short distance. Do not let air out of a warm tire to get a recommended reading; the tire will be underinflated when it cools.

Tire Grading	Traction	Temperature	Treadwear*
Highest	A	A	200 190 180 170 160
	B	B	150 140 130 120 110 100
Lowest	C	C	90 80 70 60 50

*The higher the number, the greater the mileage from the tire. Tires with treadwear grading of 150 rating will give 50 percent more miles than one graded at 100.

Tire Rotation

Bias and Belted Tires   **Radial Tires**

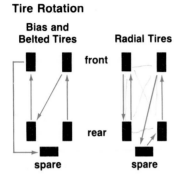

front

rear

spare   spare

Rotation and Replacement

Have your tires rotated and balanced every 10,000 to 15,000 miles to promote longer tire life and more even wear. The illustration above shows tire rotation patterns for bias, belted, and radial tires.

Replace a tire when you see smooth bars across the tread, as shown in the picture below. The wear bars indicate that only 1/16-inch tread remains. A worn tire has poor traction, especially on a wet roadway, and is more likely to fail.

Tire Quality Grading   All tires sold in the United States must meet standards for treadwear, traction, and temperature, as shown in the chart. A tire's performance is measured under controlled conditions on specific test surfaces.

The traction grade represents a tire's ability to stop on a wet roadway. A tire graded "C" has poorer traction performance than a tire graded "A." The temperature grade represents a tire's resistance to heat that builds up while driving. Substantial heat can cause a tire to wear sooner and can lead to sudden tire failure. Keep safety in mind as you compare and decide which tire offers the best value for the kind of driving you do.

Wheel Alignment and Other Tire Problems   Uneven wear often indicates problems in wheel alignment, balance, or improper inflation. A tire worn only in the center is usually overinflated. Worn edges often indicate underinflation. Wear on one edge only, or a "cupped" shape, results from poor wheel alignment.

You can extend the life of your tires by avoiding fast starts, stops, and turns. Check the tires when your car is serviced or during your routine inspection. Look for weak spots, cuts, blisters, rocks caught in the tread, and uneven wear. Have needed repairs or adjustments performed before the tires become unsafe.

Review It

1. What are warning signs for repair of each system listed?
   ► power train
   ► ignition and electrical
   ► lubrication
   ► steering and suspension
   ► cooling
   ► fuel and exhaust
   ► brake
2. How is each jumper cable marked? When trying to start a car that has a dead battery, which cable should be attached first? Which cable should be removed first?
3. What is the construction of a bias tire? a belted tire? a radial tire?

The care that a car receives to avoid trouble later is *preventive maintenance*. Preventive maintenance includes not only day-to-day care, but the periodic attention a car needs at the times listed in the owner's manual.

The schedule of service for certain maintenance jobs is extremely important. The car's warranty might not stay in effect if service is not done at the scheduled times. Preventive maintenance saves money and is less expensive than repairs which result from lack of service.

Before Starting the Engine

Before entering the car, note whether any tire is softer or lower than the other tires. A slow leak in a tire can cause an emergency as you drive. It is easier and safer to change the tire at home than on a busy street or remote highway.

Before starting the engine, clean the windshield, windows, and lights if they are dirty, as this driver is doing. Check windshield wipers and, at least once a month, also the windshield washer fluid. Make sure all lights and the horn operate. When you turn on the ignition (without starting the engine), check that gauges and warning lights come on.

After Starting the Engine

Check all instruments again after you start the engine. All warning lights should be off. If the fuel gauge shows less than half, plan to fill the fuel tank soon. Test the feel of the brake pedal as you begin to drive. The pedal should be firm, not soft or spongy, and should not be lower than 2 or 3 inches from the floor.

While Driving

Glance at the instrument panel to note any unusual readings or warning signals. Notice whether there are any unusual sounds, odors, vibrations, or thumps. These warnings indicate that something is wrong with your car. Have any change in steering, handling, braking, or acceleration checked promptly.

How to Operate a Pump

1. Remove cap from tank.

2. Remove nozzle from pump.

3. Turn pump lever on. Numbers will register zero.

4. Place nozzle in gas tank. Squeeze nozzle.

5. Turn pump lever off. Hang up nozzle.

6. Put cap back on.

At a Fuel Stop

Many drivers fill their own fuel tanks at self-service stations. Operating instructions are displayed near the service-station fuel pump. Smoking is not allowed around a fuel station. Always turn off the engine while filling the fuel tank. These pictures show how to operate a service-station fuel pump.

Type of Fuel to Buy   If your car requires unleaded or diesel fuel, this information usually is displayed on the instrument panel, around the fuel cap, and in the owner's manual. Use a fuel with sufficient octane rating to prevent engine knocking or pinging during normal driving. Octane ratings are displayed on fuel pumps. Using a higher octane costs more, yet does not increase power or mileage.

Gasohol is a blend of unleaded gasoline and ethyl alcohol. Gasohol sometimes has a higher octane rating and might cost less than super unleaded gas. Check your owner's manual to see if using gasohol is recommended.

Selecting a Qualified Mechanic

Your life and the lives of others can depend on the judgment and skill of your mechanic. Select your mechanic *before* your car breaks down. Should your car break down unexpectedly, you might not take the time to gather recommendations, think, and make a wise choice.

Family members, friends, neighbors, and an auto-shop teacher might offer suggestions on how to find a qualified mechanic. Some repair shops display certificates earned by mechanics who pass specialized courses and tests as this picture shows. In most cases, you can be assured of competent help in such shops.

Scheduled Service

Most cars need service at least once a year. Your owner's manual includes a schedule which lists time or mileage intervals for tune ups and other service. Keep a record of all service, repairs, replacement parts, and their receipts. Records will help you develop and maintain a proper maintenance schedule.

Service Checklist Your owner's manual is the best guide to preventive maintenance for your car. Sometimes you might not have the owner's manual and cannot get a replacement. In this case, you might use this schedule as a general guide.

▶ **Every Week** Run the air conditioner for about five minutes.

▶ **Every Two Weeks** Check levels of engine oil and battery fluid (if necessary). Check for system leaks by observing the surface of a place where you regularly park, such as a garage or driveway.

▶ **Every Month** Check air pressure in tires (include spare). Check level of windshield washer solution.

▶ **Every Three to Six Months (or 6,000 miles)** Change oil and oil filter. Lubricate. Check levels of brake and power-steering fluid. Check differential.

Automobile diagnostic centers or clinics, such as this clinic, test cars electronically and mechanically to find problems. The car owner is told whether any part or system fails to work or meet acceptable standards.

When selecting a diagnostic clinic, you might decide to select one that does not offer repair services. If the business does not profit from repairs, regardless of the diagnosis, it will not try to sell you unnecessary parts or repairs. You or your mechanic can repair or replace defective parts based on the information from the diagnosis.

Review It

1. What is preventive maintenance?
2. What maintenance checks should you make before and after starting the engine?
3. How can you find a qualified mechanic?

▶ **Every Year** Have a tune up and have the brakes checked. Have the front wheel bearings repacked, if necessary. Check air filter for possible replacement. Have your car winterized if your climate requires it.

▶ **Every Two Years** Replace radiator hoses and fan belts. Flush cooling system and replace coolant (once a year for high-use cars). Have automatic transmission checked.

State Inspections and Car Clinics

Some states require that every car be inspected once or twice each year. Inspections can uncover many safety-related defects before they become potential hazards. Some state laws require that any serious defects be repaired before the car can be licensed. Other states require inspection before the car can be sold or registered. Many states and cities require inspection of emission-control systems.

17–3 Improvements for Saving Fuel

Increases in fuel prices, government standards, and changing trends in the needs of car buyers have influenced the design of cars. Most newer cars are designed to increase fuel economy. Radial tires roll with less resistance than other types of tires. Even the design of wheel covers can contribute to increased fuel economy.

Design Improvements

Cars are designed to use space efficiently. The designs of many cars are streamlined to make them less wind-resistant. Streamlining helps increase engine performance and fuel efficiency.

Smaller Size Notice in the picture how the average new car is about two feet shorter than its predecessor made several years ago. The smaller car weighs less and so needs less power to move it. As a result, a smaller, lighter-weight engine can be used to help increase fuel economy. While interior space has changed, many newer cars can carry five passengers in safety and comfort.

Front-Wheel Drive Many new cars have front-wheel drive; the front wheels provide the power that makes the car move. A car with front-wheel drive has better traction than a car with rear-wheel drive. The car is pulled by the front wheels rather than pushed by the rear wheels.

Engine Improvements

Smaller engines are designed to produce sufficient power and fuel savings for smaller cars. Lightweight materials such as aluminum and plastics are frequently used. Electronic ignitions and computer-controlled carburetors help engines burn fuel efficiently under all driving conditions.

Fuel-Injection Systems An engine can have an electronic fuel-injection system rather than a carburetor. This system delivers the exact amount of fuel to the engine's cylinders to give maximum engine power and fuel efficiency.

Turbocharging In a non-turbocharged engine, the engine exhaust usually is released directly into the atmosphere. A turbocharger uses engine exhaust to produce additional power. In normal driving conditions, the turbocharger idles. When extra power is needed, such as when entering an expressway or passing, the turbocharger increases engine power.

Streamlined, smaller, lighter-weight cars are more fuel efficient.

past		present
6 or 8 cylinders	Engine	4 or 6 cylinders
212 inches	Length	180 inches
77 inches	Width	67 inches
53 inches	Height	53 inches
4,100 pounds	Weight	2,900 pounds
14 to 22	Miles per gallon	20 to 30

These figures are averages only.

Transmission Improvements

Transmitting engine power to the drive wheels is the job of the transmission. Any power lost in the transmission reduces fuel economy. A variety of transmission improvements has resulted in greater fuel economy.

Five-Speed Transmission

Many manual transmission cars now have five forward speeds. The fifth gear, an overdrive gear, lets the engine run more slowly at highway speeds. Fuel economy is improved.

Automatic Overdrive   Like

fifth gear in a five-speed manual transmission, an automatic-overdrive transmission lets the engine run more slowly at highway speeds. When extra power is needed, the transmission shifts to a lower gear automatically.

Calculating Miles per Gallon

Most drivers are concerned with getting the most miles from each gallon of fuel. In addition, checking fuel economy can warn you of possible mechanical problems.

Follow these steps to calculate miles per gallon:
1. Fill fuel tank. Record the odometer reading.
2. Drive normally until the tank is about half full.
3. Fill the fuel tank again. Record the odometer reading.
4. Subtract the second odometer reading from the first reading.
5. Divide the number of miles driven by the number of gallons required to fill the fuel tank again.
6. The result is miles per gallon (mpg).
Example:
► 17,703 (second odometer reading) − 17,514 (first odometer reading) = 189 miles
► 189 miles ÷ 7 gallons = 27 mpg

Obtain average mpg after filling the fuel tank several times over a period of a few weeks. Stop-and-go driving and short trips in city driving are less fuel efficient than driving at a moderate speed for a longer distance. Note in this chart how speed is related to fuel mileage.

Review It
1. How have design changes in car shapes, engines, and transmissions helped improve fuel economy?
2. Use this information to calculate mpg:
first odometer reading: 41,250
second odometer reading: 41,500
gallons to fill tank: 10

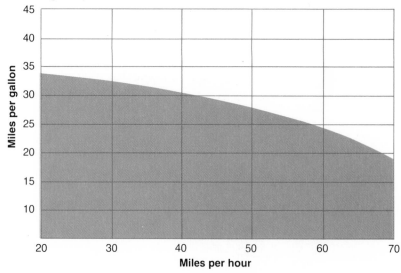

Higher speeds are less fuel efficient.

Miles per gallon vs. Miles per hour

Advancements in Traffic Safety

A wide variety of innovative tire designs is available. Terms such as all-weather, all-season, and all-terrain describe tires that have been engineered for specific driving needs.

All-terrain tires are built to provide traction for off-roadway driving as well as everyday driving. All-weather and all-season tires are designed for good traction during normal driving conditions, in rain, and to some degree, in snow. Snow tires are specifically designed to provide good traction on snow-covered roadways.

Use advertising information and test results from independent agencies to better evaluate a tire. A tire might be labeled as having a life as short as 25,000 miles or as long as 60,000 miles. A tire's advertised lifespan does not guarantee that you will get that many miles of driving from the tire. The manufacturer issues a warranty that guarantees the tire against specific defects or failures for that number of miles. Should the tire fail, the manufacturer's local dealer should repair the tire at no charge if you present the tire's warranty certificate.

Chapter Summary

1. Recognize and respond promptly to your car's warning signs that repairs, adjustments, or parts replacement might be needed. (17–1)
2. If a car's battery is dead, you might be able to jump start the car by using a car with a charged battery of the same voltage. (17–1)
3. Bias-ply, belted, or radial tires are used on most cars. Replace a tire when its wear has become a safety factor. (17–1)
4. Preventive maintenance is the care a car receives to avoid trouble later. (17–2)
5. Perform preventive maintenance checks and service before starting the engine, after starting the engine, when stopping for fuel, and when having the car serviced. (17–2)
6. Select a qualified mechanic to service and repair your car before it breaks down. You usually find competent help in repair shops that display training certificates earned by mechanics. (17–2)
7. Engineering improvements to increase fuel economy include car shape and design, and engine and transmission improvements. (17–3)
8. Calculate miles per gallon at each fuel stop by subtracting the previous odometer reading from the present one. Divide the miles driven by the number of gallons needed to fill the fuel tank. (17–3)

Think About It
How can you better prepare yourself to become a responsible driver who understands the basic workings of your car?

Decision Making

1. You are nearing this red light. As you step on the foot-brake pedal, it goes very near to the floor. How can you correct the problem soon after leaving the light? What repairs could be essential before you continue driving your car?

2. One of your headlights is not working. What should you do to correct the problem?

3. These people are attempting to start a car that has a dead battery. What steps should they take to start the battery safely?

4. You need a tire to replace one that has just failed. You do a lot of long-distance driving. What guidelines should you use in deciding what kind of tire to buy?

Chapter 17 Test

Multiple Choice   Copy the number of each sentence below on a sheet of paper. Choose the letter that best completes each statement or answers each question.

1. How does cold weather affect a car battery?
   (a) increases power   (b) decreases power
   (c) increases weight   (d) decreases
   weight   (323)
2. When jumping a dead battery, which terminals are connected first?
   (a) positive terminal on each car   (b) negative terminal on each car   (c) both terminals on dead battery   (d) both terminals on good battery   (324)
3. On many cars, the brake system includes
   (a) front disc and rear drum brakes.   (b) front drum and rear disc brakes.   (c) disc brakes on one side only.   (d) no parking brake.   (328)
4. Maintaining a car to prevent future trouble is
   (a) not necessary on a new car.   (b) more expensive than repairs.   (c) preventive maintenance.   (d) warranty service.   (331)
5. The job of the turbocharger is to
   (a) reduce pollution.   (b) increase fuel economy.
   (c) reduce engine power.   (d) increase engine power.   (335)

Completion   Copy the number of each sentence below. After each number, write the letter of the word or words that complete the sentence correctly.

6. The _____ ignites the fuel-air mixture in an engine cylinder.   (322)
7. The _____ connects the drive shaft and rear axles in a rear-drive car.   (322)
8. The _____ has gears that enable the engine to deliver power to the drive wheels.   (322)
9. The _____ carries power from the transmission to the differential.   (322)
10. The electric current from the _____ turns the electric starter motor.   (323)
11. Servicing that includes cleaning or replacing the spark plugs and checking emission controls, air filter, and fuel filter is a _____.   (323)
12. The _____ support the car.   (325)
13. The _____ is part of the cooling system.   (326)

14. A _____ replaces a carburetor and delivers a precise amount of fuel to each cylinder.   (327)
15. A _____ uses brake shoes to press against the inside of a brake drum.   (328)

a. battery
b. differential
c. disc brake
d. drive shaft
e. drum brake
f. fuel-injection system
g. spark plug
h. springs
i. thermostat
j. transmission
k. tune up

Vocabulary   Copy the number of each phrase below. Match the definition in List A with the term it defines in List B.

List A
16. generates electrical current   (323)
17. device that helps control tire bounce   (325)
18. device that forces oil through engine   (325)
19. device for cooling engine fluid   (326)
20. device that mixes fuel and air for combustion   (327)
21. stopping device in which pads squeeze a rotating steel disk   (328)
22. container for brake fluid   (328)
23. tire in which cords crisscross at an angle   (329)
24. bias-ply tire with reinforcement   (329)
25. tire with strengthening belts of steel   (329)

List B
a. alternator
b. belted tire
c. bias-ply tire
d. carburetor
e. disc brake
f. drum brake
g. master cylinder
h. oil pump
i. radial tire
j. radiator
k. shock absorber

Chapter 18
Driving for Pleasure

You're the Driver!

The time has finally arrived. You and your family are taking a vacation that involves long-distance travel. All of you have spent much time planning and preparing for this vacation.

What are the problems of driving a car that is loaded for long-distance travel?

What would be the best places and times for you, a beginning driver, to drive?

How will you stay alert when you drive?

How would the car handle differently if you were pulling a trailer?

What steps can you take to make this trip more enjoyable?

Knowing how to plan for and drive long distances can make the trip enjoyable for your entire family. Proper planning pays off in reduced costs, fewer or no inconveniences, and less worry.

By planning properly, whether for local or long-distance travel, you can improve your chances for a safe and pleasurable trip. This chapter provides information that can help you plan for both local and long-distance travel.

Objectives

18–1 Local Travel

1. List five considerations to keep in mind before local travel. (342)
2. Describe advance preparations you should make before local travel. (343)

18–2 Long-Distance Travel

3. Explain three ways in which you can use a road map to find the distance between two cities. (344)

4. Tell how to prepare in advance for a long-distance trip. (346)
5. List emergency equipment to keep in your vehicle for long-distance travel. (347)
6. List five personal items that you should take on a long-distance trip. (347)
7. State the guidelines for loading your car for a long-distance trip. (348)
8. List techniques to stay alert and concentrate on the driving task. (349)

18–3 Recreational Vehicles and Trailers

9. List the problems that you might encounter while driving a recreational vehicle. (350)
10. State the guidelines for towing a trailer. (351)
11. Explain how to back a trailer. (352)

Simple, advance preparations can make driving on local trips easier and more efficient. Arriving safely and on time are two important results of planning. Saving fuel is also an important consideration.

Short Trip Considerations

A short trip can range from shopping at a neighborhood mall to driving to the other side of a larger city. Keep in mind the following five considerations before you begin any short, local travel.

Is This Trip Necessary? The need to conserve fuel should make every driver rethink the necessity of each trip. Always ask yourself this question before driving somewhere: "Is this trip really necessary?" If your answer is "yes," could you walk, bicycle, or use public transportation like these people are doing, instead of driving?

Taking short drives for a single purpose wastes fuel. A cold engine delivers poorer mileage

and does not reach ideal operating temperatures on short trips. Plan ahead and combine a number of errands into one longer trip rather than taking several short, inefficient trips.

Allow Enough Time Once you have decided that the trip is necessary, allow extra time for any possible delays. You might be delayed by poor weather or heavy traffic.

Listen to Weather and Traffic Reports Base your travel time on weather and traffic reports. A driver who ignores weather reports is often faced with the choice of being late or driving too fast under adverse conditions. Use traffic reports to locate traffic jams and decide on route changes.

Leave on Time Be ready to leave on time. A driver who is late and in a hurry can change from a safe driver into a potentially dangerous one.

Choose Best Travel Time Traffic jams are fuel and time wasters. If you can, avoid traveling in large cities during morning and evening rush hours. Driving in rush-hour traffic can easily double your travel time.

Preventive Planning

Advance preparation, even for short trips, can prevent many problems. If your car is prepared and your route is planned, you will get to your destination more quickly, safely, and economically.

Vehicle Preparation Running out of windshield-washer fluid, driving on an underinflated tire, or having a turn-signal light fail might not sound like big problems. However, a minor problem can lead to serious trouble.

Every time you use a vehicle, make a routine pre-driving check of the tires, lights, and controls. Make a routine check under the hood each time you fill the fuel tank.

Route Selection Select a route that minimizes time and roadway hazards. Routes with uncontrolled railroad crossings or many uncontrolled intersections can minimize time, but can increase the risk of a collision. It might take less time to cross an intersection that is controlled with YIELD signs. However, this intersection can be more hazardous than one controlled with STOP signs. Reducing hazards is more important than saving time when selecting a travel route.

Know Streets and Addresses

Plan your route ahead of time. Know the names of the streets you need to follow. Write down the names and bring them with you. Your passengers can help you find street signs and address numbers as this picture shows. If you miss a street, do not make a last-second turn or stop. Drive around the block, and look for the street again.

Review It

1. What five considerations should you keep in mind before a short trip?
2. What advance preparations should you make before local travel?

18-2 Long-Distance Travel

A long car trip can become one of the most expensive ways to travel. You can reduce travel-related expenses and avoid unnecessary costs by planning ahead. Many vacations fail to serve their purpose of providing rest, relaxation, and recreation. Families often drive long distances without allowing enough time to reach their destination and return home comfortably.

Map Reading

When you plan a long trip, you need a map of the states and cities that you intend to visit. Maps are available from motor clubs, city chambers of commerce, state travel bureaus, and some service stations.

A map usually contains a *legend,* a chart that explains the markings and symbols used on the map. Most maps also include a mileage chart, town and city index, and large-scale maps of major cities.

Finding Towns and Cities

Most maps contain an index of towns and cities. Note the letter and number after the name of one of the cities in the index on the right edge of the map on page 345. Letters appear on the side edge of the map. Numbers appear on the bottom edge of the map. For example, San Antonio has the letter and

Texas

Roads and Related Symbols

Free Limited-Access Highways:
Under Construction
Toll Limited-Access Highways:
Under Construction
Other Four-Lane Divided Highways
Principal Highways
Other Through Highways
Other Roads (conditions vary — local inquiry suggested)
Unpaved Roads (conditions vary — local inquiry suggested)
Scenic Routes

90 190 80 90 Interstate Highways
ALT 17 183 18 U.S. Highways
8 18 14 83 State and Provincial Highways
4 43 147 Secondary State, Provincial and County Highways

Cumulative miles (red) between arrows
Intermediate miles (black) between intersections
One mile or less not shown

Interchanges and Numbers
(For most states mileages between interchanges may be determined by subtracting one number from the other.)

Rest Areas

TOLL Service Areas; Toll Booths

Waysides, Roadside Parks

Airports

Parks, Recreation Areas, Points of Interest

with camping facilities
without camping facilities
Campsites

Cities and Towns

Urbanized Areas
Cities and Towns; County Seats; Neighborhoods
Size of type indicates relative population of cities and towns

Scale

0 5 10 15 Miles
0 10 20 Kilometers

number O-5. First, look for O and 5 on the outside edges of the map. Then draw one imaginary line across from the letter O and another line up from the number 5. San Antonio is located close to where the two lines meet.

Determining Distances Use the *map scale* to estimate mileage between towns and cities. One inch equals a certain number of miles. On this map of Texas, one inch equals approximately 30 miles. For more exact mileage, you can use two other methods of determining distances:

▶ Use a mileage chart to determine distances between major

cities. The distance between two major cities is the point where the mileages intersect between the two locations.

▶ Colored numbers indicate distances between cities, towns, or intersections marked with colored symbols. On this map of Texas, red numbers indicate the distance between red arrowheads. Black numbers indicate the distance between intersections. Add the numbers that indicate distance to determine the mileage between places. If you follow Interstate 10, you will notice that San Antonio is 37 miles from Seguin.

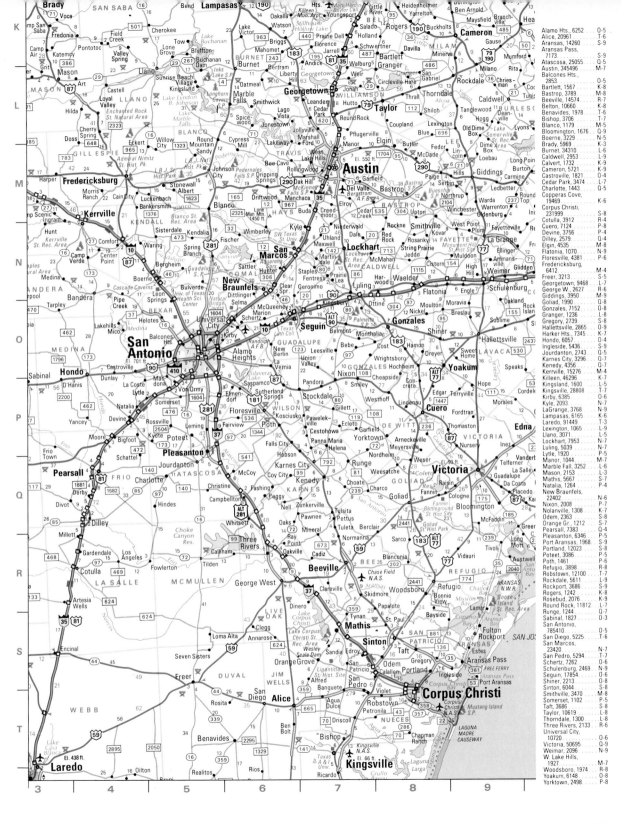

Advance Preparation

You can get assistance to help you prepare for long-distance travel. Auto clubs can suggest routes and accommodations. Mechanics can get your car in top running condition.

Routes and Accomodations An auto club can suggest routes and accommodations for your trip. The club can provide maps that show you routes to follow each day and show you the best routes to take. Some clubs provide descriptions of interesting places to visit. Auto clubs often have brochures that list recommended places to stay and eat.

Consider these points when you select your travel routes:
► How many miles will you travel in a day? Plan to drive no more than eight hours, covering 300 to 400 miles.
► What type of roadways do you want to take? Are any roadways under construction? Are there Interstate routes, two-lane highways, toll roads, bridges, or tunnels on the route?
► Will you encounter rush-hour traffic?
► What will the weather be like?
► Will there be adequate facilities for resting, eating, and lodging? For summer and holiday trips, reserve space in advance at hotels, motels, or campsites.

Vehicle Check-up Have your vehicle serviced two weeks prior to a long trip. After your vehicle is serviced, you still have time to correct any problems before you leave.

Have the following systems and parts checked:
► **Brake system** Have brake shoes or pads checked and replaced if necessary.
► **Exhaust system** On a long trip, a leaky exhaust can be deadly to car occupants.
► **Front-end alignment** A misaligned front wheel can cause excessive tire wear and a rough ride.
► **Shocks absorbers** Worn shock absorbers can affect braking and decrease ride comfort.
► **Tires** The tires should be in good condition and have plenty of tread. Check that the spare tire is inflated properly.
► **Engine systems** Check all fluid levels, including the fluid level of the battery. Check the condition of hoses, belts, and wires.

Problems that are not obvious on a short trip can become evident on a long-distance, higher-speed trip. By having your car completely checked and serviced, you can travel with more confidence.

Additional Equipment

Long-distance travel such as driving through these mountains, requires that you carry equipment not usually found in your car. You need certain equipment for emergencies. If you travel during the winter, you will need additional equipment for weather conditions.

Emergency Equipment Roadway emergencies can occur suddenly. If you carry emergency equipment, you will be ready for almost any emergency. Always carry a jack, lug wrench, tire gauge, and a spare tire. In addition, carry this emergency equipment:
► containers of oil, coolant, and windshield-washer fluid
► fire extinguisher (Type A-B-C)
► first-aid kit
► flashlight
► battery jumper cables
► spare fuses
► tools (adjustable wrench, screwdriver, and pliers).

Winter Equipment If you travel in winter or in mountainous areas, carry the following extra equipment:
► blankets and warm clothing
► tire chains or snow tires
► food, such as granola bars, nuts, and dried fruit
► window scraper and snow brush

► snow shovel
► tow line or safety chains
► transistor radio and extra batteries.

Personal Preparation

Bring these travel aids on a long-distance trip:
► change for tolls and telephone calls
► map, atlas, or travel guide
► spare set of car keys
► telephone numbers for a motor club; telephone numbers for fuel and roadway information

► traveler's checks and credit cards for major expenses.
   In addition, make these arrangements:
► Use timers to turn lights on in your home at night.
► Stop mail, newspaper, and other deliveries.
► Arrange for pet care, if needed.
► Tell your neighbors where they can reach you.

Vehicle Loading

Added weight in the trunk of a car can affect handling, acceleration, aim of the headlights, and fuel consumption. A car that is heavily loaded handles differently from a car that is carrying a light load. The car is more difficult to control, especially in an emergency situation or in a strong wind.

Follow these guidelines when loading your car:
► Avoid overloading. Check your tires and owner's manual for the maximum load per tire.
► Use the highest recommended tire pressure to accommodate the extra weight.

► Place the heaviest objects at the bottom of the trunk, as this family is doing.
► Avoid placing heavy objects in the car-top carrier.
► Keep your view to the rear clear. Do not place objects on the rear-window shelf. In a sudden stop, these objects can be thrown forward, possibly striking the occupants.
► Do not carry a spare can of fuel. It might explode in a collision.

Enjoying Your Travel

Several practices can help you enjoy long-distance travel. Keep these suggestions in

mind when you travel a long distance.

Navigation   Reading a map and following routes is called *navigating. Never try to read a map while driving.* If you are driving alone, pull off the roadway and stop before you read a map. If you have a passenger, let the passenger be your navigator. Ask your navigator to look far ahead and give information early so you can avoid having to take sudden actions. If you get lost, stop and ask directions.

Staying Alert   Use these techniques to stay alert during a long trip:
► Take a break every two hours, especially if you are traveling by yourself. Get out of your car and stretch.
► If you are traveling with another licensed driver, let that person drive for a while.
► Keep your eyes moving, scanning the mirrors and the sides of the roadway so the roadway does not "hypnotize" you.
► Adjust your car seat for greatest comfort.
► Keep air moving through the car. Use the air vents or the air conditioner or open the windows if the car gets stuffy.

Refreshments   What you eat and drink while traveling can affect your alertness. Avoid overeating when traveling. Eat light meals as this family is doing. You do not need a lot of food for energy while traveling because you are only sitting. Overeating can make you drowsy.

Avoid some kinds of foods. Foods that are very salty will make you thirsty and require you to stop. Very sweet foods might make you jittery.

Do not eat or drink while you are driving. You could spill a hot drink and burn yourself. The pain from the hot liquid might distract you from your driving task. Pull off the roadway and stop if you need refreshments.

Concentration   Follow these steps to help yourself concentrate on your driving:
► Keep at least a 2-second following distance between yourself and the vehicle in front of you.
► Read roadway signs aloud.
► Watch for mileage markers to check the accuracy of your odometer.

Do whatever you can to think about your driving task. Avoid becoming hypnotized by the roadway.

Review It

1. What are three ways you can use a road map to find the distance between two cities?
2. How should you prepare in advance for a long trip?
3. What emergency equipment should you carry in your car for a long trip?
4. What are five personal items that you should take on a long trip?
5. What guidelines should you follow when loading your car for long-distance travel?
6. What can you do to stay alert on a long-distance trip?

Sometimes you might drive a recreational vehicle or pull a trailer with your car. Therefore, you must understand what is involved in maneuvering these different vehicles.

Recreational Vehicles

A *recreational vehicle* is a type of transportation used for fun and travel. Campers mounted on pick-up trucks and self-contained motor homes are examples of recreational vehicles. These vehicles handle differently than cars. Recreational vehicles are generally harder to back, usually accelerate more slowly, and are more difficult to maneuver than cars.

Seeing   After entering a recreational vehicle, you will notice that forward visibility is much better than in a car. You can look and plan farther ahead because you sit up higher. You need this greater sight distance because stopping distance is longer and steering ability is reduced as compared to a car.

Be sure that both outside mirrors are adjusted properly before you start driving. The mirrors can help you see some objects in your blind-spot areas. For example, a driver of a wide vehicle would not be able to see the area to the right rear with a glance over the shoulder. The large mirrors on the right side of this vehicle helps a driver check the right side to the rear.

Backing   When backing, ask a passenger or bystander to direct you. Always get out of the vehicle to check for hazards before backing. Back only when necessary. Plan ahead to reduce the need to back.

Maneuvering   Lower your speed when turning a corner in a recreational vehicle. This precaution gives you extra time to maneuver around the corner. Keep in mind that you cannot accelerate, brake, or steer a recreational vehicle as easily as you can a car.

Following Distance   Increase your following distance when driving a recreational vehicle. Use at least a 4-second distance. This increased distance gives you more time to maneuver the recreational vehicle.

Handling Bigger Size   Recreational vehicles generally take up more width and height than cars. Look for signs along the roadway that warn of reduced width and height. Avoid meeting traffic on narrow bridges or near parked vehicles, pedestrians, and bicyclists. Meet where the most space is available.

Identifying Overhead Obstacles
Hitting overhead obstacles is one of the most common errors committed by recreational vehicle drivers. Recreational vehicle drivers often hit overhead structures, wires, parking garage ceilings, and tree limbs at motels, service stations, and parks. Bridges and many overhanging obstructions usually have clearance heights posted on signs.

Cross Winds Recreational vehicles are affected more than cars by cross winds. When you drive in strong cross winds, slow down or, if necessary, stop. Be prepared for wind gusts when driving out of an area that is protected by hills, trees, or viaducts.

Fatigue Recreational vehicles are harder to handle, rougher to ride in, and noisier than cars. Therefore, you probably will tire more quickly when driving a recreational vehicle. Plan to stop and rest more often, and change drivers more often than you would when driving a car.

Trailers
Pulling a trailer puts a strain on a car. Pulling a trailer can easily double the time you need to accelerate. In addition, a heavy trailer can decrease your car's:
► fuel economy by 40 to 50 percent.
► acceleration ability by 50 to 75 percent.
► top speed by up to 50 percent.
   A trailer can be an enjoyable part of your travel. Take the following precautions when pulling a trailer.

Vehicle Preparation Make these checks on your car before you pull a trailer:
► Have engine and transmission oils checked more often. The increased load on your car's engine puts a greater demand on these oils.
► Replace air, oil, and fuel filters more frequently than you would for local travel.
► Increase air pressure in the rear tires by about four pounds. However, do not exceed the air pressure limits printed on the tires.
► Check all lights on your car and the trailer.
   Towing ability varies from car to car. Check your owner's manual to make sure your car is equipped to pull a trailer. Your owner's manual also might give additional advice on preparing for towing.

Equipment A hitch and properly installed *safety chains,* as shown in the picture, are required to tow a trailer. Safety chains help keep the trailer from breaking loose from the car in case the trailer comes unhitched. Mirrors on both sides of your car, as well as brake and light hookups, are required in most states. Know how to hook up and adjust all equipment before you tow any trailer.

Load   Take these precautions when loading a trailer:
- ► Place heavy items over the axle or axles. Distribute the weight of the trailer's contents evenly on the left and right sides.
- ► Place about 10 to 15 percent of the total weight on the tongue of the trailer. The tongue is the part of the trailer that connects to the hitch.
- ► Keep heavy items out of the rear of the trailer to keep the center of gravity low.
- ► If the trailer has no brakes, keep the weight of the loaded trailer less than the weight of the towing vehicle.
- ► Pack contents firmly and close together. Secure partial loads with ropes and tie-downs.

An improperly loaded trailer is hazardous. Too much weight in the front will overload the hitch and make it more difficult for you to reduce speed. Too much weight in the rear can cause the trailer to sway, an extremely dangerous situation.

Special Driving Techniques
When pulling a trailer, remember the "two times" rule. It will take you about two times longer to pass, stop, accelerate, and turn. Follow these rules when you tow a trailer:
- ► Do not drive faster than the trailer speed limit, if one is posted.

- ► Make your turns slower and wider.
- ► If the trailer starts to sway or "fishtail," steer toward the center of the lane and gradually slow down. If the trailer has a separate set of brakes, use them first while accelerating slightly. When the trailer stops swaying, use the car brakes carefully.
- ► Allow twice as much distance when passing.
- ► Increase your braking distance. You cannot stop quickly when towing a trailer.
- ► Shift to low gear before going up or down steep hills. Go downhill at lower speeds. Vehicle stability decreases as you go downhill.
- ► Avoid traveling during very windy conditions.
- ► Never carry passengers in a trailer.

Backing   Before backing a loaded trailer, practice backing an empty trailer in a parking lot. To steer while backing a trailer, put your hand on the bottom of the steering wheel. Turn the wheel left to back left. Turn the wheel right to back right as illustrated above.

The rear of the trailer will go the same direction as your hand. Move back slowly, and make small steering corrections. Since the mirrors cannot cover all the areas to the rear, ask someone to give you directions as shown in the picture.

Hazards   Towing a trailer has some special hazards. Never follow another vehicle closely when pulling a trailer. The additional weight of the trailer makes it difficult for you to stop quickly. Use the 4-second rule to increase the space between you and the vehicle ahead.

If you are passed by a large vehicle while towing a trailer, move as far to the right as you can. This action minimizes any swaying from the wind of the large vehicle.

Review It
1. What three problems might you encounter while driving a recreational vehicle? Tell how to manage each problem.
2. What are the rules to follow when towing a trailer?
3. How should you back a trailer?

Advancements in Traffic Safety

A safety system has been developed that helps drivers of vans, recreational vehicles, trucks, and other large vehicles. The system helps drivers "see" their blind spots and avoid collisions.

The system has two parts—a small video camera and a monitor. The camera is fastened at the top center of the back of the vehicle. The monitor is inside the vehicle where the driver can see it easily. Wires connect the camera to the monitor.

When the camera is on, the driver can look at the monitor to check the blind spot directly behind and to the sides of the vehicle. The system helps the driver

avoid backing into pedestrians or other vehicles. The driver also can see if a small car suddenly pulls out from behind to pass as the larger vehicle starts to change lanes.

Chapter Summary

1. Make short trips easier and more efficient by determining if the trip is really necessary. Consider travel time, weather and traffic conditions, and the time of day you are traveling. Leave a little early to allow for unanticipated problems. (18–1)
2. Prevent many problems on short trips by routine vehicle maintenance, proper route selection, and knowing route and destination names in advance. (18–1)
3. Find the distance between two cities by using a map scale, a mileage chart, or by adding the mileage numbers between the two cities on a map. (18–2)
4. Auto clubs and mechanics can help you prepare for long-distance travel. Plan your routes and make reservations in advance. Have your car checked completely at least two weeks before departing. (18–2)
5. Carry additional emergency equipment on long trips. Add special equipment to your vehicle when traveling in the winter or in mountainous areas. (18–2)
6. Bring change, maps, extra keys, telephone numbers, and means to pay major expenses when traveling on a long trip. (18–2)
7. Avoid overloading your car for a long trip. Place the heaviest objects at the bottom when packing the trunk. Do not place heavy objects in car-top carriers. Do not block the rear window. (18–2)
8. You can better enjoy traveling when you navigate properly, take frequent breaks, stay alert, and eat lightly. Concentrate on your driving task, but do not become hypnotized by the roadway. (18–2)
9. Before driving a recreational vehicle, adjust the outside mirrors. When making a turn, slow down to give yourself more time to make the turn. When driving, increase your following distance. (18–3)
10. When pulling a trailer, adjust your driving so you can better control your own car and the trailer. (18–3)
11. To back a trailer, put your hand at the bottom on the steering wheel. Turn the wheel left to back left. Turn the wheel right to back right. Ask another person to direct you, if possible. (18–3)

Think About It
While on a long-distance trip, you learn that the roadway ahead is closed due to heavy rains. What information would you need to select an alternate route? Where could you get the information?

Decision Making

1. How can you find out in advance how weather and traffic conditions might affect your trip?

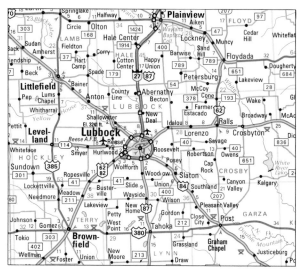

2. What main route would you take to go from Lubbock to Tahoka, Texas? How far is it and how long will the drive take? What other routes are available?

3. This driver is attempting to follow route 63 North. What mistake has the driver made? When the driver realizes the error, what should the driver do?

4. What is the problem in this picture? What is the probable cause? How might the problem have been prevented?

Chapter 18 Test

Multiple Choice   Copy the number of each sentence below on a sheet of paper. Choose the letter that best completes the statement or answers the question.

1. Which of these factors does *not* help to make a local trip easier for you?
   (a) leaving on time   (b) allowing enough time
   (c) traveling during rush hour   (d) listening to weather reports   (342)
2. Before making a long-distance trip, you should
   (a) have your car checked and serviced.
   (b) take an extra pair of gloves.   (c) load a complete tool chest.   (d) put a five gallon container of fuel in the trunk.   (346)
3. How should you read a map during a long-distance trip?
   (a) Rest it on the steering wheel.   (b) Put it on the seat to your right.   (c) Stop or have a passenger read it.   (d) Hold it to your side window.   (348)
4. What special rule should you remember when pulling a trailer?
   (a) "go slow" rule   (b) "two times" rule
   (c) "take time" rule   (d) "tire check" rule   (352)
5. To improve your view to the rear when backing a trailer,
   (a) use mirrors and ask another person to direct you.   (b) look over your shoulders.   (c) use mirrors and some markers.   (d) look over your shoulders and ask another person to guide you.   (352)

Completion   Copy the number of each sentence below. After each number, write the letter of the word or words that complete the sentence correctly.

6. To save fuel, combine several ____.   (342)
7. A short trip uses ____ per mile than does a long-distance trip.   (342)
8. A ____ can help you locate towns and cities on a map.   (344)
9. Have your car serviced about two weeks before a ____.   (346)
10. Inflate tires to the ____ recommended pressure before carrying heavy loads in your car.   (348)
11. On a long trip, eat ____ than usual.   (349)
12. When ____ a recreational vehicle or trailer, have another person direct you.   (350, 352)
13. Recreational vehicles are less stable than cars during a ____.   (351)
14. You need ____ time to pass, turn, stop, and accelerate when pulling a trailer.   (352)
15. To back a trailer to the right, turn the bottom of the steering wheel to the ____.   (352)

a. backing
b. highest
c. high-wind condition
d. less
e. long-distance trip
f. lowest
g. map index
h. more
i. more fuel
j. right
k. short trips

Vocabulary   Copy the number of each definition below. Match the definition in List A with the term it defines in List B.

List A
16. in a map legend, a line an inch or more long that indicates measurement in miles   (344)
17. boxed area on a map that explains markings and symbols   (344)
18. using signs and maps to guide a driver   (348)
19. large vehicle used for fun and travel   (350)
20. hold trailer if the hitch breaks loose   (351)

List B
a. legend
b. map scale
c. navigating
d. recreational vehicle
e. safety chains
f. trailer

Focus on Careers

State Highway Patrol Officer

Duties: Supervising drivers on major highways is the main function of the highway patrol. These officers help keep traffic flowing in a safe and orderly manner. They help roadway users in trouble, investigate collisions, issue warnings and citations, and testify in court.

Training: Most state highway patrols require at least a high-school education, plus specialized courses in police science that many community colleges and universities offer. Recruits attend an intensive training program at the state's highway patrol academy.

Opportunities: Competition for most law-enforcement positions is expected to remain high. The outlook is best for those candidates with some college training in law enforcement. Opportunities for advancement include promotion to higher levels of command.

Career Information:
Contact the State Police headquarters in your state's capital.

Highway Engineer

Duties: Highway engineers design and oversee the building, repair, and maintenance of roadways and bridges. They consider the geology of the area, as well as the environmental and social impact of any proposed roadway construction. Their duties can include presenting their plans to governmental committees, outdoor field work, and supervising construction crews.

Training: A college degree in civil engineering is required. Courses in mathematics, science (physics and geology), environmental management, and computer technology are highly recommended. Good drafting skills are necessary.

New engineering graduates often work as assistants to experienced engineers. Many engineers get a master's degree to increase their earning potential or become eligible for promotion. State licensing is usually required since the public's safety can be affected.

Opportunities: Employment opportunities are expected to improve for civil engineers. Some highway engineers can rise to administrative positions in federal, state, and local government agencies. Other engineers can become executives in engineering firms. Although most highway engineers work in urban areas, jobs in rural areas, foreign countries, or jobs involving frequent travel are also available.

Career Information:
American Society of Civil Engineers
345 E. 47th St.
New York, NY 10017

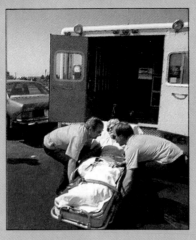

Driver-Education Teacher

Duties: Both high schools and privately owned driving schools employ driver-education teachers. These teachers use classroom instruction, and in-car instruction to teach people how to safely operate a motor vehicle.

Training: Most driver-education teachers work in public high schools that require a four-year college degree as well as a teaching certificate. Some private high schools and privately owned driving schools do not require a teaching certificate. However, some states require a special teaching license for teachers in privately owned driving schools.

Opportunities: The need for driver-education teachers is expected to remain steady. Some driver-education teachers work as consultants for government and private organizations.

Career Information:
American Driver and Traffic Safety Education Association
123 N. Pitt St.
Alexandria, VA 22314

Paramedic

Duties: A paramedic needs excellent driving skills to reach emergencies as quickly and safely as possible. Paramedics administer first aid to the sick or injured, and transport them to a nearby medical facility. Paramedics often work in a mobile intensive-care ambulance under the direction of fire department or hospital personnel.

Training: Admission to training programs usually requires a high-school diploma or equivalent education. An emergency medical technician course is followed by a 3- to 5-month training program.

Opportunities: The demand for paramedics is increasing. Salaries of publicly employed paramedics are similar to those of police officers and firefighters. Benefits are usually good.

Career Information:
National Association of Emergency Medical Technicians
PO Box 334
Newton Highlands, MA 02161

Route Driver

Duties: Route drivers use panel or light trucks to deliver products. A route driver collects payments from customers and attempts to interest them in the company's new products or services.

Training: A route driver must have orderly work habits and must be able to work without direct supervision. In most states, a route driver must qualify for a commerical driver's license.

Opportunities: Sales supervisor and route supervisor are two opportunities for advancement. As the population continues to move toward suburban areas, there will be an increased need for route drivers.

Career Information:
International Brotherhood of Teamsters, Chauffeurs, Warehousemen and Helpers of America (Ind.)
25 Louisiana Ave., N.W.
Washington, DC 20001

Automotive Mechanic

Duties: A mechanic diagnoses automotive problems and estimates the cost of both parts and labor for repairs. A mechanic also repairs vehicles, using a wide variety of tools and skills.

Training: Some high schools, trade schools, and community colleges offer courses and certification in automotive repair. Some auto dealers and large, independent repair shops offer 3- or 4-year apprenticeship programs. Such a program combines on-the-job experience with classroom instruction.

Opportunities: The need for qualified automotive mechanics is expected to be excellent since many people are keeping their cars for longer periods of time. Advancements in automotive technology should also increase the demand for qualified mechanics.

Career Information:
Automotive Service Industry Association
444 N. Michigan Ave.
Chicago, IL 60611

Sales Representative

Duties: Sales representatives usually need a car to present their company's products to local and out-of-state customers. In addition, they usually must complete an extensive amount of paperwork such as reports, expense accounts, and lists of prospective clients. Reading to study new products, the competition, and developments in the field can require much study time and self-discipline.

Training: High-school graduates are sometimes hired as sales trainees for some companies. However, up to two years could pass before the trainees actually start working as sales representatives. Sales of some products (medical supplies and chemicals, for example) can require college degrees in biology, chemistry, or pharmacy. Some companies require that sales representatives be college graduates with degrees in business or other related fields.

Opportunities: Travel is often a part of the sales representative's job. Foreign travel is a possibility with some companies. Although compensation varies a great deal, a successful sales representative can often advance to regional or national sales management positions.

Career Information:
Sales and Marketing Executives International
308 Lexington Ave.
New York, NY 10017